Women of the Commonwealth

2 WEEKS

WOMEN OF THE COMMONWEALTH

WORK, FAMILY, AND SOCIAL CHANGE IN NINETEENTH-CENTURY MASSACHUSETTS

Edited by Susan L. Porter

University of Massachusetts Press
Amherst

For the B.U. Women's Thesis Group and
other places that support work in women's history.

Copyright © 1996 by
The University of Massachusetts Press
All rights reserved
Printed in the United States of America
LC 95-21715
ISBN 1-55849-004-3 (cloth); 1-55849-005-1 (pbk.)
Designed by Milenda Nan Ok Lee
Set in Adobe Garamond
Printed and bound by Thomson-Shore, Inc.
Library of Congress Cataloging-in-Publication Data

Women of the commonwealth : work, family, and social change in
    nineteenth-century Massachusetts / edited by Susan L. Porter.
        p.   cm.
    Includes bibliographical references and index.
    ISBN 1-55849-004-3 (cloth : alk. paper). —
ISBN 1-55849-005-1 (pbk. : alk. paper)
    1. Women—Massachusetts—History—19th century.   2. Women—
Employment—Massachusetts—History—19th century.
3. Massachusetts—Social conditions.   I. Porter, Susan Lynne.
HQ1438.M4W63   1996
305.4'09744'09034—dc20   95-21715
                                                              CIP

British Library Cataloguing in Publication data are available.

This book is published with the support and cooperation of the
University of Massachusetts at Boston.

CONTENTS

Foreword
Martin Kaufman   vii

Introduction
Susan L. Porter   1

PART ONE   Women and Work

Victorian Values in the Marketplace:
Single Women and Work in Boston, 1800–1850
Susan L. Porter   17

The Feminization of Teaching in Massachusetts: A Reconsideration
James M. Wallace   43

Être à l'ouvrage ou être maitresse de maison:
French-Canadian Women and Work in Late
Nineteenth-Century Massachusetts
Paul R. Dauphinais   63

Good Men and "Working Girls":
The Bureau of Statistics of Labor, 1870–1900
Henry F. Bedford   85

The Gendered Foundations of Social Work Education
in Boston, 1904–1930
Linda M. Shoemaker   99

PART TWO   Social Reform and Political Activism

Caroline Healey Dall: Her Creation and Reform Career
Nancy Bowman   121

Josephine St. Pierre Ruffin:
A Nineteenth-Century Journalist of Boston's Black Elite Class
Rodger Streitmatter   147

Julia Harrington Duff and the Political Awakening of
Irish-American Women in Boston, 1888–1905
Polly Welts Kaufman   165

"The Simplest of New England Spinsters":
Becoming Emily Greene Balch, 1867–1961
Patricia A. Palmieri   183

Beyond Servants and Salesgirls:
Working Women's Education in Boston, 1885–1915
Laurie Crumpacker   207

Contributors   233

Index   235

FOREWORD

This book represents the continuation of the work of the Institute for Massachusetts Studies. For twenty-two years the staff of the Institute has attempted to serve the community and the state in various ways, all related to the task of preserving the historical and cultural heritage of the region. In 1972 the Institute published the first issue of the *Historical Journal of Western Massachusetts,* designed to promote an interest in state and local history. In 1980 the *Journal* expanded to focus statewide and changed its name to the *Historical Journal of Massachusetts.*

The Institute has, in conjunction with various presses, published several volumes on topics relating to Massachusetts history, some of which were initiated as part of the commemoration of the 350th anniversary of the founding of Springfield in 1986. In addition, the Institute has sponsored a number of conferences on Massachusetts history—on the Gilded Age in 1984, on education in 1988, on labor in 1989, and on sports in 1990—that were later published as collections of articles.

This volume culminates the Institute's most recent endeavor. In October 1992, the Institute held a symposium at Westfield State College on the history of women, organized by Martin Kaufman, the director of the Institute, and Susan L. Porter, assistant professor of history at Simmons College. The University of Massachusetts Press expressed interest in publishing the work presented at the conference. The Institute is pleased to see the completion of this project at the University of Massachusetts Press under the editorial guidance of Susan Porter.

The Institute for Massachusetts Studies is an integral part of the academic program of Westfield State College, and assistance and support has been provided by President Ronald L. Applebaum and William Lopes, the senior vice president for academic affairs. Lee Mangiaratti, secretary of the Institute, deserves special mention for her many contributions.

Martin Kaufman

INTRODUCTION

SUSAN L. PORTER

This volume presents a variety of new perspectives on the history of women in Massachusetts. The chapters in this book, like the submissions to the symposium on which it is based, reflect both the dimensions of the burgeoning field of women's history and the significance of the Massachusetts experience. The chronological time frame of the book reflects the interests of a diverse groups of authors in the era of industrialization, which transformed virtually every aspect of the landscape and population of Massachusetts and had an enormous impact on women's lives.

For the past twenty years many social, intellectual, and economic historians have focused their research on the nineteenth century. Often incorporating social science methodologies, they have raised questions about the dramatic economic and social changes of the period and their meanings. Much of this work has been about New England, and the Massachusetts experience in particular, because of the central role played by the colony and state in American history.

Women's historians, applying analogous methodologies, have exhibited a similar interest, although they have concentrated on gender as a means of making historically underrepresented populations more visible. In the 1960s and 1970s, many of these historians, who were themselves feminists, social activists, and political reformers, saw women's history as a means of establishing positive role models and useful paradigms that might help explain their own struggles in a patriarchal society. Through biographies of individual women, studies of women in groups, and research on women in relation to institutions, women's historians attempted to explore the histories of issues relevant to their own lives—domesticity, waged work, and social and political reform.[1]

Over time, however, the boundaries between women's history and other histories have blurred. On the one hand, the body of research in women's history has expanded to include aspects of gender relations among many diverse groups and to incorporate methodologies not only from the social sciences but also from literary theorists. In turn, the so-called traditional fields of history have also been transformed as mainstream historians have begun to employ gender as a category of analysis.[2]

The nineteenth century represents particularly fertile soil for historians because massive social and economic changes led to a fundamental reshaping of the roles played by men and women. Whereas in a pre-industrial agricultural economy men and women worked side by side to maintain a farm or shop, and child rearing was considered part of the daily duties of all members of the household, postrevolutionary economic changes eventually led to the separation of work from the home for many men and a differentiation of "spheres" by gender. Because the male sphere was "public," removed from the family dwelling, the home became the woman's arena, and her tasks in this "private" sphere, especially in the area of social reproduction, took on increased societal value and were seen as elevating her position.[3]

The ideology of separate spheres was framed and reinforced by the republican political theory that had justified the American Revolution. Republican ideology emphasized the need for virtuous, educated citizens who would guard the common welfare to prevent the greed and corruption that contemporaries believed was prevalent in Europe and had led to the decline of past republics. Some of this work, it was thought, could be accomplished in new institutions like public schools, but the primary task of inculcating values was relegated to the family. The "republican mother" in particular was viewed as the source and symbol of national values that men admired but could not always maintain in the competitive public world of business. The private sphere was to be a place apart, a refuge from the public domain, populated by supportive, frugal, virtuous wives whose contributions to the family economy were measured in moral rather than economic terms.[4]

In fact, because women were esteemed primarily for their domestic roles, women's paid labor outside the home was devalued both monetarily and conceptually. Even volunteer work in the public sphere was perceived to be of dubious respectability unless it could be construed as an appropriate extension of women's natural attributes. Over time various women made a case for their public roles, first through benevolent work with disadvantaged women and children and then through social reform movements like the temperance and abolitionist movements. Their personal experiences eventually led some of these reformers to demand women's rights and suffrage and others to seek public roles as professionals alongside men.[5]

Massachusetts is an ideal place to look at these trends. An early settlement whose population expanded rapidly in spite of relatively low agricultural productivity, Massachusetts had developed an imbalanced class structure based on merchant capitalism and had experienced land scarcity and urban poverty well before the American Revolution. The revolutionary victory brought renewed optimism that the new republic would be able to address these problems on both economic and ideological levels. Republican ideology emphasized independence—the ability to achieve self-sufficiency—and progress, the expectation that the individual and the society at large could achieve a better future. After independence, Massachusetts merchants and entrepreneurs formed insurance companies and other voluntary investment associations that allowed them to expand their trade to the far East and to inaugurate manufacturing ventures. Accumulating a level of profit unimaginable before the war, a new expanded elite was able to apply this capital to the development of mechanized industry, especially in textiles, as early as the time trade was disrupted in the War of 1812. By the 1820s this mercantile and entrepreneurial elite had succeeded in transfiguring the Massachusetts economy while securing its own wealth and status.[6]

The economic transformation of New England due to the textile industry preceded that of other regions by decades and hastened structural changes in the artisan shop, the apprenticeship system, and the nature of paid labor itself. The native-born groups that profited from these changes included not only factory-owning entrepreneurs but also a new middle class of white-collar workers and specialized artisans who worked outside the home and were expected to earn a "family wage" that would support their household. At the same time, the production of factory-made goods decreased the value of female home manufac-

4 tures and encouraged young single women to venture into the mill, the shoe shop, and other places of work where they might live away from home and be paid individually for their labor rather than as a member of a family economy. Of course, because women were paid less than men, they were particularly welcome as unskilled laborers at the same time that their work was cast as supplemental rather than primary to their family's support. Despite the cultural perceptions about women's work, however, the female contribution to the family economy was generally essential; even when unmarried women took jobs at a distance, they sent money home.[7]

As manufacturing sites proliferated, industrialists became concerned about maintaining profits in an increasingly competitive market and instituted cost-cutting measures including wage cuts and work speed-ups. Although these changes made factory work less appealing to native-born single women, they were implemented repeatedly because successive waves of immigrants—Irish, French-Canadian, Eastern European, Italian—were desperate for employment at any wage. The rapid population growth of Massachusetts from immigration and natural increase led to early efforts by female and male philanthropists and public officials to reverse the negative effects of poverty, overcrowding, poor sanitation, and other urban problems. It also spawned early efforts by working people to reverse or at least mitigate the negative effects of industrialization on their lives. In fact, Massachusetts led in social and labor reform efforts in the United States through institutions, public and private, and other collective movements.[8]

Massachusetts provides a particularly interesting site for examining new perspectives in women's history, in part because there has been so much research on the state already. As a result, new paradigms can be examined against a widely understood historical backdrop. In addition, the state in this era provides a unique opportunity for local history to interact with American history writ large; because Massachusetts, at least through the nineteenth century, was an archetype for industrial development, urbanization, immigration, and reform movements, women across the United States repeated many of the experiences described in this book.

The subjects of the chapters in this book reflect the central questions in women's history today—debates about the nature of gender difference and the interrelationships among race, class, ethnicity, and gender. Increasingly, historians have come to question the concept of a unitary "American culture" and to understand that human beings operate through overlapping value systems, or cultures, all of which influence their beliefs and behaviors. To attempt to understand the life of a woman in Boston in 1875, for example, the historian must not only locate her by gender and geography but also investigate her class, her race, her sexual identity, her religion, her age, her family situation, her skills, her neighborhood, and her ethnicity.

Historians have also begun to question the presupposition that all social groups in the United States have or have ever had a shared value system. In the past some beliefs have been seen as hegemonic because they were the ones most consistently recorded and expressed by a "dominant culture" of elite, white, Protestant men. Yet even when other groups seem to have exhibited some of these values, the historian must ask whether they were being expressed from the position of the dominant culture or deriving from an alternative set of cultural assumptions. In some way, all the articles in this volume share this thematic concern about the nature and meaning of culture.[9]

The book is divided into two sections. The first looks at the nature of women's work, waged and unwaged, in regard to gendered survival strategies within the family economy and the assumptions and actions of a market based on patriarchal power relations. These chapters consider the effects of class, ethnicity, and gender on the structure of the job market and power relations within the family.

In the first chapter, Susan Porter discusses the interaction between the job choices and cultural expectations of single, native-born, working-class Boston women over the first half of the nineteenth century. Looking at changing opportunities for these women, Porter finds that they made work choices based not only on economic advantage but also on calculations about perceived chances for marriage. Their priorities raise questions about the interpretation of Victorian values among women of different classes.

James Wallace analyzes the factors between 1840 and 1860 that account for the feminization of teaching in Massachusetts. He argues that school administrators hired more women, especially in urban areas, primarily because they could be paid lower salaries but also because they genuinely believed that women were morally superior guardians of children's virtue. Like Porter, Wallace relies on quantitative analysis to shed light on questions that have traditionally been discussed on the basis of

6   public, prescriptive, often formulaic sources. His argument shows the ways in which the doctrine of separate spheres was used to justify both the development of the first respectable female "profession" and a differential, gendered salary structure.

Paul Dauphinais also employs quantitative methods to revisit the important question of cultural assumptions about immigrant populations. Looking at French-Canadian immigrant families, who have been studied primarily in the context of "spindle cities," Dauphinais finds that family survival strategies and work patterns were quite different for those who chose to settle in more economically diverse urban areas like Fitchburg and Worcester. These families were younger and smaller, with more highly skilled male household heads; as a result, their children were able to remain in school well into adolescence. Wives stayed at home, where they participated in community-building, multiethnic religious and cultural activities that helped these cities avoid much of the ethnic conflict prevalent in textile centers.

Henry Bedford's chapter also examines cultural assumptions through a critical look at the methodology of data collection about women at the Massachusetts Bureau of Labor Statistics in the final decades of the nineteenth century. Although this agency's reports have been an invaluable source for historians, Bedford points out serious limitations. Despite the fact that all three of the agency's directors were progressive men for their era, their definitions of labor and their methods of obtaining information reveal gendered, class-biased, ethnocentric attitudes about working women.

In the final chapter of the first section, Linda Shoemaker highlights gender as a primary factor in the professionalization of social work in the early twentieth century. Like Wallace, Shoemaker analyzes the development of a sex-segregated profession as a reflection of larger societal beliefs. Using the Boston School for Social Work, a decade-long joint venture between Harvard and Simmons College, as a case study, Shoemaker argues that, despite the founders' efforts to create a broad-based, inclusive training program, they found it impossible to institutionalize a concept of social work education that could transcend their own and other prevailing attitudes about class and gender.

The second section of the book shows how new scholarship on social reformers and political activists transforms classic paradigms of feminist scholarship relating to "sisterhood"—the notion that all women have

natural affinities based on gender—and gendered socialization. While 7
all of the chapters look at women in groups, most adopt a biographical
approach to focus on the individual woman and her relationship to her
family, her class, her race, her ethnicity, and her developing and changing ideologies. Although biographies have often been used in the past as
ways of creating heroes and role models, these pieces demonstrate the
value of biography not as a means of glorification but as a doorway into
the intricacy of the individual life.

Nancy Bowman's discussion of Caroline Healey Dall, the mid-
nineteenth-century reformer and author, demonstrates the difficulty
of preserving "sisterhood" among strong-minded nineteenth-century
women for whom moral stances were a reflection of personal experience
as well as ideology. Caroline Dall rejected "private sphere" ideology for
the first time when economic exigency forced her to earn her own living
and became an activist for women's rights. Yet her personal style, which
was "unfeminine"—that is, opinionated, uncompromising, competitive, and combative—made it difficult for her to work with women's
groups, and she eventually left the movement to obtain a law degree and
become a "professional" in the male environment of the American
Social Science Association.

Rodger Streitmatter's chapter on Josephine St. Pierre Ruffin looks at
the experience of an elite African-American woman journalist and clubwoman who was able to bridge racial barriers through class affinities. As
Streitmatter demonstrates, Ruffin's newspaper provided a forum for her
to publicize the National Association of Colored Women, lobby against
racial discrimination, and promote women's rights. At the same time,
Ruffin was able to use her affiliations and friendships with white Boston
women of her class who were active in the women's suffrage and wom-
en's club movements to engage their active support on racial issues.

Like Streitmatter, Polly Kaufman examines the gendered politics of
late nineteenth-century Boston, but her chapter focuses on ethnic conflict between two early female members of the Boston School Committee, Julia Duff and Emily Fifield. In the struggle between the Irish and
the Yankees over ethnic control of the Boston School Committee, the
first Massachusetts forum in which women were allowed political representation, the issues of guardianship of virtue and gender affinities take
on new meaning.

Patricia Palmieri's piece on Emily Greene Balch, the economist and

8   social reformer who won the Nobel Peace Prize in 1946 for her work in the Women's International League for Peace and Freedom, explicates the cacophony of familial, cultural, and even institutional expectations imposed on college-educated middle-class women at the turn of the century. Palmieri argues that Balch was in her forties by the time she was able to sort these expectations out, shed those that made her uncomfortable, and finally become empowered to fully employ her considerable energy and talent.

Finally, Laurie Crumpacker's chapter looks at institutional rather than individual reformers. Crumpacker studies two programs designed by the Boston Women's Educational and Industrial Union to educate working-class women, one for domestic servants and the other for department-store salesclerks. The programs were eventually incorporated into the course of studies at Simmons College, where they followed diametrically different trajectories. Crumpacker argues that cross-class connections were most successful when the clientele was culturally similar to that of the reformers and when the clients' needs were not in conflict with those of the middle-class managers.

The ten essays in this book demonstrate the intricacy and richness of the field of women's history as it has developed over the past two decades. While they include diverse subjects and methodological approaches, the theme that resonates throughout is the complexity of gender as a unitary category. Although all the chapters discuss the traditional subjects of women's history—the relationships between the individual and her family, her workplace, her social and cultural networks, her institutional affiliations, and her civic polity—they reflect sophisticated new interpretations of the intersections between individuals and groups. As the authors have begun to break down and question a generalized concept of "woman," they have observed that, in a patriarchal society, gender has been a category for both inclusion and exclusion. As they have explored the dynamics between gender and race, ethnicity, and class, which have been seen primarily as categories for exclusion, their understandings of all groupings have become increasingly complicated. Yet, although it is clear that the category of woman is too broad to be used by itself as an analytical tool, it is also evident that, appropriately contextualized, gender remains an important lens for understanding history and culture. With this, and other lenses, historians like those repre-

sented in this volume can begin to convey an increasingly nuanced
vision of the past.[10]

This book, like any worthwhile endeavor, has benefited from collaboration and cross-fertilization. I am grateful to Martin Kaufman for inviting me to organize the symposium at Westfield State College in 1992 and to Mary Blewett and Laurie Crumpacker for their insightful comments on the papers presented there. I would like to thank Pam Bromberg, Laurie Crumpacker, Patricia Palmieri, and Susan Reverby for valuable suggestions on the introduction, Tom Dublin and Janet Golden for reading the entire manuscript and offering critiques that were both complementary and helpful, and Polly Kaufman for doing the index. Finally, I would like to thank Paul Wright, my editor at the University of Massachusetts Press, for his interest in the project and his support throughout.

Notes

1. A good example of this approach is a special issue of *The Massachusetts Review* 13 (1972) entitled "Woman: An Issue," which contained, among other things, articles on women and politics, stereotypes of women in literature, and a piece on the nineteenth-century novelist Elizabeth Stuart Phelps, subtitled, "A Study in Female Rebellion." The back cover depicted the symbol of the female antislavery movement, a kneeling, chained slave, with the motto, "Am I not a woman and a sister." For early biographies see the Feminist Press biography series edited by Robin Morgan. The first two titles, published by the State University of New York Press in 1972, were biographies of Elizabeth Barrett Browning by Mary Jane Lupton and Elizabeth Cady Stanton by Mary Ann B. Oakley. Seminal articles include Barbara Welter, "The Cult of True Womanhood: 1820–1860," *American Quarterly* 18 (1966): 151–74; Gerda Lerner, "The Lady and the Mill Girl: Changes in the Status of Women in the Age of Jackson," *Mid-Continent American Studies Journal* 10 (1969): 5–15; and Carroll Smith Rosenberg, "Beauty, the Beast, and the Militant Woman: A Case Study in Sex Roles and Social Stress in Jacksonian America," *American Quarterly* 23 (1971): 562–84 and "The Female World of Love and Ritual: Relations between Women in Nineteenth-Century America," *Signs* 1 (1975): 1–29. Some early monographs are Eleanor Flexner, *Century of Struggle: The Woman's Rights Movement in the United States* (Cambridge: Harvard University Press, 1959); Aileen S. Kraditor, *Ideas of the Women's Suffrage Movement* (New York: Columbia University Press, 1965); Anne Firor Scott, *The Southern Lady, from Pedestal to Politics* (Chicago: University of Chicago Press, 1970); Linda Gordon, *Wom-*

an's Body, Woman's Right, Birth Control in America (New York: Grossman Publishers, 1976); and Nancy F. Cott, *The Bonds of Womanhood: Woman's Sphere in New England, 1780–1835* (New Haven: Yale University Press, 1976).

2. For useful summaries of this transformation see Peter Novick, *That Noble Dream: The "Objectivity Question" and the American Historical Profession* (Cambridge: Cambridge University Press, 1988); Joyce Appleby, Lynn Hunt, and Margaret Jacob, *Telling the Truth about History* (New York: W. W. Norton, 1994); and the essays in Eric Foner, ed., *The New American History* (Philadelphia: Temple University Press, 1990). On gender and postmodern literary theory see Teresa de Lauretis, ed., *Feminist Studies, Critical Studies* (Bloomington: Indiana University Press, 1986); Joan Wallach Scott, *Women and the Politics of History* (New York: Columbia University Press, 1988); Marianne Hirsch and Evelyn Fox Keller, eds., *Conflicts in Feminism* (New York: Routledge, 1990); and Linda Nicholson, ed., *Feminism/Postmodernism* (New York: Routledge, 1990). In one of the chapters in de Lauretis, "Writing History: Language, Class, and Gender," Carroll Smith Rosenberg revisits the subject of her *Religion and the Rise of the American City: The New York City Mission Movement, 1812–1870* (Ithaca: Cornell University Press, 1971) from a postmodern perspective.

3. For the development of separate spheres see Kathryn Kish Sklar, *Catharine Beecher: A Study in American Domesticity* (New Haven: Yale University Press, 1973); Barbara J. Berg, *The Remembered Gate: Origins of American Feminism, The Woman, and the City, 1800–1860* (New York: Oxford University Press, 1978); Ruth H. Bloch, "American Feminine Ideals in Transition: The Rise of the Moral Mother, 1785–1815," *Feminist Studies* 4 (1978): 101–26; and Karen J. Blair, *The Clubwoman as Feminist: True Womanhood Redefined, 1868–1914* (New York: Holmes and Meier, 1980). For an overview of the literature on separate spheres see Linda K. Kerber, "Separate Spheres, Female Worlds, Woman's Place: The Rhetoric of Women's History," *Journal of American History* 75 (1988): 9–39. For changes in men's work see W. J. Rorabaugh, *The Craft Apprentice from Franklin to the Machine Age in America* (New York: Oxford University Press, 1986); Bruce Laurie, *Artisans into Workers: Labor in Nineteenth-Century America* (New York: Noonday Press, 1989); and E. Anthony Rotundo, *American Manhood: Transformations in Masculinity from the Revolution to the Modern Era* (New York: Basic Books, 1993). For the influence of changing work patterns on class development, see Mary P. Ryan, *Cradle of the Middle Class: The Family in Oneida County, New York, 1790–1865* (Cambridge: Cambridge University Press, 1981); Sean Wilentz, *Chants Democratic: New York City and the Rise of the American Working Class* (New York: Oxford University Press, 1984); Christine Stansell, *City of Women: Sex and Class in New York, 1789–1860* (New York: Alfred A. Knopf, 1986); and Stuart M. Blumin, *The Emergence of the Middle Class: Social Experience in the American City, 1760–1900* (Cambridge: Cambridge University Press, 1989).

4. For a useful overview see Jack P. Greene, ed., *The American Revolution: Its*
Character and Limits (New York: New York University Press, 1987). For republican theory and gender see Linda K. Kerber, *Women of the Republic: Intellect and Ideology in Revolutionary America* (Chapel Hill: University of North Carolina Press, 1980), Mary Beth Norton, *Liberty's Daughters: The Revolutionary Experience of American Women, 1750–1800* (Boston: Little, Brown, 1980); Ruth M. Bloch, "The Gendered Meanings of Virtue in Revolutionary America," *Signs: Journal of Women in Culture and Society* 13 (1987): 37–58; and Joan Gundersen, "Independence, Citizenship, and the American Revolution," *Signs* 13 (1987): 59–87. For republican ideology and education see Lawrence A. Cremin, *American Education, the National Experience, 1783–1876* (New York: Harper and Row, 1980); Carl F. Kaestle and Maris Vinovskis, *Education and Social Change in Nineteenth-Century Massachusetts* (Cambridge: Cambridge University Press, 1980); and Carl F. Kaestle, *Pillars of the Republic: Common Schools and American Society, 1780–1860* (New York: Hill and Wang, 1983). For the relationship between republicanism and corporate liberalism see Drew McCoy, *The Elusive Republic: Political Economy in Jeffersonian America* (Chapel Hill: University of North Carolina Press, 1980); Joyce Appleby, *Capitalism and a New Order: The Republican Vision of the 1790s* (New York: New York University Press, 1984); and Cathy Matsun and Peter Onuf, "Toward a Republican Empire: Interest and Ideology in Revolutionary America," *American Quarterly* 37 (1985): 496–531.

5. For women's waged work and household labor, see Alice Kessler-Harris, *Out to Work: A History of Wage-Earning Women in the United States* (New York: Oxford University Press, 1982) and Jeanne Boydston, *Home and Work: Housework, Wages, and the Ideology of Labor in the Early Republic* (New York: Oxford University Press, 1990). For benevolent, reform, and political volunteer work see Paula Baker, "The Domestication of Politics: Women and American Political Society, 1780–1920," *American Historical Review* 89 (1984): 620–47; Lori D. Ginzberg, *Women and the Work of Benevolence: Morality, Politics, and Class in the Nineteenth Century United States* (New Haven: Yale University Press, 1990), Mary P. Ryan, *Women in Public: Between Banners and Ballots, 1825–1880* (Baltimore: Johns Hopkins University Press, 1990); and Anne Firor Scott, *Natural Allies: Women's Associations in American History* (Urbana: University of Illinois Press, 1991).

6. For prerevolutionary and revolutionary Massachusetts see Robert Gross, *The Minutemen and Their World* (New York: Hill and Wang, 1976); Gary B. Nash, *The Urban Crucible: Social Change, Political Consciousness, and the Origins of the American Revolution* (Cambridge: Harvard University Press, 1979); and Gregory H. Nobles, *Divisions throughout the Whole: Politics and Society in Hampshire County, Massachusetts, 1740–1775* (Cambridge: Harvard University Press, 1983). For the era after the revolution see Harold Kirker and James Kirker, *Bulfinch's Boston, 1787–1817* (New York: Oxford University Press, 1964);

12   Francis X. Blouin, Jr., *The Boston Region, 1810–1850: A Study of Urbanization* (Ann Arbor: University of Michigan Press, 1980); and especially Robert F. Dalzell, *Enterprising Elite: The Boston Associates and the World They Made* (Cambridge: Harvard University Press, 1987).

7. For industrialization see, in addition to Dalzell, Thomas Dublin, *Women at Work: The Transformation of Work and Community in Lowell, Massachusetts, 1826–1860* (New York: Columbia University Press, 1979); Paul G. Faler, *Mechanics and Manufacturers in the Early Industrial Revolution: Lynn, Massachusetts, 1780–1860* (Albany: State University of New York Press, 1981); Jonathan Prude, *The Coming of Industrial Order: Town and Factory Life in Rural Massachusetts, 1810–1860* (Cambridge: Cambridge University Press, 1983); Christopher Clark, *The Roots of Rural Capitalism, Western Massachusetts, 1780–1860* (Ithaca: Cornell University Press, 1990); and Thomas Dublin, *Transforming Women's Work: New England Lives in the Industrial Revolution* (Ithaca: Cornell University Press, 1994).

8. For economic and demographic changes after 1820 see Peter Knights, *The Plain People of Boston, 1830–1860* (New York: Oxford University Press, 1973); Edward Pessen, *Riches, Class, and Power before the Civil War* (Lexington, Mass.: D. C. Heath and Company, 1973); and Peter R. Knights, *Yankee Destinies: The Lives of Ordinary Nineteenth-Century Bostonians* (Chapel Hill: University of North Carolina Press, 1991). For working-class resistance see Dublin, *Women at Work;* Mary H. Blewett, *Men, Women, and Work: Class, Gender, and Protest in the New England Shoe Industry, 1780–1910* (Urbana: University of Illinois Press, 1988); and Teresa Anne Murphy, *Ten Hours' Labor: Religion, Reform, and Gender in Early New England* (Ithaca: Cornell University Press, 1992). For early social reform and philanthropic movements in Massachusetts see Roger Lane, *Policing the City: Boston 1822–1840* (New York: Atheneum, 1971); Richard D. Brown, "The Emergence of Urban Society in Rural Massachusetts, 1760–1830," *Journal of American History* 61 (1974): 64–73; Anne M. Boylan, "Women in Groups: An Analysis of Women's Benevolent Organizations in New York and Boston, 1797–1840," *Journal of American History* 71 (1984): 779–97; and Conrad Edick Wright, *The Transformation of Charity in Postrevolutionary New England* (Boston: Northeastern University Press, 1990). Two general overviews of reform are David J. Rothman, *The Discovery of the Asylum: Social Order and Disorder in the New Republic* (Boston: Little Brown, 1971) and Walter I. Trattner, *From Poor Law to Welfare State: A History of Social Welfare in America* (New York: The Free Press, 1988).

9. I use the word "culture" here in the broadest sense, to describe shared assumptions and characteristics, as defined by Raymond Williams in *Keywords: A Vocabulary of Culture and Society* (New York: Oxford University Press, 1976), 76–82. I use the word "hegemonic" as defined by Antonio Gramsci and interpreted by T. Jackson Lears in "The Concept of Cultural Hegemony: Problems and Possibilities," *American Historical Review* 90 (1985): 567–93. In this reading

hegemony refers to all the ways—unconscious, subtle, and stated—that dominant social groups establish their values as universal and themselves as leaders, not through force but with consent. Cultures are not seen to be either monolithic or imposed; they are created, but they also emerge wherever there are people who share goals and values.

10. Linda Alcoff calls this approach "positionality." Linda Alcoff, "Cultural Feminism versus Post-Structuralism: The Identity Crisis in Feminist Theory," *Signs* 13 (1988): 405–36.

PART ONE

WOMEN AND WORK

VICTORIAN VALUES IN THE MARKETPLACE

Single Women and Work in Boston, 1800–1850

SUSAN L. PORTER

Lydia J——, daughter of a widow with five children, was admitted to the Boston Female Asylum, an orphanage run by women, in 1826, at the age of four. When she was eleven she was apprenticed to a Boston physician and his wife. On her eighteenth birthday, Lydia agreed to remain with the family as a salaried servant, but six months later she left "to learn the business of dressmaking." Lydia's specialized training in a needlework trade supported her until her marriage four years later and, in all likelihood, at various periods later in her life.[1]

Lydia's history is much like that of many other native-born, working-class female orphans who came of age in eastern seaboard cities in the third and fourth decades of the nineteenth century. However, her experience contrasts sharply with those of other poor orphaned young women born earlier and later in the century. This study examines the lives of 354 Boston women, born between 1792 and 1837, who shared a relatively constant childhood experience as inmates of the Boston Female Asylum (BFA), an orphanage for destitute children who had lost at least one parent. Their employment and marriage patterns illuminate the changes and continuities in women's work in the nineteenth century, and they also show the effects of a Victorian domestic ideology that became increasingly hegemonic over the first half of the century.

Working-class women registered and acted upon the economic, social, and cultural forces that ebbed and flowed in industrializing urban

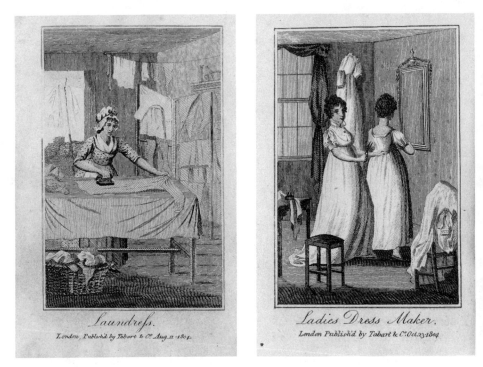

Laundress.

London, Publish'd by Tabart & C°. Aug. 11 1804.

Ladies Dress Maker.

London Publish'd by Tabart & C°. Oct. 23 1804.

Illustrations from *The Book of Trades; or, Library of Useful Arts* (London, 1804). Courtesy, Baker Library, Harvard Business School, Harvard University.

areas. Their work decisions, timing of marriage, and choice of husbands reflected a balance between their values and aspirations and their perception of market forces. Studies of working-class women have been limited by the difficulty of accessing data, especially before 1850, when censuses began to list the names of all household members; most analyses of women's work, therefore, are life-course projections based on cross-sectional evidence. This work represents part of a longitudinal study of a relatively stable population—BFA orphans from similar backgrounds who survived to adulthood.[2]

The Boston Female Asylum was a nonsectarian institution founded in 1800 and run entirely by women that admitted native-born female orphans (children with at least one dead parent) aged three to ten. The BFA was designed to offer an alternative intervention to placing very young children in families where they might be overworked or neglected. The founders hoped to reduce the vulnerability of disadvantaged young girls by educating and training them in the Asylum and then sending them during adolescence to live in the protective atmosphere of a family home.

From its inception the Asylum was overseen by a nine-member board of managers that hired a "matron" to run the home and school facility and coordinated admissions and placements. The children lived and studied in the Asylum for a minimum of two years and, generally, for several years. The Asylum program's second phase was an apprenticeship in a family that began in early adolescence and ended on the orphan's eighteenth birthday. Although during the half-century under study there were slight variations in timing, emphasis, and ideology as the board reacted to changing conditions, the program remained remarkably consistent.[3]

I have divided the orphans into four cohorts determined by decade of birth. The first cohort, seventy-five girls born between 1792 and 1805, reached maturity before 1825. The second group, ninety-two children born between 1806 and 1815, came of age between 1824 and 1833, while the ninety-six orphans born between 1816 and 1825 matured between 1834 and 1843. The final cohort, ninety-six orphans born between 1826 and 1837 (old enough to be admitted to the Asylum by 1840), entered the job market after 1844. Because the program remained relatively constant, the choices made by the orphans can be seen as responses to their perceptions of the relative advantages of the opportunities available to them.[4]

As a group, BFA orphans experienced particular disadvantages and advantages that may have affected their later work lives. On one hand, they had all lost at least one parent and could not be supported by their surviving parent or relatives. Many of them were, therefore, cut off from kin networks that might support or open doors for them as young adults. On the other hand, their Asylum experience provided the orphans with several years of physical protection (food, clothing, shelter), vocational training in sewing and housewifery, and a general education superior to that of most members of their class. It also exposed them to two sets of middle-class values—the ones the managers expressed, which emphasized self-reliance, moral fortitude, hard work, and habits of "industry and order," and the ones they exemplified, domestic comfort and stability.[5]

As a statistical analysis of the working lives of the orphans demonstrates, the BFA graduates made choices that seem to show their absorption of both the implied and expressed values of the Asylum program

Table 1   Father's occupation

| | 1792–1805 | | 1806–15 | | 1816–25 | | 1826–37 | |
Father's occupational level	N	Percentage	N	Percentage	N	Percentage	N	Percentage
Unskilled, menial	5	22.8	13	41.9	15	32.6	4	9.5
Semiskilled, service	10	45.4	9	29.0	6	13.0	10	23.8
Petty proprietors	2	9.1	1	3.2	5	10.9	2	4.8
Skilled	5	22.7	7	22.6	17	37.0	20	47.6
Clerical	0	0.0	1	3.2	3	6.5	2	4.8
Proprietors, ship captains	0	0.0	0	0.0	0	0.0	4	9.5
Totals	22	100	31	100	46	100	42	100

Sources: BFA Admissions Registers; Boston Directories, 1798–1850.
Note: Percentages may not add up to 100 due to rounding. Occupational classifications are based on Peter Knights, *Plain People of Boston, 1830–1860* (New York: Oxford University Press, 1973), 149–56.

and the ability to adapt them to their own uses. As they came of age, most assessed the opportunities available and used them to advantage. They changed jobs at will, were geographically mobile, and married well. Although they could not always avoid the kinds of tragedies that had befallen their families of origin, they did, in almost all cases, rise above the poverty they had suffered as children.

The BFA inmates came from families that were representative of Boston's working class. Like almost half of Boston's population, these families were poor or "near poor."[6] As has always been the case in poor households, both parents worked at jobs in and out of the household in their attempts to clothe and feed their families. Early in the century, when skilled crafts were regulated, most of the fathers followed unskilled or semiskilled occupations, with more than half the fathers of children born before 1816 working as day laborers, common sailors, or soldiers.[7] Although increasing numbers of fathers in the last two cohorts practiced "skilled" trades (Table 1), the combined effects of a volatile market, a devalued trade structure, and a high mortality rate made it difficult for mechanics and their families to avoid downward mobility.[8]

Mothers, like other antebellum working-class women, also earned money in and out of their homes. Most of their income probably came from outwork—taking in washing and ironing or sewing and mending—but because it was part-time and sporadic, they viewed this work as indistinguishable from their other domestic labor. Only 15 percent, or a total of fifty-nine, of the orphans' mothers identified themselves by wage work categories, and more than one-third of those described themselves simply as "labourers" (twenty-one or 35.6 percent of those

who list an occupation), while most of the rest were domestic servants or nurses (twenty-five or 42.5 percent).[9] For many mothers the struggle to make ends meet proved fatal. Louisa and Caroline S——'s mother, for example, took in laundry to augment the income of her husband, a painter "labouring for the support of his five children." She was killed when her dress caught fire "as she was sitting up at a late hour to finish some clothes she had been ironing." Mrs. S——'s demise was particularly dramatic, but many other mothers, especially widows, sickened and died from overwork as they struggled to keep their households intact by taking in needlework or laundry (seven or 11.9 percent).[10]

Economic and seasonal employment fluctuations in nineteenth-century Boston led to financial insecurity for working-class families, but high disease and mortality rates among adults and children made personal tragedy inescapable in all walks of life. Widowhood and orphanage were common; a death occurred in one of every eleven Boston families in any given year. Financially secure families could weather misfortune, but poor widows and widowers faced economic disaster when deprived of a spouse.[11]

The inmates of the Asylum, by definition, came from marginal families further disrupted by the death of a parent. Alternatives to institutional life for the orphans who came within the purview of the BFA were grim. Widowed mothers, in particular, with mean wages of $1.50 per week including board (for a domestic servant), could afford to support only one child at the typical Boston board rate of one dollar per week. Older children could be indentured or left to provide for themselves by picking chips (dried horse manure used for fuel) or selling matches on the street.

The foremost relief the BFA offered, then, was physical security—food, clothing, and shelter. Although frugal, these provisions allowed the orphan the luxury of spending her days learning "to read, write, and sew and the first rudiments of Arithmetic" in addition to "all kinds of domestic business." Some time after her eleventh birthday she would be apprenticed to a family to learn "housewifery" until the age of eighteen. When her contract expired the family was obligated to provide her, until 1841, with "two suits of clothes, one proper for Sunday, and the other for domestic business," and fifty dollars in addition to the clothing thereafter.[12]

The orphan's first paid employment came when she officially "cancelled" her articles of indenture on her eighteenth birthday. It was possible to locate 227 of the 354 BFA orphans at this turning point, and to trace 128 to at least one later place of employment. The orphan's position at eighteen most often represented the placement decision of the Asylum managers or the family of indenture rather than that of the orphan herself; her first decision making was the choice to move to a new position or remain with her family of indenture. This experience was a constant; yet the young women in each cohort made different choices that were the product of a complex interaction among market opportunities, changing ideological expectations, and each individual's perception of her needs and preferences.

Asylum graduates from the first cohort had few employment choices outside domestic service. The factory system had not yet become a readily available alternative. Although household production of cloth was in decline, the making of garments was still largely a home industry that used the labor of family members, servants, or a hired tailor or dressmaker. In this culture, most young women shared the work pattern of Mary O——, who, as one manager approvingly commented, "served her apprenticeship in an excellent family and . . . remained with these kind friends on wages several years."[13]

At eighteen years of age, 85.1 percent (forty of the forty-seven orphans for whom information is available) of the young women born before 1806 were living in households as domestic servants (five, or 10.6 percent, were living with relatives). Of the thirteen who can be traced further, all were servants in homes, twelve as general domestics and one as a cook. Eight of these thirteen women lived in the household of their apprenticeship on wages for lengthy periods before moving on. The two women who can be traced to a third job served for two years and five years before taking new jobs, also in domestic service. In addition, the geographical persistence rate was high (73.3 percent). Most of the children (85.0 percent) had been indentured in the Boston area and remained there as adults, while those sent elsewhere were equally likely (80.0 percent) to stay in the vicinity of their original placement. Their work lives consisted of a series of lateral moves. One woman from this cohort, Sally H——, worked for forty-one years as a "domestic and nurse" before retiring to Boston's Home for Aged Indigent Females.[14]

In comparison to other employment records these times of employment are remarkably long. Servants in that era were notoriously "unfaithful," and employers were often notoriously exacting. Boston attorney Willard Phillips, for example, kept an account of his servants for eighteen months from January 1818 to July 1819. During this interval, he hired nineteen servants, twelve female and seven male, fired sixteen and had three quit. The average time a female domestic stayed in his employ was 8.7 weeks (median 6 weeks), and males left even more quickly (mean 5.5 weeks, median 4.5 weeks). For Phillips, hiring, training, and discharging servants was a constant occupation.[15]

Yet, although the Asylum graduates were remarkably stable in contrast to Phillips's employees, they did not remain as long-term family retainers to their indentured mistresses. More than three-quarters (78.5 percent) left the household of their indenture within two years. Despite their lack of options, eventually the young women seemed to recognize that they might receive more respect and higher wages in a household where they were perceived as adults rather than children. In a new environment the young woman would be seen as an experienced servant rather than the "sweet, red-cheeked little girl" that one mistress's son later recalled. At least, she would labor in a household of her choice; at best, she could achieve a position of higher responsibility or income or find a position where she was treated more like a member of the family.[16]

In the early decades of the nineteenth century, as Faye Dudden has documented, domestic workers were often seen as "help" who worked along with their mistresses, ate with the family, and slept in the same part of the house, rather than as part of a "staff" that had little cross-class contact. Because servants were always in short supply, well-trained domestics could bargain effectively for privileges or money. The former BFA inmate could hope to become, like Mary M——, "a young woman of highly respectable character and situation."[17]

Respectability, negotiating skills, and good "situations" were important for self-supporting single women over the long term. The orphans born before 1805 remained unmarried for long enough to test these attributes. As far as can be determined, only half of the surviving women ever married (thirty-seven of seventy-five), while those who did, wed late in their twenties, after almost a decade of adult singlehood (mean age 28.1, median 26.2), a significantly later age than the general population.[18]

By the mid-1820s, the demand for servants increased as foreign trade and industrial investments transformed Boston from a stagnant town to a prosperous city. Between 1830 and 1860, Boston attracted both artisans and unskilled immigrant labor as a market developed for increasingly elaborate articles of conspicuous consumption—from elegant housing and lavishly carved and inlaid furniture to expensive and delicately worked ladies' clothing.[19]

During this period native-born women found new employment opportunities in the sewing trades, other crafts, and the new textile mills like Lowell's. These occupations offered women not only nondomestic work environments but also the chance to live with peers in a boardinghouse, to dress as they liked, to have leisure time, and to spend their earnings as they chose. Female immigrants, especially from Ireland, provided a ready source of domestic help, but nativist prejudice put the native-born at an advantage in the domestic and artisan job market, even when economic downturns affected the availability of jobs and competition contracted wages.[20]

By 1825 asylum graduates had many career options that had not existed for earlier generations of women workers.[21] None of these occupations was particularly lucrative, and few were genteel, but they did at least offer the worker a choice of the environment and conditions in which she would labor. She could choose to live alone (probably with peers in a boardinghouse) or with a family. She could work in a factory or shop, at home, or in someone else's household. If she learned a trade she could set her own hours and wear what she liked. Such options offered a sense of independence, even though they did not allow for radically different standards of living.

The occupational choices of the Asylum graduates born between 1805 and 1825 reflect the plethora of choices available to native-born working-class women. Jane C—— was typical of the middle cohorts. When she turned eighteen in 1834, her Cambridge mistress asked Jane to remain as an employee because "her character merits continued approbation." But Jane did not see herself as a long-term domestic; like Lydia J—— she left her employer after several months in order to apprentice herself to a needlework trade.[22] Like most of the women in the earlier cohort, Jane and Lydia remained in service for a short time after indenture, but unlike the earlier group, those who can be traced opted for new kinds of jobs thereafter. Fewer than one-third remained in domestic service (five of seventeen, or 29.4 percent), while twice as many (ten or 58.8 percent) became tradeswomen. One woman became an officeworker, and another, who had been adopted, worked as a teacher.[23]

More than a quarter of the Asylum graduates (nineteen of sixty-five,
29.2 percent of those for whom an occupation could be determined)
decided to take advantage of new employment opportunities immediately after their eighteenth birthdays. Eleven (16.9 percent) apprenticed to learn or found jobs as skilled workers in the sewing trades
(dressmaker, tailor, needleworker, mantua maker). Two entered other
skilled trades and six (9.2 percent) went to work in factories, where,
although wages were only slightly higher than in domestic service, hours
were clearly delimited and autonomy was guaranteed.[24]

The middle cohorts of Asylum graduates were, in addition, more
mobile than the earlier group. They stayed at the households of their
indenture only long enough to put aside some savings. Almost three-
quarters of the girls (sixty-one of eighty-three, 73.5 percent of those who
can be traced to a second address) left their places of indenture within a
year, and nine out of ten changed positions before they were twenty.

The women born between 1805 and 1825, even those who stayed in
service, relocated more often than their earlier counterparts. As the
century progressed, the young woman who finished her indenture was
increasingly unlikely to stay in the town or city where she had served her
term. In the second and third cohorts, when fewer than two-thirds (59.0
percent) were sent to Boston and surrounding towns, only slightly more
than half (51.7 percent) stayed where they had been sent, with many
girls returning to Boston, their childhood home.[25]

The girls born between 1805 and 1825 could expect to participate in
enough years of full-time work to make the investment in a trade apprenticeship worthwhile. As in the first cohort, only half (85 of 170) of
the women are known to have married, and those who did worked for
five or six years before they tied the nuptial knot (median age at marriage 23.3, mean 24.7).

With the maturation of the middle cohorts between 1825 and 1845, a
new and different pattern of life for the young Asylum graduate had
emerged. She was more likely to return to Boston, where more skilled
employment opportunities were available, than to stay where she had
been indentured. She probably would not spend her entire work life in
domestic service; instead she might live in the peer culture of a boardinghouse, engage in specialized crafts training, and plan for an independent future.

In a letter to the managers, one orphan expressed this independent mentality. Caroline H——, a child who was admitted to the Asylum in 1830 after her mother drowned herself in a "fit of desperation," thrived in the Asylum and was chosen (as a few girls were, over time) to spend her apprenticeship helping the matron in the institution. As she later recalled, on her eighteenth birthday, "the ladies of the Asylum very kindly offered to give me a trade, but I preferred living at service; lived in that capacity nearly two years and then thought I would try my fortune at something else. I procured a situation in a printing office which I liked very much."[26]

By the 1840s the shifting employment patterns of Asylum graduates had convinced even the BFA managers that their wards were better off in trades than in service. Thus, in the 1840s, the managers repeatedly offered to support graduates during their trade apprenticeships, and by 1851 they had modified the Asylum program to emphasize needlework. Although the managers recognized that "coarse" sewing was poorly recompensed, they were convinced that for "those whose practiced fingers can expertly and ingeniously perform the nicer and more difficult exercises of the needle, the facilities now offered for obtaining fine work, and increased demand for it, allow little cause of complaint either for want of employment or of scanty remuneration." The panic of 1837 and the influx of Irish immigrants had combined to increase competition in both the sewing trades and domestic service, depressing the value of piecework and wages. Although historians have not been able to analyze hierarchies in the sewing trades, they have argued that, in this market, native-born women used their advantage to monopolize nonservice jobs, leaving domestic work to the Irish. If this held true for BFA orphans, the pattern of abandoning domestic service for trades exhibited by many of the orphans in the second and third cohorts should have strengthened in the final cohort.[27]

However, girls born after 1825 made decisions that differed considerably from those made by earlier Asylum graduates. Mary B—— was typical. Admitted at the age of four, she was "well brought up" by her apprenticeship family in Medford, a Boston suburb. When she turned eighteen in 1846, she left the family for another domestic position in which she earned "good wages at respectable service." By 1850 she had left Boston to become a servant in the family of a young bootmaker and his wife in Stoughton, a rural community thirty miles from Boston. Late that year she married a Stoughton farmer and set up her own household. Like earlier Asylum graduates, Mary made deliberate em-

Table 2 Comparison of first and second jobs

| | First job | | | | Second job | | | |
| | 1806–25 | | 1826–37 | | 1806–25 | | 1826–37 | |
Occupation	N	Percentage	N	Percentage	N	Percentage	N	Percentage
Domestic servant	46	70.8	30	81.1	5	29.4	5	71.4
Skilled trade	12	18.5	2	5.4	10	58.8	1	14.3
Factory worker	6	9.2	3	8.1	0	0.0	1	14.3
Office, clerical	1	1.5	0	0.0	1	5.9	0	0.0
Teacher	0	0.0	2	5.4	1	5.9	0	0.0
Totals	65	100	37	100	17	100	7	100

Sources: BFA Records; Public Marriage Records; U.S. Census (1850).
Note: The domestic servant category includes cooks and nurses. Skilled trades represent dressmakers, tailors, needleworkers, mantuamakers, bookbinders, and basketmakers.

ployment choices based on her personal goals and assessment of opportunities. Although the Asylum managers encouraged their graduates after 1840 to enter trades and regularly offered to pay for specialized training, most of the young women, like Caroline H——, "preferred living at service." Thirty of thirty-seven of the orphans (81.1 percent) in the final cohort (see Table 2) chose to remain in domestic service after completing their indentures, even though they were offered alternatives and had all received fifty dollars in cash when they fulfilled their contracts. Only two of the women entered the sewing trades for their first job (5.4 percent as compared to 18.5 percent in the previous cohort), and most stayed in service when they changed jobs.[28]

Despite the fact that the changing market had led to increased diversification in women's employment opportunities, the women of the last cohort chose domestic service. The mobility demonstrated by this group was primarily geographical; job changes for orphans born after 1825 entailed locational changes of greater distance and more variety than in previous groups. Fewer girls born after 1825 stayed in the place where they had been indentured, even when that place was Boston, as the persistence rate decreased to 46.9 percent. Young women like Mary B—— may have seen rural areas or small towns as more advantageous for their present work needs and future comfort. The division of labor remained more egalitarian in small households, and less stratified localities might offer better social opportunities.

While it is impossible to explain these changes fully, several factors may have persuaded the women born after 1825 to stay in service rather than to train for trades. Certainly they would have recognized that, despite the optimism of Asylum managers about the sewing trades, most needleworkers were miserably underpaid and had little security. The panic of 1837 had led to decreased wages for women's work, and if, in addition, immigrant girls in Boston, like those in New York, were beginning to flood the market, price reductions for piecework would have made skilled trades even less appealing.[29]

While the Asylum manager's explicit encouragement of needlework is clear, and the orphan's perception of the market is imaginable, it is more difficult to assess the influence the orphan's relations may have had on her job choices. None of the orphans was ever entirely cut off from her surviving kin, but early Asylum placement policy discouraged indenture to relatives. Eventually, however, the Asylum managers began to permit some children whose families had stabilized to return home for indenture, to be apprenticed to relatives who were financially secure artisans, and, when problems arose with a placement (as they often did), to finish their indenture with relations. The S—— twins, for example, had been admitted to the Asylum in 1833, at the age of five, after their mother died and their father, a sea captain, was lamed in an accident. By 1838, however, their "father had . . . recovered his health and married a very worthy woman. He finds himself able to maintain his family, now comfortably settled in Hingham. He wants his children bound to him instead of strangers."[30]

At the age of eighteen, 20.3 percent of the girls in the third cohort (fifteen of seventy-four) and almost half of those in the fourth cohort (twenty-nine, or 46 percent of sixty-three for whom information exists) were living with kin (Table 3).

By the 1840s, economically secure families kept their daughters at home until they married. Victorian ideals centered on the home and family rather than the marketplace.[31] As far as can be determined, very few of the children who lived with their relatives engaged in full-time employment outside the household. Only two of these orphans in the third cohort and one in the fourth claimed an occupation when they turned eighteen, and only five of those born between 1815 and 1825 and six of those born after 1825 ever took jobs outside the household.[32]

Hannah and Mary S—— spent their youths in a home where they were daughters rather than servants. When they became adults they remained, performing domestic labor or, perhaps, sporadic outwork for their families. Their help was undoubtedly welcome; most relatives'

Table 3   Indenture to relatives by placement

Year of birth	First placement (percentages)	N	Last placement (percentages)	N
1792–1805	6.7	75	10.6	47
1806–15	5.4	92	9.3	43
1816–25	14.6	96	20.3	43
1826–37	29.2	96	46.0	63

Sources: BFA Records; U.S. Census (1850).

households were headed by couples with children and many contained boarders and other nonnuclear family members.[33]

In a secure domestic environment, the hopes of the S—— twins and other orphans seemed to center on the primary Victorian domestic ambition—marriage. Hannah S—— married a Dedham shoemaker at the age of eighteen, while Mary wed a Boston carpenter at twenty-one. When the census taker called on Mary less than a year later, she was already a mother in her own home (shared with her brother-in-law and his wife) in East Boston. Marriage was not a goal that required work experience; in fact, youth and naïveté were advantages in the marriage market. In marriage the skills, discipline, and efficiency the orphan learned in the Asylum would be applied to promote her own family's happiness and independence rather than that of her employer.

For the orphans of the third cohort, growing up with relatives seemed to encourage early marriage; those who were apprenticed to relatives married significantly earlier than the rest; young women of the last cohort living with kin also married young. This pattern was predictable for the women whose families could provide for them, but, surprisingly, the orphans born after 1825 who could not count on family support tied the nuptial knot almost as quickly (Table 4).

While earlier Asylum graduates had married significantly later than the general population (with the exception of those bound to relatives in the third cohort), the girls born after 1825 wed at ages close to first marriage norms. As Thomas Dublin suggested in *Women at Work*, a higher age at marriage for working women demonstrated independence. Working women lived away from their families, knew something of the world, and could make rational judgments about prospective husbands and the choices open to them. The lower marriage age and employment patterns of the final cohort may reflect the opposite—a desire for domestic security rather than independence.[34]

VICTORIAN VALUES IN THE MARKETPLACE

Table 4   Age at marriage

	Sent to relatives		Not sent to relatives	
	Median (Mean) Age	Number	Median (Mean) Age	Number
1816–25	22.0 (22.9)	13	24.0 (26.4)	34
1826–37	22.0 (22.1)	15	22.6 (23.4)	33

Sources: BFA Records; Public Marriage Records.

Most of the orphans needed to support themselves when they came of age. Perhaps because they had a domestic future in mind, these graduates chose jobs in service. As Alice Kessler-Harris has observed, after 1840 "women did not cease to work but . . . their wage work was overlain with ambiguity." Service would provide experience in a domestic environment, honing the skills that would, it was hoped, be applied after marriage.[35] Well-educated native-born women would be able to bargain well in the servants' market, perhaps avoiding the more unpleasant household duties, or at least earning higher wages than untrained immigrants. If marriage could not be achieved, then at least the woman would be living in a home, the proper, respectable place for a Victorian woman.

By 1840 the respectability that the Asylum had always touted took on new meaning as domestic ideology linked marriage, home, and family with propriety and morality and condemned those who were forced to remain in the labor force. Females who worked were no longer considered "independent"; they were seen as lesser women. Because men were expected to support their dependents on a family wage, women's earnings were regarded as supplemental, and wages and working conditions in female occupations deteriorated.[36]

Given these developments it is not surprising that the orphans of the final cohort preferred marriage over work. The unmarried working-class woman could support herself, but she was unlikely to prosper or achieve security. Prolonged illness, in fact, often led to destitution, especially among orphans who lacked kin networks for support. Lucinda E—— and Theresa C——, for example, were forced by illness to leave their respective jobs in service and a factory. "Only able to perform such light duties in a family as claim but small compensation," they quickly exhausted their savings. The BFA managers obtained free hospital beds for them and paid their board until they died.[37]

Female Asylum graduates of all cohorts may have seen marriage as a chance for security. If an orphan chose her husband carefully, he might provide her with financial as well as emotional security. A husband would give the woman who had grown up in an institution a home, a partner in life, and a source of protection against the world.

Most Asylum graduates did pick their husbands wisely. They married skilled artisans who were trained in trades that required a significant time investment to learn and would pay a reasonable return. Seventy-one of 120 husbands (59.2 percent of those whose occupations are known) were tradesmen. Thirty-one were in the building trades, nineteen in the clothing trades, and the rest were engaged in the manufacture of products ranging from furniture to horseshoes.[38] Fewer than one orphan in ten married an unskilled worker (eleven, or 9.2 percent). One in seven married men who were proprietors of either a store or a farm (14.2 percent). Four women married men in higher-status professions—a minister, two merchants, and a sea captain (3.3 percent). Thus, the training that the orphans received in the Asylum may have helped them attain mobility through marriage.

The poverty and tragedy the orphans experienced before they entered the Asylum may have left them determined to achieve security. As Caroline H——, daughter of an alcoholic hackman, happily reported two years after her marriage to a housewright, "I have a very kind husband and am comfortably settled." About 87 percent of the orphans (thirty-nine of the forty-five orphans for whom information about both fathers' and husbands' occupation exists) married men whose occupations carried equal or higher status than those of their fathers, while 36 percent married husbands of significantly higher economic standing.[39]

These statistics were true for all the Asylum graduates, but the last cohort, more attuned to a domestic ideology than their earlier counterparts, seemed to see marriage as an alternative to work. Because, so far as can be determined, only half the BFA orphans wed, this may not have been the most advantageous strategy. Choosing positions that offered marriage opportunities rather than skills toward a wage-earning future might not serve lifelong workers well, and even those who married could find it difficult to supplement the family wage or sustain their own family of orphans if their husbands should die, desert them, or become incompetent.[40] As all orphans knew, marriage was no guarantee of security.

In addition, marriage of any kind, upwardly mobile or not, was increasingly unlikely for eastern seaboard women, as female-male sex ratios, already uneven in 1800, became more and more skewed. As an 1853 article in the *New York Daily Tribune* warned, "to tell our . . . poor Young Women . . . that the end of their existence is to be good wives and mothers, is to insult them most stupidly. . . . It is a decree of Fate that a very large proportion of the Young Women of our older and more easterly States must remain single, while necessity and self-respect alike forbid that they shall eat the bread of idleness."[41]

The idea that widespread dispersion of domestic ideology could mean that working-class women might aspire to retirement rather than wage work raised the spectre of social disorder among middle-class groups of all stripes who saw "industry and order"—useful, structured work—as the economic and social foundation on which the republic either stood or foundered.

Noting the domestic orientation of later Asylum graduates, the BFA angrily remarked in 1857:

ill-judged remarks are sometimes thoughtlessly made to this class of children, which might lead them to suppose marriage the chief end of their existence, a mistake which some of them are quite likely enough to fall into of their own accord. Persons who speak thus do not appear to consider that in most cases the chances of their circumstances being improved by marriage is at best a doubtful one; and at all events, the thing of most importance to impress on their minds is, that they are to grow up faithful, true-hearted women in the station to which Providence has called them, whatever that may be.[42]

The managers' stated concern, of course, was that their wards might see marriage as a panacea. Years of experience showed that it was almost impossible for unskilled women to provide for themselves and their dependents, and the managers remained convinced that, whatever the circumstances, tradeswomen could negotiate the labor market more successfully. Needlework might be poorly paid, but it was useful as a supplement or an emergency resource. More lucrative than other home-based services, such as washing and ironing, it could be performed in conjunction with child care and housework.

The managers' language, however, reflects the complicated meanings of womanhood in the nineteenth century as constructed for the different classes. Self-reliance was an important value for the benevolent women who founded and ran institutions. They believed, as Judith Sar-

gent Murray had argued a half-century earlier, that all women should be well trained in self-reliance, whether they married or not, through a
"useful" rather than "ornamental" education that would create good
"republican mothers."[43]

Yet there was a problem with disseminating hegemonic middle-class
expectations among the working class, as the choices made by the final
cohort make clear. The managers' mixed feelings about marriage are
revealing; they express their ambivalence about working-class men, the
distance between their own expectations and those of their wards, and
their recognition that the "station to which Providence" would call most
of their charges would not allow for Victorian standards of domestic
comfort on a family wage. The "faithful, true-hearted women" of the
working class would spend their lives being workers whether or not they
became wives.

Middle-class men and women, whether sympathetic or opposed to
charity, were determined to make poor women understand that they
could not rely on either middle-class values or institutions to support
them in hard times. Despite democratic rhetoric, there was a difference
between a "mill girl" and a "lady."[44]

In addition, young women who saw work as a temporary condition
bought into a dichotomous, gendered view that served the needs of the
proprietory classes rather than their own self-interest. As Alice Kessler-
Harris has argued, women who saw their work as short-term would
accept low wages and poor working conditions. In this way, working-
class women became doubly disadvantaged—by their own self-image
and by the conditions of work that these expectations permitted.[45]

The Asylum graduates, however, made their own decisions, using
their training in ways they, not the managers, considered proper. The
middle-class values that the managers pressed upon them as children
and those they observed among their mistresses must have offered these
young women the hope that they might have lives similar to those of
their mentors, with marriages and families of their own. Their experience in the work world reinforced this ambition, leading many to make
occupational decisions aimed toward marriage rather than long-term
work. Thus, the orphans of the fourth cohort adapted the values taught
in the Asylum to their desires, whether or not they realistically reflected
their long-range needs.

Asylum graduates stood on the threshold between two worlds—the
one in which they were born and the one in which they grew up. As they

VICTORIAN VALUES IN THE MARKETPLACE

entered the workforce they made choices that reflected their attempts
to order and reconcile these worlds into life experiences that reflected
the best of both. For the first cohort this meant bargaining effectively
for domestic jobs on the basis of skills rather than paternalism; for
the second and third, it meant leaving service to become independent
tradeswomen. The fourth cohort recognized that all waged workers'
independence was illusory and chose to work in domestic environments
that seemed more "respectable." In all cases, their judgments were accu-
rate reflections of the marketplace and its increasingly ambivalent message for women.

As the "cult of domesticity" filtered down to the working class
through the penny press and magazines, the dualism experienced first-
hand by Asylum orphans spread among other working women, who,
although they may have understood that the market used rather than
served them, could only continue to struggle along in the hope that they
might escape. Middle-class employers and reformers retaliated by cast-
ing increasingly shrill aspersions on poor women for refusing to see
themselves as long-term workers at the same time as they continued to
align respectability with domesticity. The experience of the BFA orphans
thus provides a case study of the conflict between hegemonic cultural
values and the strictly economic values of the marketplace.[46]

Notes

1. A slightly different version of this chapter was published in *Social Science History* 17, no. 1 (Spring 1993), 109–34. Meeting notes, Oct. 1826, May 1840, Dec. 1840, Boston Female Asylum Record Book 3, Massachusetts State Library. Record of Marriage, Commonwealth of Massachusetts, Division of Vital Statistics. For more on the Boston Female Asylum, see Susan L. Porter, "The Benevolent Asylum—Image and Reality: The Care and Training of Female Orphans in Boston, 1800–1840" (Ph.D. diss., Boston University, 1984).

2. Thomas Dublin's study of Lowell mill girls is based on employee records from the Hamilton Company in July 1836 and vital statistics from three New Hampshire communities that sent operatives to Lowell. Carol Groneman's research on working women in New York City's sixth ward and Laurence Glasco's work on the life cycles of ethnic groups in Buffalo rely on the 1855 census. Peter Knights, in his pioneering longitudinal work on mobility in Boston between 1830 and 1860, bypassed women entirely. Thomas Dublin, *Women at Work: The Transformation of Work and Community in Lowell, Massachusetts, 1826–1860* (New York: Columbia University Press, 1979); Carol Groneman,

" 'She Earns as a Child—She Pays as a Man' ": Women Workers in a Mid-
Nineteenth-Century New York City Community," in Richard L. Ehrlich, ed.,
Immigrants in Industrial America (Charlottesville: University Press of Virginia,
1977); Laurence A. Glasco, "The Life Cycles and Household Structure of
American Ethnic Groups: Irish, Germans, and Native-Born Whites in Buffalo,
New York, 1855," *Journal of Urban History* 1 (1975): 339–64; Peter Knights,
Plain People of Boston, 1830–1860 (New York: Oxford University Press, 1973).

3. The Asylum admitted both Protestant and Catholic children until 1829,
when the Catholic bishop insisted that no more children of his faith enter an
institution where the children used Protestant texts and attended Protestant
services. Meeting notes, Nov., Dec. 1829, BFA Record Book 3.

4. Orphans were traced by linking information obtained from the records of
the Boston Female Asylum (meeting notes and Registers) with other public
and private records. The only discernible bias in this method is the low success
rate for subjects with common names. Because many of the orphans had such
names, the success rate was greatly reduced. The study discusses the 354 girls
who survived to the age of eighteen, of 359 who were indentured. Record
Books 1–5 and the Registers are in the collections of the Massachusetts State
Library, Massachusetts State House, Boston. Public records used include unpublished vital statistics for Boston, 1629–1848, available at the Boston City
Registrar's Office, Boston City Hall; published volumes of vital records for 180
towns in Massachusetts under the title *Vital Records of [the Various Towns and
Cities], Massachusetts;* and the "Records of Births, Deaths, and Marriages, 1841–
1903" kept at the Massachusetts Division of Vital Statistics, Boston. In addi-
tion the U.S. Census (1850), Records Pertaining to Boston Churches, 1629 to
1850 (Boston City Registrar's Office), and the Records of the Home for Aged
Women (Schlesinger Library on the History of Women in America, Radcliffe
College) were useful. For a further discussion of methodology, see Porter, "The
Benevolent Asylum—Image and Reality" appendix A.

5. This is not to deny that, as Christine Stansell and others have argued,
working-class women had a separate culture that may have operated outside of
middle-class values. Christine Stansell, *City of Women: Sex and Class in New
York, 1789–1860* (New York: Alfred A. Knopf, 1986).

6. Allan Kulikoff argues that by 1790, the poor and "near poor," those "living
at or near the minimum level of subsistence," made up 37 to 47 percent of the
population; "near poor" includes widows, seamen, laborers, and poor artisans.
Allan Kulikoff, "The Progress of Poverty in Revolutionary Boston," *William
and Mary Quarterly,* 3d ser., 28 (1971): 383–84. Although BFA children were
required to be native born, many of their parents were recently arrived immigrants and migrants.

7. As Peter Knights emphasizes, many workers were recent migrants with
few connections in the city; this group was most likely to come within the
purview of the BFA. Statistics about family backgrounds are based on the total

36   number of 386 orphans who entered the BFA between 1800 and 1840, not the 359 who were indentured or the 354 who lived to be eighteen. Eleven of twenty-two fathers in the first cohort (50.0 percent), eighteen of thirty-one in the second cohort (58 percent), eighteen of forty-six in the third cohort (39 percent), and twelve of forty-two in the last cohort (28.6 percent) worked as laborers, sailors, or soldiers. Sailors and soldiers were categorized as semiskilled, laborers as unskilled. Knights, *Plain People of Boston,* esp. chapter 5.

    8. As the BFA became financially secure, it admitted all eligible children, not just the most desperate cases; thus families of slightly higher economic status are more heavily represented. However, as recent work on apprenticeship has shown, by 1830 occupational classifications had become less indicative of income and status than earlier. W. J. Rorabaugh, *The Craft Apprentice: From Franklin to the Machine Age in America* (New York: Oxford University Press, 1986) and Bruce Laurie, *Artisans into Workers: Labor in Nineteenth-Century America* (New York: Noonday Press, 1989), especially chapters 1 and 2.

    9. Jeanne Boydston, "To Earn Her Daily Bread," *Radical History Review* 35 (1986): 6–25; Jane H. Pease and William H. Pease, *Ladies, Women, and Wenches: Choice and Constraint in Antebellum Charleston and Boston* (Chapel Hill: University of North Carolina Press, 1990); Mary H. Blewett, *Men, Women, and Work: Class, Gender and Protest in the New England Shoe Industry, 1780–1910* (Urbana: University of Illinois Press, 1988), chapter 4; Thomas Dublin, "Women and Outwork in a Nineteenth-Century New Town: Fitzwilliam, New Hampshire, 1830–1850," in Stephen Hahn and Jonathon Prude, *The Countryside in the Age of Capitalist Transformation: Essays in the Social History of Rural America* (Chapel Hill: University of North Carolina Press, 1985), chapter 2.

    10. Meeting notes, Aug. 1838, BFA Record Book 4.

    11. Maris Vinovskis, "Mortality Rates and Trends in Massachusetts before 1860," *Journal of Economic History* 32 (1972): 204, 213. Carol Strole, in "'Beyond One's Control': Life Course and the Tragedy of Class, Boston, 1800 to 1900," *Journal of Family History* 11 (1986): 43–54, argues that class affected mortality rates in ways that increased the level of orphanage before maturity for working-class females.

    12. "Announcement," *Boston Gazette,* October 27, 1800. Public poor relief for orphaned children usually meant an early indenture. Indenture contract for Mary T——, September 26, 1820, Shattuck Family Papers, Massachusetts Historical Society. In 1841 the managers voted to "substitute . . . the sum of $50 for the clothing now required at the end of the apprenticeship." Meeting notes, Nov. 1841, BFA Record Book 1.

    13. Rolla Milton Tryon, *Household Manufacturers in the United States, 1640–1860* (Chicago: University of Chicago Press, 1917), p. 244, also pp. 242–302. See also Edith Abbott, *Women in Industry* (New York: D. Appleton and Company, 1910). [Abigail Frothingham Wales,] *Reminiscences of the Boston Female Asylum* (Boston: Eastburn's Press, 1844), 47. It was possible to obtain some employ-

ment information for 135 Asylum graduates (37.2 percent of the total number
of girls who were alive and unmarried at the age of 18, N = 363). The primary
sources for this data are the Asylum records and public marriage records for the
state of Massachusetts (which list address and ask for occupation) and the 1850
U.S. Census. Fifty-three women were unemployed and living with relatives
(14.6 percent) when their indentures expired. Work information, therefore,
was available for 43.5 percent of those who were working. While such evidence
as exists indicates that most of these women moved on to other paid work, it is
extremely difficult to create employment histories. Data are available for only
13.2 percent of the women for a second job (forty-eight) and for seven women
for a third job. The 386 cases in this study represent not a sample but the entire
population of the BFA from 1800 to 1840. As earlier studies have demonstrated,
the success rate for tracing men in the nineteenth century is poor; for women it
is even worse because they did not appear in censuses by name until 1850, were
not listed in city directories or tax lists except when they were widows or
proprietors, and changed their names when they married. Common surnames
presented the most insurmountable obstacle, and no attempt was made to find
women who left Massachusetts. For other tracing attempts with Boston records, see Knights, *Plain People of Boston,* and Stephan Thernstrom, *The Other
Bostonians: Poverty and Progress in the American Metropolis, 1880–1900* (Cambridge: Harvard University Press, 1973).

14. Sally H——, April 30, 1857, Register of the Home for Aged Indigent
Females, Schlesinger Library, Radcliffe College. These figures may understate
mobility because they come primarily from Massachusetts vital records. It was
difficult to trace common names and subjects who left the state. However, it is
unlikely that the error is large enough to affect the argument because it occurs
evenly across all four cohorts.

15. These domestics included three cooks, two chambermaids, and one
tailor. Wages for the servants of both sexes were within the norms, ranging
from $.75 to $1.25 per week for females and $2.00 to $2.70 per week for males
(including board, which Phillips valued at $3.00 per week for an adult male).
Nevertheless, he had difficulty finding servants to his satisfaction and keeping
those he liked. Willard Phillips, "Account of Servants, 1818–1819," written into
a copybook called *The Writer's Assistant,* by Joseph Seavy (Willard Phillips
Papers, Massachusetts Historical Society). According to Daniel Sutherland, the
situation described by Phillips was typical for the United States between 1800
and 1920. Daniel E. Sutherland, *Americans and Their Servants* (Baton Rouge:
Louisiana State University Press, 1981), pp. 9–25. For wage comparisons see
Stanley Lebergott, *Manpower in Economic Growth: The American Record since
1800* (New York: McGraw-Hill, 1964).

16. Letter from John Gray, Jan. 1845, BFA Record Book 4.

17. Faye Dudden, *Serving Women: Household Service in Nineteenth-Century
America* (Middletown, Conn.: Wesleyan University Press, 1983). Mary M——

38　　had been apprenticed in Westminster, but six years later she was living in Westborough. Meeting notes, Sept. 1828, BFA Record Book 3.

18. For statistics on marriage age from 1845, see Thomas Monahan, "One Hundred Years of Marriages in Massachusetts," *American Journal of Sociology* 56 (1951): 541. Monahan calculated mean age at marriage for women between 1845 and 1854 as 23.42 years, median 22.4. The mean and median for the sixty-two orphans who were wed during the same period are 24.4 and 22.6. There are no comparable figures for the earlier period, but the typical marriage age in one rural early nineteenth-century town was the mid-twenties. Nancy Osterud and John Fulton, "Family Limitation and Age at Marriage: Fertility Decline in Sturbridge, Mass., 1730–1850," *Population Studies* 30 (1976): 481–89. Marriage statistics were calculated primarily from Massachusetts vital records; rates may be understated because of common names and the difficulty of tracing those who left the state. However, because this issue is constant across the four cohorts, the error should not affect the argument.

19. For a recent treatment of Boston during this period, see William H. Pease and Jane H. Pease, *The Web of Progress: Private Values and Public Styles in Boston and Charlestown, 1828–1843* (New York: Oxford University Press, 1985).

20. This change has been well documented. See, for example, Oscar Handlin, *Boston's Immigrants* (New York: Atheneum, 1974); Edward Pessen, *Riches, Class and Power before the Civil War* (Lexington: D. C. Heath and Company, 1973); Walter Muir Whitehill, *Boston: A Topographical History* (Cambridge: Harvard University Press, 1968), chapters 4–7; Kulikoff, "The Progress of Inequality"; Robert A. McCaughey, "From Town to City: Boston in the 1820's," *Political Science Quarterly* 88 (1973): 191–213.

21. Edith Abbott found more than one hundred industrial occupations that employed women in 1837, including "the manufacture of boxes, bedcords, and clothes lines, blacking, children's carriages, cards, chocolate, cordage and twine, candles and soap, cork cutters, cigars and tobacco, chairs, chair stuff, crackers, carpets, curtains, cheese and butter, copperas, furs, furniture, flax, flint glass, fishing nets, gimlets, hair cloths and hair beds, hosiery, hooks and eyes, india rubber, lead, lead pencils, lace, letter boxes, locks, looking glasses, paper hangings, pails, rakes, stocks, tacks, types, thread and sewing silk, umbrellas, window blinds; and women were also engaged in millinery, tailoring, and mantuamaking, making of instruments, wool-pulling, gold-beating, silk and wool dying, lithographing, bed-binding and upholstering; and they were also employed as silversmiths, and in publishing houses" as bookbinders and typesetters (Abbott, *Women in Industry,* 66; see also 65–81).

22. Meeting notes, Aug. 1834 and July 1835, BFA Record Book 3. Jane supported herself as a tradeswoman for ten years until she married a Boston plumber. Marriage may have released her from the wage-earning workforce; according to Knights, her husband's trade placed her in the upper half of Boston's economic strata. Knights, *Plain People of Boston,* table 5-1, 84.

23. I have collapsed the two middle cohorts for the purposes of this discussion because their employment and marriage patterns were very similar.

24. In the second cohort, three young women took factory jobs and four entered needlework trades (in all, twenty-one were traced). In the third cohort, three took positions as operatives, while seven entered sewing trades, one became a bookbinder, and another a basket maker (total: forty-three). Lebergott values the labor of a domestic at thirty-two cents per day in New England (including the value of board) and that of a female factory worker at thirty-two to forty-one cents per day (*Manpower in Economic Growth*, table A-31). Wages for needlework varied according to the skill of the worker and the delicacy of the work produced. Plain sewing paid a full-time wage of only a dollar per week in the 1830s, but other skilled women were reported to earn as much as seventy-five cents per day. Carol Lasser, "Mistress, Maid, and Market: The Transformation of Domestic Service in New England, 1790–1870" (Ph.D. diss., Harvard University, 1981), 73, Pease and Pease, *Ladies, Women, and Wenches*, 45–46.

25. Of eighty-nine orphans who could be traced, twenty-two indentured in Boston and surrounding towns remained, eleven left the city (five to live in adjacent towns), and nineteen returned to the city.

26. Caroline H——, meeting notes, April 1830, BFA Record Book 3; letter to the Managers Dec. 1844, BFA Record Book 4.

27. See Caroline H——, letter to the Managers, Dec. 1844, BFA Record Book 4. Annual Report, Sept. 1851, BFA Record Book 4. Stansell, *City of Women*, chapter 8; Kessler-Harris, *Out to Work*, 46–56; Dudden, *Serving Women*, 59–71.

28. Meeting notes, Dec. 1846; letter to the Managers, Dec. 1844; BFA Record Book 4. Two women made lateral moves that no orphan in the previous cohort had chosen, one becoming a cook and the other a nurse. The only domestic servant for whom a third position is known comes from this cohort. Teaching appears in this cohort because several children were adopted after 1830 and were given advanced schooling. While teaching was the only middle-class occupation open to women in this period, historians have primarily regarded it negatively. From a working-class viewpoint, however, poorly paid teaching was more respectable and less physically taxing than equally poorly paid manual labor. See, for example, Richard Bernard and Maris Vinovskis, "The Female School Teacher in Antebellum Massachusetts," *Journal of Social History* 10 (1977): 332–45.

29. Groneman, "She Earns as a Child"; Christine Stansell, *City of Women*, 110–13; Alice Kessler-Harris, *Out to Work*, chapter 3. For Boston wages and occupational choices see Pease and Pease, *Ladies, Women and Wenches*, 45–50. For two revealing contemporary analyses of the employment market at a slightly later date, see Virginia Penny, *The Employments of Women: A Cyclopedia of Woman's Work* (Boston: Walker, Wise and Company, 1863) and "Needle and

Garden, The Story of a Seamstress Who Laid Down Her Needle and Became a Strawberry-Girl," *Atlantic Monthly* 15 (January–October 1865).

30. Meeting notes, Nov. 1837 and April 1838, BFA Record Book 3.

31. The literature documenting this change is voluminous. For two very different examples, see Mary P. Ryan, *Cradle of the Middle Class: The Family in Oneida County, New York, 1790–1865* (Cambridge: Cambridge University Press, 1981) and Frances Cogan, *All American Girl: The Ideal of Real Woman-hood in Mid-Nineteenth-Century America* (Athens: University of Georgia Press, 1989). On differential ethnic employment statistics, see Glasco, "Life Cycles and Household Structure."

32. Three in the third cohort entered domestic service and two entered sewing trades. In the final group, five entered service and one became a teacher.

33. Of the thirteen households of relatives that were traced in the 1850 Census, only five were nuclear. Five contained boarders, two held extended family, and three housed a servant. Three had children more than ten years younger than the orphan.

34. Dublin's sample of Hamilton mill hands, whose birth dates are compara-ble to the BFA's second cohort, married at a mean age of 26.3 (median 25.2), figures similar to the ones for Asylum women. Dublin, *Women at Work*, 52.

35. Kessler-Harris, *Out to Work*, 52. Julie Matthaei submits that Victorian girls saw "labor force participation as an 'adolescent stage' which, they hoped, would pass." In 1897, Lucy Salmon found that girls chose domestic service because it was more "natural" and had some of the qualities of a mother-daughter relationship. Julie A. Matthaei, *An Economic History of Women in America: Women's Work, the Sexual Division of Labor, and the Development of Capitalism* (New York: Schocken Books, 1982), 150; Lucy M. Salmon, *Domestic Service* (New York: Macmillan Company, 1897), 137.

36. Kessler-Harris, *Out to Work*, 67–72.

37. Meeting notes, Jan. 1839 and Dec. 1844, BFA Record Book 4. Another BFA orphan died in Boston's House of Industry. Eliza K—— W——, "Boston Alpha-betical Death Records, 1629 to 1848 Inclusive," 1836, Boston City Registrar's Office.

38. The list includes ten carpenters, seven house wrights, four painters, three plumbers, two masons, two stucco workers, two stonecutters, a brickmaker, seventeen shoemakers, and two tailors.

39. Letter to the Managers, Dec. 1844, BFA Record Book 4. In the first eighty years of the BFA's history, only two former inmates of the Asylum had their own daughters admitted to the institution. Meeting notes, Aug. 1838 and July 1842, Record Book 4.

40. On the basis of Massachusetts records and meeting notes, it can be determined that 46.7 percent of the orphans born before 1805 (35 of 75) mar-ried, while half of those born from 1806 to 1825 (85 of 170) and those born after 1825 (48 of 96) wed. As many orphans may have left the state—and procuring

out-of-state marriage records was difficult—this figure may be low. Matthaei,
Economic History of Women, 183.

41. *New York Daily Tribune,* June 18, 1853, as quoted in Matthaei, *Economic History of Women*, 152.

42. Annual Report, September 1857, BFA Record Book 5.

43. Judith Sargent Murray, *The Gleaner* 1, no. 17, pp. 167–68. The term "republican mother" was coined by Linda Kerber in "Daughters of Columbia: Educating Women for the Republic, 1787–1805" in Stanley Elkins and Eric McKitrick, *The Hofstadter Aegis* (New York, 1974), pp. 36–59. See also Linda Kerber, *Women of the Republic: Intellect and Ideology in Revolutionary America* (Chapel Hill: University of North Carolina Press, 1980); Ruth H. Bloch, "American Feminine Ideals in Transition: The Rise of the Moral Mother, 1785–1815," *Feminist Studies* 4 (1978): 101–26; and Mary Beth Norton, *Liberty's Daughters: The Revolutionary Experience of American Women, 1750–1800* (Boston: Little Brown, 1980).

44. Gerda Lerner, "The Lady and the Mill Girl: Changes in the Status of Women in the Age of Jackson," *American Studies* 10 (1960): 5–15.

45. Alice Kessler-Harris, "Where are the Organized Women Workers?" *Feminist Studies* 3 (Fall 1975): 92–110.

46. A contemporary novel, *Needle and Garden,* exemplifies this conflict. The protagonist, after much discourse about the inequities of needlework, leaves sewing to grow strawberries on her small family plot. Just as her business takes off, her acumen attracts a wealthy suitor who rewards her by removing her to a new world of comfort and domesticity, where gardening provides pleasure rather than a livelihood.

THE FEMINIZATION OF TEACHING IN MASSACHUSETTS

A Reconsideration

JAMES M. WALLACE

In 1845, in his eighth annual report as secretary of the Massachusetts Board of Education, Horace Mann declared:

> One of the most extraordinary changes which have taken place in our schools, during the last seven years, consists in the great proportionate increase in the number of female teachers employed. . . .
>
> This change . . . I believe to be in accordance with the dictates of the soundest philosophy. Is not woman destined to conduct the rising generation, of both sexes, at least through all the primary stages of education? Has not the author of nature pre-adapted her, by constitution, and faculty, and temperament, for this noble work? What station of beneficent labor can she aspire to, more honorable, or more congenial to every pure and generous impulse? In the great system of society, what other part can she act, so intimately connected with the refinement and purification of the race?[1]

In numerous statements of this sort over the years, Mann appealed to women to prepare themselves for teaching and encouraged school committees to hire them. Mann's rhetoric on this subject is suffused with the nineteenth-century idea that women had a special role to play in the ethical sphere—that their influence on the young, and thus on society, would be morally uplifting.[2]

Even some hard-headed school committees expressed sentimental

A New England schoolroom. Painting by Charles Frederick Bosworth, ca. 1852. Courtesy, Massachusetts Historical Society.

notions concerning the moral superiority of women teachers.[3] The committee of the town of Petersham in Worcester County reported on the effectiveness of the women who had taught in their winter schools in 1840–41, closing with these words:

This superior success in teaching is not owing to a better knowledge of the sciences taught, but to a superior manner, a more agreeable way of giving instruction. A female is a more gentle and amiable being; possessing more of the tender impulses of kindness and affection;—she more easily wins the attachment of the young scholar to her; and where that is once gained, the scholar is easily taught and easily governed.[4]

We may assume that these men and others who made similar statements sincerely believed that society would gain morally by the increased employment of female teachers and hoped that their arguments would be effective in persuading committees to hire and keep women teachers. Districts did in fact feminize their teaching staffs. In 1844

Mann reported that during his first seven years as secretary the number
of male teachers in the state had increased by only 159, while the number
of female teachers had grown by 990.[5] The percentage of women in the
total teaching force had thus increased from 60.2 percent to 64.5 percent. A look into the future would have shown even greater changes
forthcoming: women would make up 81.5 percent of the Massachusetts
teaching staff by the beginning of the Civil War and over 90 percent by
the last decade of the century.[6]

This trend toward a female teaching force, which Mann observed
and encouraged, was no isolated phenomenon, although in this respect—as in many others—Massachusetts led most states.[7] In 1846, 56
percent of Connecticut teachers were women; by 1857 this figure had
increased to over 70 percent. The proportion of women teachers in New
Jersey increased from less than a third to over half between 1842 and
1852.[8] The western states underwent a similar transformation, although
more slowly. Not until 1862, when many male teachers had gone to the
Civil War, did Iowa and Ohio have majorities of women teachers.[9] In
Indiana in 1855 fewer than one-fourth of the teachers were women; not
until 1890 did the figure approach one-half.[10]

How may we account for this shift from a largely male teaching force
to one in which women predominated? How responsive were practical
school committees to the sentimental appeal which Mann and other
humanitarian reformers employed? What role was played in this shift by
economic, social, and other factors?

Historical developments just prior to this time provide background
for understanding the feminization of teaching. As Nancy Cott explains,

the period between 1780 and 1830 was a time of wide- and deep-ranging
transformation, including the beginning of rapid intensive economic
growth, especially in foreign commerce, agricultural productivity, and
the fiscal and banking system; the start of sustained urbanization; demographic transition toward modern fertility patterns; marked change toward
social stratification by wealth and growing inequality in the distribution of
wealth; rapid pragmatic adaptation in the law; shifts from unitary to plu-
ralistic networks in personal association; unprecedented expansion in primary education; democratization in the political process; invention of a
new language of political and social thought; and—not least—with respect
to family life, the appearance of "domesticity."[11]

THE FEMINIZATION OF TEACHING IN MASSACHUSETTS

46   This was the context within which feminization occurred. While it
is easy to establish that the change in the teaching staff took place,
it is impossible to determine conclusively the motives of those responsible for making the change. But an examination of data from the
period 1840–60 indicates that certain economic and social transformations accompanied the feminization of teaching. This leaves open
the question of the role played by the rhetoric of Mann and others.
That rhetoric may have helped remove some of the psychological fric-
tion that would have inhibited the change. If so, the school committees were in the enviable position of having their cake and eating it
too—of doing that which economic pressure dictated and what would
project an image to educational leaders of high-mindedness and public-
spiritedness.

        But this rhetoric may have represented something more significant: a
response to the familial and social reorganization that—though already
occurring in the colonial period—was accentuated by the growth of
industry and cities in the nineteenth century.[12] The leaders of the common school revival and the local committees responsible for hiring
teachers shared the hope that a feminized teaching staff would infuse
maternal warmth into education and that the schools might restore
some of the social cohesion that seemed to be disappearing in an increasingly atomistic, competitive society.

        Women teachers were not unknown, of course, even during the colo-
nial period. The practice of having women conduct "dame schools" for
the smaller children had been brought by the settlers from England.[13]
There are records of women teaching in the more formal and official
town summer schools of Connecticut as early as 1695.[14] And, in Massachusetts, with the growth in the late eighteenth century of the district system, women were increasingly hired as teachers in the summer
schools.[15]

        The expansion of educational opportunities for girls after the Ameri-
can Revolution was a precondition for a feminized teaching force.[16]
Also important was the growth of the graded school, in which women
usually taught the younger children. Women teachers first taught in
the winter schools in communities that separated classes for older and
younger pupils. As other communities observed the success of this ex-
periment, they adopted both practices—the division of pupils by age
and the employment of female teachers.[17] Women's acknowledged success as mothers, and in their work in institutions such as orphanages and

WOMEN AND WORK

reform schools, may also have enhanced the confidence of school committees as they employed women teachers.[18]

The development of separate summer and winter sessions gave women their first significant entry into the educational system. Generally the smaller children, whose labor was not needed on the farm or in the home, attended the summer sessions. The older children worked during the summer and attended winter schools, usually (before about 1840) taught by men. Having women as teachers in the summer schools released men for more remunerative work during that season. Men still dominated the winter schools, however, partly because of the fear that women could not control the older and more unruly students who attended during the winter season.[19]

When it was found that women could handle summer school successfully, they soon came to outnumber male teachers during that session. In Essex County, Massachusetts, for example, as early as 1837, 81 percent of the summer teachers, but only 18 percent of the winter teachers, were women.[20] It became common to refer to the summer session as a "woman's school" and the winter term as a "man's school."[21] In the state as a whole, women were already dominant in the summer session by 1840; by 1860 they constituted 92 percent of the summer staff and 72 percent of the winter staff.[22]

Between 1840 and 1860, then, the winter schools underwent the same transformation the summer schools had undergone earlier. In some ways this change was even more significant because it meant that a sizable proportion (nearly three-fourths) of the staff was teaching in both sessions. This was a major step in the development of a corps of people whose primary occupation was teaching.[23] Thus, by 1860, teaching had evolved from being a male-dominated vocation through an intermediate stage in which men and women both taught on a part-time basis, to the more modern situation in which women compose the majority of a full-time teaching force.

This study identifies some of the factors associated with the feminization of the teaching staff in Massachusetts and suggests which of those factors were most influential. The general hypothesis is that the feminization of teaching was associated with urbanization and industrialism; those communities that feminized most rapidly were the larger, denser, wealthier towns and cities in which men could find alternative employment and in which high male salaries encouraged school boards to hire women teachers.[24]

There have been a number of quantitative studies of the feminization process, drawing on different locales and time periods. The findings of my own research are consistent with the conclusions of several of these studies; however, my findings may enrich earlier inquiries by providing further evidence of correlations between feminization and other developments.

Several methodological points require explanation: (1) the selection of the locale for the study; (2) the use of winter school data, rather than that from both winter and summer terms; (3) the period of time used as the limits for the study; and (4) the choice of specific variables.

Massachusetts was chosen as the site for the study because school data is available for early periods and because it was one of the earliest states to feminize its teaching staff. Many of the forces causing the transformation in Massachusetts later operated in other states. Essex, Worcester, and Berkshire were chosen as counties representing conditions in eastern, central, and western Massachusetts. Together they include over a third of the towns in the state.[25]

The winter schools, rather than both sessions, were chosen partly because they feminized during a period for which data is available. Including both sessions would have created inaccuracy because an increasing number of teachers taught in both terms and were counted twice in Board of Education data.

The years 1840–41 and 1860–61 were chosen as the limits of the study because they provide a long enough period over which to measure change; a decided increase in the female teaching staff took place; the use of 1860–61 as the final date avoids the effect of the Civil War on teaching staffs; and 1840 and 1860 were census years, for which economic and population data are available.

In order to test several hypotheses the following variables were selected:

1. *Women teacher ratio:* The ratio of women teachers to the total staff in the winter schools was the critical variable.

2. *Population:* A positive correlation was anticipated between the population of a community and the degree of feminization of its teaching staff.

3. *Density:* A similar positive correlation was expected between population density and feminization. The more urban communities, where men could command higher salaries in other occupations, might face economic pressure to employ women teachers.

4. *Agriculture:* A negative correlation was anticipated between feminization and the percentage of the population engaged in agriculture. Agricultural communities would offer fewer economic opportunities for men, particularly in the winter.

5. *Male teacher salaries:* A positive correlation was expected between feminization and male salaries. As male salaries increased, districts would be more motivated to employ less expensive women teachers.

6. *Female teacher salaries:* Expectations here were mixed. One might anticipate that low female salaries, suggesting an oversupply of women available for teaching, would be associated with a high degree of feminization. However, the more prosperous communities, which feminized because of high male salaries, might also have had to raise female salaries to stay competitive with millwork and other women's occupations.

Data bearing on the above variables were gathered primarily from the annual reports and returns of the Massachusetts Board of Education and from United States Census reports for the years cited. Information on these variables was developed for 1840–41 and 1860–61. Correlations were computed between each of these variables and all others. The basic correlation between the proportion of female teachers and each of the other variables is given in Table 1.

When the above coefficients are placed in rank order, a pattern becomes evident (see Table 2).

Taking any correlation above .25 as significant, we find four of the 1840 variables above that point: female salaries, male salaries, density, and total population. These same four variables come first in the 1860 ranking, but their order has changed. Male salaries are now first, population second, female salaries third, and density fourth.

When we put these rankings together, the levels of male and female salaries correlate about equally with degree of feminization. The level of female salaries comes first in 1840, while the level of male salaries is first in 1860. Perhaps a slight edge may be given to male salaries in that— while this variable ranks second in 1840—in neither case does it drop more than .01 below female salaries. Female salaries, however, slip to third place in 1860, .07 below male salaries. Without consulting other evidence at this point, we may conclude that—in this place, and at this time—a high level of male salaries, and the accompanying desire of communities to minimize school costs, was the single most effective force in the feminization of teaching.[26]

Table 1   *Correlation* Coefficient with Proportion of Female Teachers

	1840–41	1860–61
Population	.27	.36
Density	.33	.31
Agriculture	−.16	−.28
Male Salaries	.39	.38
Female Salaries	.40	.31

Sources: Annual Reports and Returns; Massachusetts Board of Education; U.S. Census.

These figures also indicate that those communities that most completely feminized their teaching staffs also tended to pay the highest female salaries, probably because these were the most industrialized areas in which alternative employment (often millwork) for women was most available.

Density occupies third place in the 1840 ranking (.33) and fourth in 1860 (.31). Population is in fourth place (.27) in 1840 and second in 1860 (.36). The proportion of the population engaged in agriculture occupies fifth place in both rankings, though it is only statistically significant in 1860 (−.28). Correlations for all three of these variables support the original economic hypothesis that feminization was associated with urbanism and with nonagricultural occupations. This ties in closely with the conclusions derived from the salary variables: those urban communities that offered alternative economic opportunities to men tended to encourage women to enter teaching. Conversely, in those agricultural towns that offered few job opportunities for men, especially in the winter, feminization proceeded most slowly.[27]

The growing numbers of pupils enrolled in school no doubt speeded feminization, as committees sought means of keeping costs down during the expansion process.[28] Some communities saw cost savings by employing female teachers as a way to provide more schooling by lengthening school terms.[29] Thus the desire to keep schools open for longer periods and to serve a larger clientele doubtless encouraged many towns to make greater use of female teachers.

These findings are consistent with those of other scholars. Michael Katz, writing about Massachusetts in this period, said that "school committees were faced with a rapid increase in the numbers of children because of immigration, a scarcity of men because of industrial and commercial opportunities, and a consequent probable enormous rise in school costs. In this situation schoolmen, like industrialists, sought to

Table 2   Rank Order of Correlations and Variables   51

Rank	Corr.	Variable	Corr.	Variable
1	.40	Female salaries	.38	Male salaries
2	.39	Male salaries	.36	Population
3	.33	Density	.31	Female salaries
4	.27	Population	.31	Density
5	−.16	Agriculture	−.28	Agriculture

Sources: Annual Reports and Returns; Massachusetts Board of Education; U.S. Census.

increase the 'marginal productivity' of labor through training, feminization, innovation, and reorganization."[30]

Geraldine Clifford has written that "only in 'hard times' and in stagnant locales was the supply of acceptable men likely to approach the schools' needs."[31] But the impact of "hard times," such as the depression of 1857, is difficult to assess since, as we have seen in Massachusetts at least, teaching was already feminized (over four-fifths of teachers were women by 1861) and few men were willing to work for the meager wages received by women teachers.[32]

The correlations derived from this study support the conclusion that industrialization and urbanization were the dominant factors in the feminization of the Massachusetts teaching force. But the quantitative data tell us only that there was a relationship between teacher salaries and feminization, not the nature of that relationship. We may consider a continuum of four possibilities:

1. Because they could save money by doing so, districts would have feminized their teaching staffs even if this had not been considered an educational reform.

2. Districts were primarily guided by the financial advantages of feminization but were somewhat influenced by social and moral considerations.

3. School committees were mainly concerned with the educational advantages of a feminized staff, and economic factors were significant only in encouraging them to do that which their collective consciences dictated.

4. Communities were entirely guided by ethical considerations and were completely uninfluenced by practical matters such as teacher salaries or the wealth of the community.

We may reject the two extremes of this continuum on the premise that neither "economic man" nor "moral man" ever existed in pure form.[33] What support may we find for the idea that moral considerations played a partial role in feminization?[34] Examining the motives of people who left sketchy records, and who may have deluded themselves about their intentions, allows only speculation but is nevertheless an opportunity to consider some potentially fruitful material and ideas.

It is clear from the evidence we do have that massive social and economic changes contributed to the sense of social unease that emerged along with the superficial optimism of mid-nineteenth-century America. Many Americans felt considerable fear about the social and moral effects of industrialization, competition, and urbanization. In *Cavalier and Yankee* William Taylor wrote that during the 1820s, 1830s, and 1840s Americans lived in an "age of anxiety" and felt dark forebodings as they contemplated existing social trends:

If men were naturally self-centered and rapacious, bent on pursuing their own private ends, and nature was an amoral or neutral force, then what was there in the classless and open society of America to prevent its becoming a social jungle the equal of which the civilized world had never seen? What was to preserve the sanctity of the home and family, upon which it felt depended the stability of society, from the forces which were daily tearing it apart?[35]

These were problems that many people felt and that some were able to put into words. Often the vague dissatisfaction was expressed in terms of loss—of the gradual erosion of old religious values, moral standards, and strength of character. Few, however, were willing to follow mavericks like Thoreau in rejecting the advantages of industrialism in the East or cheap land in the West. Most saw material and technological development as inevitable but wanted to bring into the new era the values they believed had characterized an earlier, simpler time.

The great need, then, was for institutions and forces to counteract the centrifugal tendencies of society—to promote social cohesion in the new economic order. The obvious place to begin was with the family, particularly the mother. Sylvia Hoffert has suggested that a

clearly articulated ideology of motherhood, corollary to the cult of domesticity . . . offered childbearing women the opportunity to demonstrate their patriotism by rearing paragons of civic virtue. It was by developing moral

sentiments in children, shaping their temperaments, and preparing them
to fulfill the responsibilities of citizenship that mothers could ultimately, if
indirectly, fulfill an important public and political role that would allow
them to "hold the reins of government" and shape "the destiny of our great
nation."[36]

As many women assumed this "mission of republican motherhood"
within the family, still others extended their role into the more public
realm of the common school.[37] Commenting in 1836 on the transition
from agriculture to industry, a committee of the Massachusetts House
of Representatives made the following statement:

It becomes the solemn and indispensable duty of the representatives of the
people to provide seasonably and effectually that those institutions which
have given New England her peculiar character for general intelligence and
virtue be not changed with the changing employment of her people . . . [for
it] requires no spirit of prophecy to foresee and to know that the collection
of large masses of children, youth, and middle-aged persons of both sexes
into compact villages, is not a circumstance favorable to virtue.[38]

Clearly these men feared the social effects of the new industrial world
that was being created; their hope was that the character-building forces
in society, such as families and schools, would "be not changed" in the
process and would maintain unabated their power to sustain social
unity.

Horace Mann was the most eloquent advocate of a social and moral
role for the common school. In 1848, in his final report as secretary to
the Massachusetts Board of Education, he proclaimed:

These wonders, [education] has done in its infancy, and with the lights of a
limited experience; but, when its faculties shall be fully developed, when it
shall be trained to wield its mighty energies for the protection of society
against the giant vices which now invade and torment it;—against intem-
perance, avarice, war, slavery, bigotry, the woes of want and the wickedness
of waste,—then, there will not be a height to which these enemies of the
race can escape, which it will not scale, nor a Titan among them all, whom
it will not slay.[39]

The school, then, was a source of hope to those determined to resist
the "giant vices" of the new society; women were another. In a reaction

54   against the "masculine vices" of the developing social order—aggressive-
ness, insensitivity, competition, acquisitiveness—many saw in women
the instruments of salvation. Former president John Quincy Adams
asked in the House of Representatives in 1838:

Why does it follow that women are fitted for nothing but the cares of
domestic life . . . for promoting the welfare of their husbands, brothers,
sons? . . . I say that the correct principle is that women are not only
justified, but exhibit the most exalted virtue, when they do depart from the
domestic circle, and enter upon the concerns of their country, of humanity,
and of their God.[40]

The influences of the schools and of high-minded women, then, were
to be stabilizing forces in a rapidly moving society. They were to serve
what was later called a "counter-cyclical" function in the social order.[41]
They were not to mirror passively the dominant trends of American life
but were to strengthen those that were worthwhile and resist those that
were destructive. Taking Sara Josepha Hale, then the editor of *Godey's
Lady's Book,* as a leading exponent of this view during this period,
William Taylor wrote:

The role which she evolved for the American woman was a compensa-
tory one. In an America, she reasoned, where a man was forced to make his
way and fulfill himself by the accumulation of property, the woman was left
with a positive and dynamic role to play. She was destined to be the active
agent of culture and moral perception. . . . The woman should be an
example, a compensating influence to overcome the terrible and apparent
dangers which existed in a society given over without reservation to the
pursuit of wealth. The destiny of America, she concluded, was therefore
largely in the hands of its women.[42]

As a more open, competitive economy effectively prevented the re-
establishment of the close patriarchal family, many turned to the school
to fulfill some of the moral functions that the family no longer seemed
able to meet. Women leaders as well as the common school reformers
had such functions in mind in their advocacy of the greater use of
women teachers, and there is evidence that some school committees
shared this viewpoint. While reporting that women teachers were as
good as men in knowledge and discipline, the thrust of the argument in

favor of women teachers (aside from economic ones) was that women's moral and emotional qualities were superior.

The school committee of Worcester, Massachusetts, declared in 1841 that "females make better teachers than males. Their patience, delicacy, quickness of apprehension, and sympathy with the young mind, more readily fit them for the task."[43] And in the same year, the committee in Raynham said that "the prominent faculty in the adult female is love, or affection. . . . Female teachers . . . can lead those, in whose minds little beside affection is active, by the affections."[44]

It is, of course, impossible to assess precisely the role such factors had in the shift to a largely female teaching force. However, we can assume that Mann and other reformers used social and ethical arguments for feminization, not only because they believed in them personally but because they expected them to be effective.[45] They anticipated that their readers and listeners would share their concerns about deteriorating social cohesion and agree with their prescriptions. And there is evidence in school reports that some committees took positions similar to Mann's.

But why did some communities respond to such concerns earlier than others? Although economic factors were probably dominant in the shift to a feminized teaching force, ethical and social factors were apparently more influential in some communities. Doubtless some committees used sentimental rhetoric to rationalize their parsimonious propensities; others may have been deeply concerned about social disorganization and so feminized their staffs without regard to cost.

Feminization of the teaching staff may well have been a necessary step in the development of the teaching profession. In hiring men, communities were often drawing from a limited labor pool or—in the case of college students—from a temporary one.[46] There was justifiable dissatisfaction with the dismal quality of men teachers. But with women teachers the supply exceeded the demand, and committees could be more selective. Committees came to feel that in hiring women, they were making a longer school term possible and getting higher quality instruction in the bargain.

The competition for positions—even at low pay—encouraged some women to take advantage of the programs offered by the proliferating normal schools.[47] Thus, with a feminized teaching staff, schools gradually improved, salaries increased, and eventually, in the twentieth century, teaching again began to attract men.

THE FEMINIZATION OF TEACHING IN MASSACHUSETTS

56   Scholars like Carl Degler have noted the relationships among the education of women, the feminization of teaching, and the women's rights movement.[48] The feminization of teaching may well have promoted the growth and success of the women's rights movement generally. In 1844 Horace Mann held out the hope that through woman's influence as a teacher she might not only serve as an uplifting force in society but achieve some of her own rights as well: "How otherwise can she so well vindicate her right to an exalted station in the scale of being; and cause that shameful sentence of degradation by which she has been so long dishonored, to be repealed?"[49]

Clearly, some leaders saw the feminization of teaching as one means of elevating the status of women. They no doubt saw that those who had been successfully taught by women were poorly positioned to declaim dogmatically on the mental inferiority of females and thus hoped that they might be more open-minded about the quality of the sexes.[50]

But conservative school trustees would not have been so sanguine. Mary Blewett has noted the irony of the fact that school committeemen, hoping that women teachers would promote social equilibrium, "must have been surprised at the consequences of their decisions to hire women." By so doing, they

created a growing cohort of single, self-supporting educated women, some of whom became like Susan B. Anthony [in neighboring New York State] involved in reform activities such as temperance, anti-slavery, and woman suffrage. In Lowell in the mid-1840s, a few teachers joined mill girls to wear the bloomer costume on the city streets until they were sufficiently discouraged by insults. This was female moral superiority really gone public and freed for a while from the restraint of family and husband. And this was reform, even revolution to some, but certainly not social stability. The women's rights movement inside the teaching profession, especially at its annual state conventions where women demanded the right to speak and vote did nothing to soothe the anxieties felt by the middle class while urban, industrial America was being formed.[51]

Feminization has been interpreted by historians with varying degrees of optimism and pessimism. In the 1930s and 1940s scholars like Elsbree and Monroe described feminization positively and saw it as an important stage in the professionalization of teaching. More recently, revisionist scholars have seen feminization—and the common school revival of

WOMEN AND WORK

which it was a part—as a development that subordinated women in a hierarchical school system that was itself an instrument of an emerging and unjust market economy. And in the last few years scholars like Michael Apple and Nancy Hoffman have observed that feminization eventually led to efforts on the part of women teachers to empower themselves that were at least partially successful.[52]

Feminization was one of the major movements in the history of teaching—the largest and only sizable public profession in America— and, indeed, the *only* paid middle-class profession for women in the nineteenth century. It is clear that there were important links between the changing teaching force and economic developments like urbanization and pre–Civil War industrialization. The common school "revival" and other reform movements, including the formalization and bureaucratization of schools, were at least in part a response to these developments. The feminization of teaching was possible because the ideology of republican womanhood convinced school reformers and school committees that women were good teachers as well as an inexpensive labor supply. In the process of feminization the modern occupation of teaching was born, with important implications for women's empowerment.[53]

Notes

I am grateful to Daniel Calhoun for his guidance on an early version of this study, to Christa Winter for her assistance with questions of methodology, and to Mary H. Blewett, Susan Porter, and anonymous reviewers for helpful and specific editorial suggestions.

1. *Eighth Annual Report of the Secretary of the Board of Education* (Boston: Board of Education, 1845), 60. (Hereafter, these will be cited as *Annual Report,* with dates.)

2. The classic study of this belief is Barbara Welter's "The Cult of True Womanhood," chapter 2 of *Dimity Convictions: The American Woman in the Nineteenth Century* (Athens: Ohio University Press, 1976).

3. Madeleine Grumet critiques nineteenth-century educational sentimentalism in *Bitter Milk: Women and Teaching* (Amherst: University of Massachusetts Press, 1988), 56.

4. *Abstract* of the Massachusetts School Returns for 1840–1841 (Boston: Board of Education, 1841), 113 (hereafter cited as *Abstract,* with dates).

5. *Eighth Annual Report* (1844), 60.

6. *Twenty-third Annual Report* (1861), *Fifty-third Annual Report* (1891).

7. Geraldine Joncich Clifford, "Man/Woman/Teacher: Gender, Family, and

58   Career in American Educational History," in *American Teachers: Histories of a Profession at Work*, ed. Donald Warren (New York: Macmillan, 1989), 295. The research on feminization is voluminous and will be cited very selectively below. Clifford's notes identify much of the relevant literature.

8. Willard Elsbree, *The American Teacher: Evolution of a Profession in a Democracy* (New York: American Book Company, 1939), 202.

9. Elsbree, *American Teacher*, 206.

10. Paul Monroe, *Founding of the American Public School System* (New York: Macmillan, 1940), 1:487. John Rury identifies regional variations in feminization in "Who Became Teachers? The Social Characteristics of Teachers in American History," in Warren, *American Teachers*, 16–17.

11. Nancy Cott, *The Bonds of Womanhood: "Woman's Sphere" in New England, 1780–1835* (New Haven: Yale University Press, 1977), 3.

12. For perceptions of social disintegration, see Michael B. Katz, *The Irony of Early School Reform: Educational Innovation in Mid-Nineteenth Century Massachusetts* (Cambridge: Harvard University Press, 1968), part 3.

13. Nancy Hoffman, *Woman's "True" Profession: Voices from the History of Teaching* (New York: Feminist Press, 1981), 6.

14. Elsbree, *American Teacher*, 67–68.

15. Monroe, *Founding*, 1:116–23.

16. Myra H. Strober and David Tyack identify "preconditions" and "precipitants" for feminization in "Why Do Women Teach and Men Manage: A Report on Research on Schools." *Signs: Journal of Women in Culture and Society* 5 (Spring 1980): 494–503. Among these factors are bureaucratization and the growth of the graded school, neither of which was a variable in this study. However, they and Michael B. Katz make persuasive cases for the influence of these developments. See Katz's *Irony of Early School Reform*, part I.

17. Myra H. Strober and Audri Gordon Lanford, in "The Feminization of Public School Teaching: Cross-sectional Analysis, 1850–1880," *Signs: Journal of Women in Culture and Society* 11 (1986): 212–35, write that "the proportion of women in teaching increased not because of urbanization per se but because of the formalization of school systems and the decrease in the female/male salary ratio, which tended to occur in urban settings" ("Feminization," 217). Age grading was one of the first steps in the formalization process.

18. The Boston Female Asylum, for example, was "run entirely by women." Susan L. Porter, "Victorian Values in the Marketplace: Single Women and Work in Boston, 1800–1850," *Social Science History* 17, no. 1 (Spring 1993): 110; Katz, *Irony of Early School Reform*, 193.

19. Strober and Tyack, "Why Do Women Teach and Men Manage?" 497–98.

20. *Abstract* (1838), 3–28.

21. Newton Edwards and Herman Richey, *The School in the American Social Order* (Boston: Houghton Mifflin, 1963), 249–50.

23. This may be seen as a partial reversion to the colonial situation in which many schoolmasters considered teaching to be their primary occupation, even if for only a few years. See Rury in Warren, *American Teachers,* 11–14.

24. This is a common explanation for the trend under study here. See, for example, Carl Kaestle and Maris Vinovskis, *Education and Social Change in Nineteenth-Century Massachusetts* (New York: Cambridge University Press, 1980), 200–207.

25. One hundred nine towns or groups of towns were included in this study. Several communities that were either divided or joined to other towns during this period were grouped together in order to keep the data comparable. There were 307 towns in Massachusetts in 1840–41. See *Abstract* (1841), 111.

26. Another plausible explanation, not measured by the data presented here, is that most remaining men teachers in feminized communities taught in the upper grades or high school and were paid higher salaries partly on that account. On this and related issues, see also Jo Anne Preston, "Feminization of an Occupation: Teaching Becomes Women's Work in Nineteenth-Century New England" (Ph.D. diss., Brandeis University, 1982), chapter 3.

A note on methodology may be helpful here. The study began with ten variables each for 1840–41 and 1860–61 and ten for the proportion of change between these two years. Since the degree of change in the population and density variables was identical (area remaining the same), only nine variables were used in the group representing change between these years. Thus twenty-nine variables were used in the study. Zero-order correlations were computed between each of these twenty-nine variables and all others. In the interest of brevity and clarity, the least significant variables have been omitted from this chapter.

27. These interpretations support those of Strober and Lanford in "The Feminization of Public School Teaching" 234–35.

28. Keith E. Melder discusses this in reference to Massachusetts and other states in "Woman's High Calling: The Teaching Profession in America, 1830–1860," *American Studies* 13 (Fall 1972), 21–22.

29. See, for example, *Abstract* (1841), 8, 91.

30. Katz, *The Irony of Urban School Reform,* 60. See also Clifford, "Man/Woman/Teacher," 299, 306, and 336, note 84.

31. Clifford, "Man/Woman/Teacher," 306.

32. Elsbree, *American Teacher,* 205–6.

33. If "economic man" had existed he could doubtless have been found on a nineteenth-century New England school board.

34. See Strober and Tyack, "Why Do Women Teach and Men Manage?" 495.

35. William R. Taylor, *Cavalier and Yankee* (New York: Braziller, 1961), 98. I am grateful to Michael B. Katz for recommending this useful source.

36. Sylvia Hoffert, *Private Matters: American Attitudes toward Childbearing and Infant Nurture in the Urban North, 1800–1860* (Urbana: University of Illinois Press, 1989), 2. Hoffert is quoting from an 1859 article in a women's magazine. (See her note 4, page 11). Nancy Cott credits William R. Taylor with the first use of the term "domesticity" in its current historical sense: *The Bonds of Womanhood*, 1n.

37. Hoffert, page 2, citing Linda Kerber, *Women of the Republic: Intellect and Ideology in Revolutionary America* (Chapel Hill: University of North Carolina Press, 1980).

38. Quoted in Arthur W. Calhoun, *A Social History of the American Family* (1918; reprint, New York: Barnes and Noble, 1960), 2:196.

39. *Twelfth Annual Report* (1848) in *The Republic and the School: Horace Mann On the Education of Free Men*, ed. Lawrence Cremin (New York: Teachers College Press, 1957), 80.

40. Quoted in Alice Felt Tyler, *Freedom's Ferment: Phases of American Social History to 1860* (Minneapolis: University of Minnesota Press, 1944), 429.

41. David Riesman adapted the concept of counter-cyclical forces from economics. See his *Constraint and Variety in American Education* (New York: Doubleday Anchor, 1958), 147–48.

42. Taylor, *Cavalier and Yankee*, 119.

43. *Abstract* (1841), 137–38.

44. *Abstract* (1841), 255.

45. Richard M. Bernard and Maris A. Vinovskis make a strong claim for the impact of Mann's rhetoric in favor of feminization: "Due largely to the propaganda of Mann himself, many of the patterns developed in Massachusetts subsequently re-emerged elsewhere." "The Female School Teacher in Ante-Bellum Massachusetts," *Journal of Social History* 10 (Spring 1977): 332.

46. Jurgen Herbst, *And Sadly Teach: Teacher Education and Professionalization in American Culture* (Madison: University of Wisconsin Press), 23.

47. Bernard and Vinovskis describe the growth of Massachusetts normal schools during this period: "The Female School Teacher," 332–36.

48. Carl Degler, *At Odds: Women and the Family in America from the Revolution to the Present* (New York: Oxford University Press, 1980), chapter 13.

49. *Eighth Annual Report* (1844), 60–61.

50. Mann's thoughts on female mental equality were progressive for the time. See John Rury and Glenn Harper, "The Trouble with Coeducation: Mann and Women at Antioch, 1853–1860," *History of Education Quarterly* 26 (Winter 1986): 481–502.

51. Mary H. Blewett, "Comment on Nineteenth-Century Women and Work," Symposium on the History of Women in Massachusetts, Westfield State College, October 24, 1992. Blewett's sources for the bloomer reference were the *Lowell Advertiser* and the *Lowell Courier* between June 16 and July 5, 1851.

52. See the studies cited earlier by Elsbree, Monroe, Katz, Melder, Preston, and Strober and Lanford. Also Michael Apple, "Teaching and 'Women's Work': A Comparative Historical and Ideological Analysis," *Teachers College Record* 86 (Spring 1985), 455–73; also Hoffman, *Woman's "True" Profession*, 15–17.

53. See Clifford's conclusions and extensive notes (329–43) in "Man/Woman/Teacher" for a thoughtful discussion of current and needed research in this area.

ÉTRE À L'OUVRAGE OU ÉTRE MAITRESSE DE MAISON

French-Canadian Women and Work in Late Nineteenth-Century Massachusetts

PAUL R. DAUPHINAIS

During the second half of the nineteenth century waves of immigrants came to Massachusetts, first from Ireland, then from Quebec, and eventually from eastern and southern Europe. Many of these people found jobs in factories where the work was mechanized, as in the textile industry, and skill requirements were minimal. The low pay required that not only men but also women and, sometimes, children seek waged labor. Historians have often interpreted the numbers of nineteenth-century immigrant women wage earners as a function of male skill level and the need for additional sources of income. Irish women often became domestics, while women of other nationalities sought millwork.[1]

Millwork was especially predominant among French-Canadian women. Some historians have seen this pattern as the extension of the rural French-Canadian tradition of employing the entire family, particularly young wives and daughters, in the mills. This, in turn, has been interpreted as a carryover of the division of labor on the farm. However, this cultural interpretation fails to take into account the economic structure of a given immigrant destination area.[2] By looking at the industrial makeup, wage structure, and employment possibilities of a city in relation to the number of wage-earning French-Canadian girls and women and the positions they held, it is possible to illuminate the varying family strategies in the French-Canadian immigrant community.

Much of the work on waged women between 1850 and 1900 has fo-

Children outside Amoskeag housing; child in front identified as Fred Normandin. Photograph by Lewis Hine, 1090. Courtesy, Library of Congress, National Child Labor Committee Collection.

cused on textile centers, the "spindle cities" of New England. Cities such as Lowell, Lawrence, Holyoke, and Fall River, Massachusetts; Woonsocket, Rhode Island; Manchester, New Hampshire; and Biddeford, Maine, have been examined by numerous researchers. In each of these cities textiles was the dominant industry and French-Canadians, particularly girls and women, made up a large portion of the workforce. However, by the turn of the century, there were numerous "cities or towns where the economy was dominated by diverse industries," but few studies have examined the working girls and women in these multi-industrial centers.[3]

This chapter will look at the relative weight of market forces and family values in two Massachusetts cities, Fitchburg and Worcester, to discover the various roles women played in immigrant families. During the second half of the nineteenth century both of these cities exhibited well-diversified economies. Fitchburg's industrial base centered on paper, metals, and machinery and, after 1880, a sizable textile sector. Worcester's economy was based on metal and machinery work and the boot and shoe industry. In population Worcester was larger than any of the spindle cities, while Fitchburg was smaller than most.

Thomas Dublin has noted that, during the nineteenth century, the steady expansion of a local economy increased economic opportunity, while a healthy economy improved the local sex ratio and marriage opportunities of immigrants. Cities dominated by the textile industry did not experience steady growth. Although they may have done well during years when their products were in demand, these cities were among the hardest hit during recessions and depressions with rapid workforce turnover as strikes, layoffs, and market fluctuations forced immigrant workers to seek jobs in other industrial centers. Dublin has further suggested that individual persistence or mobility during the nineteenth century was a function of the economic setting and social composition of an industry or city. Jay P. Dolan noted that French-Canadian families in textile mills experienced minimal social mobility because local economies dominated by a single industry retarded upward mobility. According to Frances Early, those *canadiĕns* who did settle in textile centers had limited opportunities; most became common laborers and low-paid mill operatives, and many members of each household were employed. The money from nonhousehold heads often kept the creditors at bay and allowed the French-Canadian family to make ends meet.[4]

In the spindle cities there were more French-Canadian women (mostly young and single) than French-Canadian men in the textile factories and in the French-Canadian population at large (Table 1). In Fitchburg and Worcester, however, French-Canadian men, many of whom were single, outnumbered French-Canadian women.[5] The economic and social composition of the textile industry may have influenced the numbers of women in these cities. The absence of large textile mills that would provide unskilled work for the entire family may have made Fitchburg and Worcester unattractive to large families with no specialized skills or trades. The numerous skilled trades in a more diversified economy, however, could have made Fitchburg and Worcester attractive to younger families with fewer children and single men who were skilled or seeking to learn a skill. Potential immigrants in Quebec were often informed about which cities offered better opportunities. Félix Albert, for example, was advised by his brother to stay away from Fall River because there were numerous strikes there and work would be more steady in Lowell.[6] Some French-Canadian families found that the problems they left behind in Quebec differed little from those they encountered in New England. Bettina Bradbury has shown that, in

Table 1   Number of French-Canadian Men and Women in Selected
Massachusetts Cities, 1875, 1885, 1895

City	1875	1885	1895
	Men/Women Male/Female Ratio	Men/Women Male/Female Ratio	Men/Women Male/Female Ratio
Fall River	2312/2712 .85 to 1	3835/4384 .87 to 1	8182/8897 .91 to 1
Lawrence	801/1123 .71 to 1	853/1068 .80 to 1	2245/2392 .94 to 1
Holyoke	1322/1490 .88 to 1	2435/3632 .68 to 1	2930/3417 .86 to 1
Lowell	1557/2223 .70 to 1	2901/3537 .82 to 1	6092/6751 .90 to 1
Worcester	1192/1057 1.13 to 1	1490/1304 1.14 to 1	2106/2113 .99 to 1
Fitchburg	321/271 1.18 to 1	400/341 1.17 to 1	1487/1412 1.05 to 1

Source: Massachusetts Bureau of Statistics of Labor, *Census of Massachusetts* (1875), 1:300–304; 1885, 1:89–407; 1895, vol. 2.

Quebec, "as old trades were deskilled and production reorganized unskilled laborers, women and children, all competed for the same jobs." Increasing mechanization often decreased job opportunities for men and lowered wages. In a number of industries, entire families were forced to work for wages in order to survive. In fact, there was insufficient industry in Quebec to accommodate the entire population that sought work. In hard times wages fell while hours rose, and, as waves of migrants took jobs in an already overcrowded labor pool, wages in the Montreal and Quebec City regions, the industrialized areas of Quebec, became increasingly depressed.[7] Much the same can be said about New England, particularly in regard to the textile cities.

Although Armand Chartier proposed that the French-Canadian *mentalité* produced a resignation to arduous factory work, local economic structure, not a cultural predilection, may have encouraged a large female labor force in some cities. The depressions of the late nineteenth century forced numerous women, even those from the "comfortable classes," to seek wage work.[8] Despite the common perception that wage-earning French-Canadian women were usually young and single, quite often married women would work several months a year to augment the household income. Mary Dancouise remembers bringing her mother's lunch pail to work at the Amoskeag Mills in Manchester, New Hampshire. Dancouise's mother worked for Amoskeag for forty uninterrupted years.[9]

In large families children over ten years of age would often work in the mills. According to an 1885 U.S. Senate report, French-Canadian newlyweds in Fall River sentenced themselves to a life of poverty for twelve years until their children could join them in the mills.[10] Fall River was not the only city where this could be expected. When Mary Dancouise was first born her parents sent her back to Canada so that her mother could work in the mills. She was brought back to New Hampshire when she was twelve years old so that she could take care of her younger siblings while her mother continued working in the mills.[11] In other textile centers women worked or took in boarders after marriage to contribute to the family economy. Many women who worked as girls did not stop after marriage regardless of age.[12]

In 1875 Lowell's female workforce outnumbered the male force by nearly two thousand, and Fall River, Lawrence, and Holyoke demonstrated similar patterns.[13] While wage rates in these cities varied greatly, in each case the textile industry was the single largest employer for both men and women. As Table 2 demonstrates, wage rates for women in textiles were particularly low. Competition for a limited number of jobs meant that women in the spindle cities earned less than the state average for women in cotton goods or woolens. Only in Worcester and Fitchburg, which had a number of small, independently owned woolen mills, were women's wages above the state average.

The average wage in Fitchburg and Worcester in 1875 was much higher than in the textile centers. Blacksmiths, carpenters, stone workers, and woolen mill operatives all received better pay in Fitchburg and Worcester. For the most part these were male-dominated trades. The one exception was in the cotton textile industry, which in Worcester and Fitchburg was comparatively small. Wages for machine work were also lower than in the textile centers, but significantly more people in Worcester and Fitchburg worked in this industry than in other cities.

By the 1880s the primary textile center workforce consisted of poorly paid women. Wages in these cities were generally lower than elsewhere, and skilled positions were limited. Using Lowell as an example of such centers, one can see a significant contrast between textile cities and diversified cities such as Fitchburg and Worcester in 1885 (Table 3).

Table 2   Annual Wages in Selected Massachusetts Cities, 1875 (in Dollars)

	Blacksmithing	Carpentry	Machinery	Stone Work
State average	636.21	658.63	652.46	627.30
Lowell	566.20	710.95	550.50	722.85
Fall River	654.36	716.80	687.00	324.50
Fitchburg	682.03	734.84	635.00	737.56
Holyoke	714.00	—	662.20	—
Lawrence	599.76	519.39	710.00	—
Worcester	714.24	720.90	612.00	623.76

	Cotton Goods		Woolens	
	Men	Women	Men	Women
State average	480.61	285.84	420.67	293.78
Lowell	535.50	238.68	384.30	263.34
Fall River	388.96	263.04	408.96	290.00
Fitchburg	287.00	186.55	492.42	308.76
Holyoke	424.41	238.04	400.32	235.94
Lawrence	454.50	249.92	469.86	218.79
Worcester	494.00	170.52	637.53	315.52

Source: Massachusetts Bureau of Statistics of Labor, *Census of Massachusetts* (1875).

There were significantly fewer women working in all wage brackets but particularly among those who earned less than seven dollars per week. In addition, men tended to receive better wages. In Lowell there were roughly the same number of male workers in all wage brackets under twelve dollars per week, but the number of men fell dramatically as wages increased. In Worcester the absolute number of men earning more than ten dollars per week was greater than in Lowell, reflecting the higher wages in boot and shoe making and the metals and machinery sector, both of which were important in Worcester.

The overwhelming majority of working women in Lowell were employed in the textile mills as unskilled workers. Two-thirds of all women engaged in waged labor made less than seven dollars a week. Fierce competition for unskilled jobs made it possible for the mills to hire the cheapest labor force available—immigrant women. In cities with large textile sectors the numbers of unskilled jobs depressed the average wage for men and women. In 1885 in Lowell more than half (52.5%) of the entire workforce made less than six dollars per week.[14]

By comparison the industrial structure of Fitchburg and Worcester discouraged a large female workforce. This was due to the fact that there

Table 3   Weekly Wages in Lowell, Fitchburg, and Worcester, 1885 (in dollars)

	<5.00	5.00–5.99	6.00–6.99	7.00–7.99	8.00–8.99	9.00–9.99	10.00–11.99	12.00–14.99	15.00–19.99	>20.00
A. Lowell										
Men (54%)	1,103 (14)	930 (12)	828 (11)	860 (11)	740 (10)	1,168 (15)	746 (10)	637 (8)	487 (6)	149 (2)
Women (46%)	4,285 (66)	1,131 (8)	744 (5)	173 (3)	67 (1)	49 (.7)	18 (.2)	21 (.2)	1 (.01)	2 (.01)
TOTAL	5,388 (38)	2,061 (14.5)	1,572 (11)	1,033 (7)	807 (5.7)	1,217 (8.6)	764 (5)	654 (4.6)	488 (3.5)	151 (1)
B. Fitchburg										
Men (76%)	94 (6)	50 (3.5)	72 (4.5)	129 (8)	139 (9)	182 (11)	225 (14)	406 (25)	234 (14)	81 (5)
Women (24%)	235 (47)	88 (18)	74 (15)	51 (10)	8 (1.6)	21 (4)	7 (1.4)	7 (1.4)	0 (0)	0 (0)
TOTAL	329 (15.6)	138 (6.5)	146 (7)	180 (8.5)	147 (7)	203 (10)	232 (11)	413 (19.6)	234 (11)	81 (4)
C. Worcester										
Men (83%)	404 (6)	184 (3)	258 (4)	385 (5.5)	353 (5)	715 (10)	1,624 (23)	1,722 (25)	1,054 (15)	229 (3)
Women (17%)	484 (35)	249 (18)	239 (18)	161 (11.8)	86 (63)	64 (5)	37 (3)	28 (2)	3 (.2)	6 (.4)
TOTAL	888 (10.7)	433 (5)	497 (6)	546 (6.6)	439 (5)	779 (9)	1,661 (20)	1,750 (21)	1,057 (12.7)	235 (3)

Source: Massachusetts Bureau of Statistics of Labor, *Census of Massachusetts* (1885), 1:248–61.
Note: Numbers represent totals in each category; figures in parentheses are percentages.

were more skilled jobs in both of these cities; in addition, leading industrial sectors like the metals and machinery industries employed men at all skill levels. Men's wages were higher and peaked at higher levels than in Lowell. In both Fitchburg and Worcester over two-thirds of the men earned more than nine dollars each week (the comparative figure for Lowell was less than one-half). Men in Fitchburg and Worcester were more able to support a family on their own wages, which seemed to keep more women off the mill floor. As Table 2 shows, fewer worked and those who did earned slightly more than those in Lowell. While only 17% of all wage-earning women earned six dollars or more each week in Lowell, 35% in Fitchburg and 47% in Worcester did so. This is partly because there were fewer textile jobs available in Fitchburg and Worcester. In 1885 both the industrial structure and the higher wage rates of Fitchburg and Worcester seem to have contributed to limiting the number of women in the workforce.

The propensity to employ poorly paid women in textile centers continued throughout the nineteenth century. In New England's spindle cities in 1900 few women worked in any other occupation (Table 4). In Fall River, Lawrence, and Lowell 91%, 94% and 79% respectively of the wage-earning women labored in the cotton mills.

There were remarkable similarities in female employment among the spindle cities in 1900. Generally, despite the fact that women outnumbered men in the textile mills, they received lower aggregate wages. This was particularly noticeable in Lowell; although there were 22% more women than men in the textile industry, they earned only 79% as much as the men. In Holyoke 13% more women earned only 79% of the wages of their male counterparts in the textile industry. But wages in the textile centers in 1900 were lower for both genders. Although Lowell had approximately six thousand more workers than Worcester, the working population of Worcester earned an additional $1.1 million in wages. During the same year Woonsocket's workforce was 15% larger than that of Fitchburg, but overall wages were lower.[15] As the textile industry began to migrate south, maintaining low wages was one way for northern factories to remain competitive. The large pool of immigrants also helped to keep wages down in spindle cities. This led to wage pooling by immigrant families.

In 1900 women represented between 32.5% and 42% of the laboring population in textile cities. In Fitchburg and Worcester, however, women composed only 25% and 18% of the workers respectively. De-

spite the fact that Worcester was the second-largest city in Massachusetts, it had fewer wage-earning women than Holyoke, with only one-
fourth the population. Clearly wage pooling by immigrant families
remained necessary in textile cities until the end of the century.

By the turn of the century, French-Canadian women in textile cities also worked outside the home in places other than factories. In
1895 seven of twenty-three dressmakers in Woonsocket were French-
Canadians (four single, three married); twenty of eighty in Manchester,
New Hampshire; and ten of thirty-nine in Fall River, Massachusetts,
between 25 and 30% of the total number of dressmakers in each city.
Independent French-Canadian businesswomen were rarer in Fitchburg
and Worcester. In Fitchburg only one of twenty-five dressmakers was a
French-Canadian woman, and in Worcester only four of seventy-nine.[16]
Like their unskilled counterparts, skilled French-Canadian women in
these cities tended to stay out of the employment market.

Overall there appears to be a correlation between economic structure
and the number of women in the labor force. In monoindustrial cities
greater numbers of paid women labored in the mills, worked as dressmakers, and engaged in other income-producing pursuits in order to
make cash contributions to the family economy. In the more diversified
economies of Fitchburg and Worcester fewer adult women worked outside the home. Because wages for men in these cities were higher than in
the textile centers, the number of women engaged in wage labor may
have been smaller.

During the nineteenth century there was also a high incidence of
child labor in the textile cities. Diversified economies affected child
labor, with long-term ramifications. Children in textile centers appear
to have gone to work more often and at earlier ages than children in
cities such as Worcester and Fitchburg.

Bruno Ramirez notes that in any given year between 1880 and 1900
over ten thousand children worked in New England's textile mills, with
substantially higher numbers in the pre-1890 era. Other authors have
emphasized cultural traits as the reason for child labor among French-
Canadians, minimizing economic necessity. Children worked when
families required their income.

In 1870, 70% of Lowell's French-Canadian children, primarily between the ages of eleven and fifteen, worked away from home. Most of
the children came from households where the father worked as an
unskilled laborer. Child wage-earners were crucial to keeping unskilled

ÉTRE À L'OUVRAGE OU ÉTRE MAITRESSE DE MAISON

French-Canadian families in Lowell above the poverty line. The wages of working children contributed a substantial portion of the family income; two children working in the textile mills could earn almost as much as their father. Families of skilled workers, because they made more, were less reliant on children's wages.[17]

In other textile cities many French-Canadian children also worked in the mills and did not attend school. James Hanlan has determined that, in Manchester, second-generation children went to school until the age of ten, when they entered the mills.[18] In Holyoke, during the 1880s and 1890s, the few French-Canadian children who did go to school attended public rather than the parochial schools, since the public schools required only twenty weeks' attendance compared to the thirty-eight required by church schools. Eighteen additional weeks of income from work in the mills might have been crucial to these families. Those French-Canadian children who went to parochial schools were from families that did not need the additional income they might have earned.

Because they were heavily dependent on child labor, textile companies often pressured city school officials to relax attendance rules; the companies often prevailed because they were so important to continued community prosperity.[19] Of the 1,227 French-Canadian textile workers in 1878 Holyoke, 58% were female. Well over half of those under the age of fifteen were female, and 60% of all French-Canadian textile workers under twenty years of age were female.[20] In Fall River, school absenteeism was 60% during the 1860s. In 1865 the law governing the minimum working age was essentially ignored; nearly 20% of all children between the ages of ten and fourteen did not attend a single day of school. City directories listed 66% of the city's minors as mill workers.

Fall River's school superintendent was forced from office when he spoke out against the abuses that contributed to these statistics. In 1878 one-half of all French-Canadians were listed as illiterate; the rate for other ethnic groups averaged 14%. Ten years later the illiteracy rate of French-Canadians in Fall River was still 50%. Although parents were often condemned for keeping their children out of school, little was said about the low wages that required children to work in order to sustain the family.[21] The household economy needed the contributions of every family member.

Women were culturally the hub of the French-Canadian family, whose job it was to inculcate values in the children at home. While it was not always possible for French-Canadian immigrant mothers to stay home in industrial New England, in Fitchburg most could. In 1860 Fitchburg had twenty-seven French-Canadian families that included sixteen girls between the ages of five and fifteen and thirty-five women ranging from sixteen to sixty-four years old. Fourteen of these *canadiennes* earned wages, all but two of whom were over the age of fifteen. Ten of the twelve adult women engaged in waged work came from three families in which the male heads of household were either textile operatives or unemployed. Two women were alone in the city, only one of them married, and nine were between the ages of sixteen and twenty-five.

In 1870 the number of French-Canadian females over the age of five had risen to eighty-eight, nineteen between the ages of five and fifteen and sixty-nine between sixteen and sixty-seven. Despite the increase, only eleven worked for wages outside the home; none of these was married, only one was under sixteen, and seven of the eleven were between the ages of seventeen and nineteen.[22]

In 1880, of 314 employed French-Canadians in Fitchburg, only 33 were women over the age of twenty. Few women with skilled husbands worked, while nearly three-fourths of the working wives or daughters were related to unemployed men, laborers, chair makers, or textile workers. Most of the French-Canadian female population was young (70% were under the age of thirty), and those who worked were employed primarily in the textile mills (85%). Most of these women married after age twenty and stopped working.[23]

In Fitchburg forty-nine French-Canadian minors, male and female, were employed, more than half of them in the textile mills. Eleven of these individuals were fourteen years old while the rest were between the ages of fifteen and twenty. Six of the forty-nine working minors did not have parents, siblings, or spouses in the city; only one of these was a woman, nineteen-year-old Exhilde Vallient, who worked as a servant.[24] The relatively high wages may have allowed children to stay in school longer than elsewhere. The industrial structure may have minimized the need for a cheap labor force in Fitchburg and allowed more women and children to stay out of the mills.

Fitchburg, unlike the spindle cities, had one of the lowest unemployment rates in Massachusetts during the 1880s. Unemployment frequency, the percentage of the workforce unemployed at some point during a given year, hovered at 15 percent in 1885, while in Fall River,

Lawrence, and Lowell the unemployment frequencies were 51.5 percent, 34.5 percent, and 32.9 percent respectively. Although the mean duration of unemployment was similar in all these cities—4.1 months in Fitchburg, 5.2 in Lawrence, 3.9 in Lowell, and 3.7 in Fall River—the likelihood of losing one's job was significantly smaller in Fitchburg.[25]

It is clear that more household heads earned higher wages more regularly in Fitchburg than in the textile centers; in addition, the data indicate that women and children did not perform wage work as often as their counterparts in the spindle cities did. Perhaps these factors meant that the wages of women and daughters may not have been required to keep the typical family out of poverty. Families with working wives or daughters were often on the lower end of the economic spectrum; other families may have seen the extra income as a hedge against unemployment or a boost to their standard of living. Certainly, in Fitchburg women and daughters did not provide a substantial portion of the family's income as in the textile cities.[26] Higher wages and a lower incidence of unemployment reduced the need for income from wives and even daughters in Fitchburg, yet two-thirds of daughters did work. Perhaps these daughters hoped to earn money for dowries or clothing or saw work as a step toward marriage or independence.[27]

The patterns in Worcester were similar. As in Fitchburg, the regularity of employment for men had important ramifications for women. Few adult French-Canadian women were employed in 1880. Of the 307 married French-Canadian women in the city in 1880 only five worked for wages outside the home, and none of these couples had children. Two incomes might help these couples buy a house, expand a business, return to Quebec, or protect them against possible disaster in an uncertain urban industrial environment.

French-Canadian females were most likely to work between the ages of sixteen and twenty; in fact, 75% French-Canadian girls in this age group were employed. Only one of the eight married women in this age group was employed. Girls with unemployed fathers entered the workforce earlier. Of the eighty-seven females under the age of sixteen who might have been in school, three girls under the age of fourteen and twenty-five girls between fourteen and sixteen had jobs: seven in the boot and shoe industry, six in dressmaking, six in the small woolen and cotton mills, and the remainder in a variety of occupations. The likelihood of women being employed declined with age; less than one-tenth of French-Canadian women over the age of twenty worked outside the home in Worcester in 1880.[28]

The pattern was similar in Fitchburg twenty years later. A sample of 20% of the population in 1900 includes 160 French-Canadian women, of whom 34 were employed, primarily as textile operatives. Some 1,757 women over the age of sixteen worked in Fitchburg in 1900. Twenty-two of the thirty-four wage-earning French-Canadian women in this sample were under the age of twenty-two and only one was married. Only five of the thirty-four employed women in the sample were married. Four were alone in the city. Six women had fathers or husbands who worked as day laborers.[9] While the numbers of wage-earning French-Canadian women remained low, those who did work appear to be somewhat older. This may be due to the tightening of school truancy policies or successful adaptation to the economic environment.

In Fitchburg in 1900, as earlier, there were significantly fewer women earning wages outside the home than in the textile centers. As before, these two cities also had a more diversified occupational profile for men; male heads of French-Canadian households and single men over the age of twenty tended to work in metal and machinery trades or in shoe making.[30]

It is clear that there were fewer French-Canadian women in Fitchburg and Worcester than in the spindle cities throughout the period studied. This could be explained in two ways. First, migrants to these communities were families at a different stage in their life cycles than those who went to textile centers. U.S. census information indicates that immigrant families in Fitchburg and Worcester were generally younger than those migrating to the textile cities; in fact many were newly married couples who had their first child within a year of their arrival. A French-Canadian census taken by the immigrants themselves also seems to indicate that families in Fitchburg and Worcester were smaller and possibly earlier in their life cycle.[31]

Second, the relative skill level of immigrant males was higher in Fitchburg and Worcester. Those with specific skills may have chosen these cities because they offered higher earning potential. Between 1870 and 1900 one-third of the French-Canadian workers in Worcester and more than 20% of the French-Canadian workforce in Fitchburg was employed in the building trades (carpenters, masons, painters) and in metals and machinery work (blacksmiths, foundry workers, machin-

ÊTRE À L'OUVRAGE OU ÊTRE MAITRESSE DE MAISON

76 ists). These occupations were among the best paying in Massachusetts and required more skill than textile jobs.[32] French-Canadian families with numerous children and few trade skills, on the other hand, would have been more attracted to the job market in the spindle cities.[33]

The economic diversity offered by Fitchburg and Worcester implied not only better wages but also less competition among ethnic groups for jobs. Both may have decreased the levels of ethnic tension that have been documented in textile cities. Mary Cunion remembers French-Canadians and Irish millworkers hitting each other with shovels in the Amoskeag mills. "Irish confetti" pelted French-Canadians newly arrived in Biddeford, Maine, in the 1880s. This "confetti" was actually bricks thrown at the new immigrants, who would be taking jobs from the already established Irish.[34]

Violence on the shop floor and in the streets was not a feature of life in Fitchburg and Worcester. When the French-Canadians arrived they did not displace earlier immigrants. In Worcester an orphanage established by French nuns was supported by the Irish, and it distributed aid to children of both nationalities. Even the small Armenian community in the 1890s contributed food to the orphanage.[35]

Women, largely out of the waged workforce, were also more apt to cooperate across ethnic lines. As early as 1873 the Saint-Jean-Baptiste Society of Fitchburg attended the Catholic fair given by the Irish of Saint Bernard's parish in the same city en masse.[36] Children who stayed in school longer had greater contact across ethnic lines, and this contact was more likely to be cooperative than confrontational. When they entered the workforce this spirit continued. In 1880, for example, it was reported that "Most all young ladies employed in Fitchburg woolen mills are wearing green today in honor of St Patrick." Most places employing French-Canadians in 1889 were closed on New Year's Day, a day with only slightly less significance for the French-Canadians than that of Saint-Jean-Baptiste Day.[37] Women and children were a prominent part of picnics in Worcester, where they had their own games and competitions and entire families boarded trains for excursions to the beach and to Montreal for Saint-Jean-Baptiste Day trips.[38]

Family strategies in Fitchburg and Worcester mirrored those of the textile centers, but the occupational structure allowed for a different implementation of these strategies. In general, household heads were able to earn a family wage; this had important implications for wives and children.

When unemployment, the death of a spouse, or the desire to accumulate savings made it necessary, women, as in other cities, entered the labor force, but this happened less frequently than in other cities with less diversified industry. Child labor was rarely required to provide for necessities. Indeed, some of the occupations most often practiced by French-Canadians in Fitchburg and Worcester paid quite handsomely.[39] Between 1870 and 1900 most young couples that came to these two cities were headed by a skilled worker.[40] Men working in skilled occupations—masons, blacksmiths, machinists, carpenters, and those running stationary engines—made approximately twenty dollars each week while laborers and factory operatives earned nine dollars per week.[41] More often employed in the skilled trades, men in Fitchburg and Worcester were better able to earn sufficient wages to support a family. Higher incomes also allowed families to provide their offspring with a more comprehensive education. Education seems to have been valued, especially for girls, who attended school for significant periods in Fitchburg and Worcester. Daughters worked when their father was unemployed, but few worked for prolonged periods until they were fifteen years old.

In monoindustrial cities like the spindle cities, family work patterns were influenced by the dominant industry. The behavior of migrants in New England's spindle cities has been well documented. Women of all nationalities, in addition to wage work, increased household income through nonwage labor; they took in laundry and/or boarders to provide much-needed cash.[42] Yet census material for Fitchburg and Worcester indicates that few French-Canadian families took in boarders. Throughout the period studied nearly all household residents of French-Canadian families in these two cities were family members. Some aunts, uncles, or in-laws may have paid for room and board, but it is significant that very few French-Canadians were listed as boarders. In diversified manufacturing centers such as Fitchburg and Worcester, more economic opportunities may have permitted a freer expression of cultural preferences.[43]

The relatively secure job opportunities and higher wages in Fitchburg and Worcester may have led French-Canadian immigrants to employ different family strategies than in the spindle cities. In Fitchburg and Worcester, women and children worked less often, usually to offset income lost due to the unemployment of the male household head.[44] Those women and children who were employed over the long term seem to have been either alone in the city or members of households headed by women. But working women and children were the exception, not the rule.

French-Canadian immigrant women played two roles. Those who engaged in wage work were essential contributors to the family economy. In families headed by unskilled workers, the wages brought in by women may have provided the majority of the family income. Whether these women enjoyed their role as workers is unknown, but the lower wages they would accept encouraged mill managers to hire them.

In nontextile cities French-Canadian women seem to have contributed to the family economy primarily through household labor, except for young girls between school and marriage. Equally important, they may have provided a stimulus for ethnic interaction that decreased the ethnic tension in Worcester and Fitchburg. They may have been able to spend more time with their children, as both mother and child were likely to remain off the shop floor. Those who did work apparently cooperated with women of other nationalities on the shop floor as well as in the neighborhood.

Children in Fitchburg and Worcester, who stayed in school longer, had greater exposure to children of other nationalities in an environment less competitive than that of the shop floor. After prolonged exposure to other ethnic groups in school, these children might have been more likely to cooperate with other ethnic groups, particularly if they did not compete for the same jobs in an economy dominated by a single industry. In addition, because they remained in school longer than their contemporaries in the spindle cities, they entered more skilled occupations. With more education and access to better jobs, these children could better provide for themselves in the future. The structure of French-Canadian families and the economic success they enjoyed reproduced themselves better in Fitchburg and Worcester.

Were Fitchburg and Worcester isolated exceptions? Was the French-Canadian experience in these two cities unique? In order to gain greater and more meaningful insight one must study the economic and demographic context. Context is the key to gaining a deeper understanding of the roles immigrant women played in the family economy during the nineteenth century. The contributions of women to the family economy may vary by immigrant group, as a cultural interpretation might suggest, but the context in which these families operated tells us much about the adaptations immigrant women made to their environment.

1. Roy Rosenzweig, *Eight Hours for What We Will: Workers and Leisure in an Industrial City, 1870–1920* (Cambridge: Cambridge University Press, 1983), 18.

2. The cultural interpretation assumes a natural predilection toward behavior that has been ingrained by years of adaptation to a specific environment. In the case of nineteenth-century French-Canadian immigrants to New England, years of farming on small, poor farms led to a certain *mentalité* regarding work.

3. Frances H. Early, "The Settling-in Process: French-Canadian Beginnings in an American Community, Lowell, Massachusetts, 1868–1886" (Ph.D. diss., Concordia University, 1979); Early, "The Rise and Fall of Félix Albert: Some Reflections on the Aspirations of Habitant Immigrants to Lowell, Massachusetts in the Late Nineteenth Century," in *The Quebec and Acadian Diaspora in North America,* ed. Raymond Breton and Pierre Savard (Toronto: Multicultural History Society of Ontario, 1982); Early, "The French-Canadian Family Economy and Standard of Living in Lowell, Massachusetts, 1870," *Journal of Family History* 2 (Summer 1982): 180–97; Early, "Mobility Potential and the Quality of Life in Working-Class Lowell, Massachusetts: The French-Canadians ca. 1870," *Labour/Le Travailleur* 2 (1977); Tamara Hareven and Randolph Langenbach, *Amoskeag: Life and Work in an American Factory City* (New York: Pantheon, 1978); Hareven, "Family Time and Industrial Time: Family and Work in a Planned Corporation Town, 1900–1914," *Journal of Urban History* 1 (May 1975): 365–89; Hareven, "Family and Work Patterns of Immigrant Laborers in a Planned Industrial Town, 1900–1930," in *Immigrants in Industrial America,* ed. Richard Ehrlick (Charlottesville: University of Virginia Press, 1977); Hareven, *Family Time and Industrial Time: The Relationship between the Family and Work in a New England Industrial Community* (Cambridge: Cambridge University Press, 1982); Louise Lamphere, *From Working Daughters to Working Women: Immigrant Women in a New England Industrial Community* (Ithaca, N.Y.: Cornell University Press, 1987); Bruno Ramirez, "French-Canadian Immigrants in the New England Cotton Industry: A Socioeconomic Profile," *Labour/Le Travailleur* 11 (Spring 1983): 125–42.

4. Alexander Keyssar, *Out of Work: The First Century of Unemployment in Massachusetts* (Cambridge: Cambridge University Press, 1986), 118–19. Keyssar bases his argument on his analysis of Massachusetts Bureau of Statistics of Labor (MBLS) reports. Thomas Dublin, "Rural-Urban Migrants in Industrial New England: The Case of Lynn, Massachusetts, in the Mid-Nineteenth Century," *Journal of American History* 73, no. 3 (December 1986): 623–64, 643; Jay P. Dolan, *The American Catholic Experience: A History from Colonial Times to the Present* (New York: Doubleday, 1985), 154; Félix Albert, *Immigrant Odyssey: A French-Canadian Habitant in New England,* trans. Arthur L. Eno, Jr., with an introduction by Frances H. Early (Orono: University of Maine Press, 1991), 19, 20.

ÊTRE À L'OUVRAGE OU ÊTRE MAITRESSE DE MAISON

5. Massachusetts Bureau of Statistics of Labor, *Census of Massachusetts* (1885), 1:89–407.

6. Albert, *Immigrant Odyssey*, 12.

7. Bettina Bradbury, "Women and Wage Labor in a Period of Transition: Montreal 1861–1881," in *Canadian Labor History: Selected Readings,* ed. David J. Bercuson (Toronto: Copp Clark Pitman, 1987), 27–42, 31. See also, Fernand Harvey, "Technologie et organisation du travail à la fin du XIX^c siècle: la cas du Québec," *Recherches Sociographiques* 18 (September–December 1977): 397–414, 413; Yves Roby, "L'évolution économique du Québec et l'émigrant," in *Vie française: L'émigrant québécois vers les États-Unis 1850–1920,* ed. Claire Quintal (Quebec City: Le Conseil de la vie française en Amérique, 1982), 147; Albert Faucher and Maurice Lamontagne, "History of Industrial Development," in *French Canadian Society,* ed. Marcel Rioux and Yves Martin (Toronto: Macmillan, 1978), 1:257–70; Brian Young and John Dickinson, *A Short History of Quebec: A Socio-Economic Perspective* (Toronto: Copp Clark Pittman, 1988), 111; Paul-André Linteau, René Durocher, and Jean-Claude Robert, *Histoire du Québec contemporain* (Montreal: Boréal Express, 1979), 147. Uneven regional development is addressed by Bruno Ramirez, *On the Move: French-Canadian and Italian Immigrants in the North Atlantic Economy 1860–1914* (Toronto: McClelland and Stewart, 1991), 91; and Gilles Paquet and Jean-Pierre Wallot, *Lower Canada at the Turn of the Nineteenth Century: Restructuring and Modernization,* Canadian Historical Association Historical Booklet 45 (Ottawa: Canadian Historical Association, 1988), 19.

8. Armand Chartier, *Histoire des Franco-Américains de la Nouvelle-Angleterre, 1775–1990* (Sillery, Quebec: Editions Septentrion, 1991), 82; Arthur M. Schlesinger, *The Rise of the City, 1878–1898* (New York: Macmillan, 1933), 149; Page Smith, *The Rise of Industrial America: A People's History of the Post-Reconstruction Era* (New York: McGraw-Hill, 1984), 683.

9. Hareven and Langenbach, *Amoskeag,* 51.

10. Yves Roby, *Les Franco-Américains de la Nouvelle-Angleterre, 1776–1930* (Sillery, Quebec: Editions Septentrion, 1990), 73.

11. Hareven and Langenbach, *Amoskeag,* 51.

12. Roby, *Les Franco-Américains de la Nouvelle-Angleterre,* 75, 76. In this case children of wage-earning mothers testified to the continued employment of their parent after marriage. See also Hareven and Langenbach, *Amoskeag,* 255; Hareven, *Family Time and Industrial Time,* 78; Keyssar, *Out of Work,* 151–65; Early, "French-Canadian Beginnings," 113.

13. Massachusetts Bureau of Statistics of Labor, *Census* (1875), 2:497–571. The 9,555 working women of 1875 Lowell over the age of fifteen received $1.3 million less in wages for the year than their 7,699 male counterparts.

14. Massachusetts Bureau of Statistics of Labor, *Census* (1885), 1:248–61. There were 6,612 people making less than six dollars per week and 5,416, or 82%, of these workers were female. The women in these low wage cate-

gories accounted for 83% of all women in Lowell who were engaged in waged
work.

15. Bureau of the Census, *Twelfth Census of the United States, 1900* (Washington, D.C.: Bureau of the Census, 1904), vol. 8, part 2, 382–825.

16. *New England Business Directory and Gazetteer, 1896* (Boston: Sampson, Murdoch, and Co., 1896).

17. Bruno Ramirez, in "French-Canadian Immigrants in the New England Cotton Industry: A Socioeconomic Profile," *Labour/Le Travailleur* 11 (Spring 1983): 125–42, uses data from an Immigration Commission report of 1908–9. He estimates from this report that 17,704 children worked in New England's textile mills in 1880, 10,165 in 1890, and 10,819 in 1900. While Irish immigrants also required their children to work, a substantial portion of those working children were French-Canadian. Frances Early, "The French-Canadian Family Economy," finds that 39 percent of the income of French-Canadian families with working children was contributed by those children, 22 percent by children under sixteen. By the turn of the century Ramirez finds that children contributed one-third of the French-Canadian family's income in Lowell. See also Early, "Mobility Potential and the Quality of Life in Working-Class Lowell, Massachusetts"; and Stephan Thernstrom, *Poverty and Progress: Social Mobility in a Nineteenth Century City* (Cambridge, Mass.: Harvard University Press, 1964), 22.

18. James P. Hanlan, *Working Population of Manchester, N.H., 1840–1886* (Ann Arbor, Mich.: UMI Research Press, 1981), 124, 165.

19. Peter Haebler, "Habitants in Holyoke" (Ph.D. diss. University of New Hampshire, 1976), 69, 130, 133, 135.

20. Haebler, "Habitants in Holyoke," 68. See also Roby, *Les Franco-Américains,* 68–69.

21. Philip T. Silvia, "Neighbors from the North: French-Canadian Immigrants vs. Trade Unionism in Fall River, Massachusetts," in *The Little Canadas of New England,* ed. Claire Quintal (Worcester, Mass.: French Institute/Assumption College, 1983), 51–52.

22. U.S. Manuscript Census, Fitchburg, Mass., 1860, 1870. The majority of the females for 1860, a total of thirty-four, were born in Canada while seventeen were born in various New England states of French-Canadian parents. All of those born in New England were under the age of fifteen. All of the French-Canadian women who earned wages in 1870 were born in Quebec. Only eight of the eighty-eight were not born in Canada.

23. U.S. Manuscript Census, Fitchburg, Mass., 1880.

24. U.S. Manuscript Census, Fitchburg, Mass., 1880. Those in textiles were concentrated in woolen mills, with a handful in cotton and less than three each in worsted or duck mills.

25. Keyssar, *Out of Work,* 50, 120–21, 328–29. Keyssar differentiates unemployment frequency from the unemployment rate by defining the latter as the

number of workers unemployed at any one specific time during the year. Unemployment frequency for Fitchburg was roughly 15 percent for all male age cohorts except for the 50–59 age group, which had an unemployment frequency of 19.3 percent. As noted earlier, Keyssar developed his statistics from census and MBLS reports.

26. See Haebler, "Habitants in Holyoke," 170; Ramirez, *On the Move*, 119, 125; Albert, *Immigrant Odyssey*, 11.

27. U.S. Manuscript Census, Fitchburg, Mass., 1880.

28. U.S. Manuscript Census, Worcester, Mass., 1880. In Worcester, as in Fitchburg, French-Canadian women wage earners accounted for less than 10% of all working French-Canadians in the city in 1880. The vast majority of the 580 French-Canadian women, 447, were born in Quebec. Only in the sixteen-to-twenty age cohort did the native born of French-Canadian parents outnumber the Quebec born. Among the 98 wage-earning women only 4 were married. Slightly less than one-half, 47, were born in the United States of French-Canadian parents with 41 of these under the age of twenty. As in Fitchburg these female wage earners were young women who worked following the end of school and before marriage.

29. U.S. Manuscript Census, Fitchburg, Mass., 1900.

30. Paul R. Dauphinais, "Structure and Strategy: French-Canadians in Central New England, 1850–1900" (Ph.D. diss., University of Maine, 1991), 101–59; Yves Roby, *Les Franco-Américains de la Nouvelle-Angleterre*, 68.

31. U.S. Census, Fitchburg, Mass., 1880, 1900; *Rapports des centres au comité executif de la convention de Franco-Américain*, Nashua, N.H., 1888.

32. U.S. Census, Fitchburg, 1870, 1880, 1900; U.S. Census, Worcester, 1870, 1880, 1900; Fitchburg City Directory, 1890; *Le Worcester Canadien*, 1891.

33. Massachusetts Bureau of Statistics of Labor, *Census* (1885), 1:89–407.

34. Hareven and Langenbach, *Amoskeag*, 45; Jacques Downs, *The Cities on the Saco* (Norfolk, Va.: The Danning Co., 1985), 100. See also Constance M. Green, *Holyoke, Massachusetts: A Case Study of the Industrial Revolution in America* (New Haven, Conn.: Yale University Press, 1939), 369; Haebler, "Habitants in Holyoke," 96, 369; Early, "The Settling-in Process," 231; Brian Mitchell, *The Paddy Camps: The Irish of Lowell, 1821–61* (Urbana: University of Illinois Press, 1988), 144.

35. Sister Marie-Michel-Archange, *By This Sign You Will Live* (Baie-Saint-Paul, Quebec: Little Franciscans of Mary, 1955), 36, 97, 347.

36. *Fitchburg* (Mass.) *Sentinel*, October 11, 1873.

37. *Fitchburg Sentinel*, March 17, 1880, January 1, 1889. Saint-Jean-Baptiste Day celebrates the patron saint of Quebec and is today a holiday of great importance in that province.

38. Rosenzweig, *Eight Hours for What We Will*, 28; Dauphinais, "Structure and Strategy," 160–202.

39. Massachusetts Bureau of Statistics of Labor, *Census of Massachusetts* (1875), 2: 415–18, 468–69, 507, 552–53, 596–97, 634.

40. U.S. Manuscript Census, Fitchburg, Mass., and Worcester, Mass., 1870, 1880, 1900; Fitchburg City Directories, 1878–90.

41. Keyssar, *Out of Work*, 45.

42. See, for instance, Louise Lamphere, *From Working Daughters to Working Women*.

43. Virginia Yans McLaughlin, "Patterns of Work and Family Organization: Buffalo's Italians," in Theodore K. Rabb and Robert I. Rotberg, eds., *The Family in History: Interdisciplinary Essays* (New York: Harper and Row, 1971), 111–26.

44. Ramirez, "French-Canadian Immigrants in the New England Cotton Industry," 138.

ÉTRE À L'OUVRAGE OU ÉTRE MAITRESSE DE MAISON

GOOD MEN AND "WORKING GIRLS"

The Bureau of Statistics of Labor, 1870–1900

HENRY F. BEDFORD

Conceived in 1869 to deflect mounting demands for substantive labor reform, the Massachusetts Bureau of Statistics of Labor began with a vague mandate, no precedent, a tiny budget, and Henry Kemble Oliver, a determined director. The Massachusetts General Court provided modest salaries for him and his deputy, George E. McNeill, and appropriated five thousand dollars to support the first public agency in the nation established to provide reliable statistical information about the life and work of "the working classes." The legislative directive—"to collect . . . and present . . . statistical detail" and to investigate "industrial, social, educational, and sanitary conditions" in the Commonwealth—gave Oliver, McNeill, and their successors a wide field for research.[1]

Oliver brought to his appointive post a suspicion of industrial employers nurtured most recently during two years spent monitoring noncompliance with laws requiring school attendance and restricting the working hours of children. Once a teacher in Salem, he had founded an academy for young women there and then managed profitable textile mills in Lawrence, whose owners discharged him, according to local rumor, because he coddled employees. McNeill had promoted legislation to limit the hours of industrial labor and forcefully argued against management's insistence that it alone should determine wages. Employers, doubtful that officials with those preconceptions would con-

"The Girls I Used to Work with on Winter Street." Courtesy, the Boston Public Library, Print Department.

duct impartial research, resisted their inquiries and almost succeeded in eliminating the Bureau after Oliver alienated the state's banks in 1873 and precipitated his own dismissal. His replacement was Carroll D. Wright, a failed merchant but a successful patent attorney and two-term state senator who subordinated his own interpretation of evidence to the task of compiling it. Horace Wadlin, Wright's deputy and successor, followed his mentor's example after Wright became the first United States Commissioner of Labor in 1888.

All three nineteenth-century directors interpreted the Bureau's charter to require investigation of the ways working people lived, as well as the ways they earned their living, and to educate the public, as well as elected officials, about the circumstances of a growing number of their fellow citizens. In the years after the Civil War, as Oliver noted in 1871, a "large . . . majority" of the state's residents were female, a demographic fact that made research "regarding women's work and wages highly important."[2] As a matter of course, the agency included female employees in its industry-wide studies of wages, hours, and working conditions, and in surveys of intermittent employment. Since women constituted a substantial fraction of those engaged in the production of textiles or shoes, for instance, they were not merely incidental to such research. But concentration on one industry or factory tended to make gender distinctions seem no more significant than other differences the Bureau noted, such as age, ethnicity, or skill.

Other inquiries the directors initiated did emphasize gender, with extensive data about jobs commonly thought of as peculiarly female: teacher, retail clerk, cook, and maid. Tables revealing compensation and other specifically economic facts measured only one aspect of any worker's life. The agency arranged census returns to inform public discussion about the effect of employment on marriage, health, and fertility, and gathered information about the living conditions of working women, their leisure activity, and their household and family responsibilities.[3]

By the standards of the late nineteenth century, the men who directed the Bureau had a progressive outlook on the social and economic questions of the day. Carroll Wright ordinarily let statistical detail rather than explicit advocacy convey his point of view and persuade others. Oliver was less patient, as his proposals for improving the conditions of female factory operatives demonstrate. He favored increasing the minimum age of first employment to insure more formal education for girls. He urged the legislature to reduce and limit the hours of daily and weekly labor in mills, to require equal pay when men and women performed the same tasks, and to enact political equality. He suggested that municipalities, social agencies, and civic-minded individuals open boardinghouses to provide dignified lodging and healthy meals for single working women. He thought employers ought to improve factory conditions and modify work rules for women and girls in order to ensure the health of the present and future children of Massachusetts.

Oliver's sympathetic, programmatic response to what he obviously believed to be injustice stemmed from conviction as much as from research and analysis. He concluded an early survey, for instance, by enumerating the "disabilities . . . peculiar to" working women, an unfortunate phrase that seemed to blame them for their own victimization.[4] The "disabilities" he specified were in fact social assumptions about female roles "peculiar to" society at large and probably not subject to correction through research conducted at the Bureau of Statistics of Labor. The men who assigned that research, furthermore, sometimes manifested those same attitudes. Families supported solely by a working woman's wages, for instance, were never the focus of their investigations; instead, they examined the marginal amounts women contributed to the budgets of male-centered households. While Oliver, Wright, and their successors occasionally questioned the economic orthodoxy of the day, they did not challenge marital and domestic arrangements that they and most of their contemporaries presumed to be immutable. Their reports, shaped by traditional assumptions about gender, often betrayed the Victorian condescension that later characterized many middle-class progressives—the obligation of good men to protect weaker women.

Although the Bureau's directors seem to have believed that a woman's work ought to be performed in her home for her family, and rewarded with deference and affection instead of cash, they acknowledged that present reality in Massachusetts did not meet that ideal. Their own surveys showed thousands of female employees in mills and factories, offices, classrooms, and shops, as well as in kitchens, laundries, and nurseries. In 1889, reviewing the Bureau's work over its first twenty years, Horace G. Wadlin pointed proudly to the concern for and inclusion of working women in studies that began with the very first report in 1869. That volume, Wadlin noted, examined "the effect of factory life upon women, the conditions of working women in Boston, and the result of night work upon women and children." The Bureau later broadened the inquiry with investigations of boardinghouses, divorce, involuntary unemployment, the effectiveness of the 1874 law limiting to ten the daily hours of female factory workers, and the impact of factory work and higher education on health. In 1884, an essay entitled "The Working Girls of Boston" included a sober presentation about the city's prostitutes.[5]

In the nineteenth century, serious study of the work women performed in the home, whether or not compensated, was about as rare as dispassionate discussion of prostitution. Domestic labor was not ordinarily the focus of the Bureau's research, but the agency's published reports at least remarked the economic importance not only of paid cooks and nannies but also of women who prepared their own meals and tended their own children. In taking that work into account, the Bureau was several steps in advance of the legislature that established it and much of the public whose economic life it charted.

To facilitate consideration of what it called "House Work," and to complement data about women who received wages, the Bureau devised a taxonomy of domestic chores. The unpaid effort of those who managed households and bore children was not initially the object of research. But hired female domestics, the Bureau believed, lived "as a rule, in greater comfort" than other employed women; "their food is better, lodgings more comfortable, and their wages enable them to dress neatly and comfortably and to save something." Although maids and seamstresses earned no more than three or four dollars a week, the Bureau noted that work in households staffed by more than one servant was "often not arduous compared with other vocations." Yet the situation was "always confining," an uncharacteristic acknowledgment of the worker's own reaction to her situation. "Many who try this kind of labor," especially those the Bureau called "American girls," abandoned service for the "discomforts and privations" of "the shop-girl," who enjoyed "greater freedom and independence."[6]

The Bureau did not discuss restrictions on the autonomy of married women who worked in their own homes. Indeed, Carroll Wright did not even number them among the workers he counted in the Massachusetts census of 1885. That survey included house*keepers*, who received a wage for service, and house*workers*, who assisted with family chores and were not otherwise employed, among the 300,999 women engaged in industry. But house*wives*—the 372,612 adult females for whom family was the sole occupation—were omitted. Horace Wadlin advanced an unconvincing explanation for this statistical artifact after Wright departed to become United States Commissioner of Labor.

"Houseworkers," Wadlin argued, could be differentiated from "housewives" because the former preempted jobs that unemployed women or immigrants might have filled. In addition, unlike those Wadlin labeled housewives, some houseworkers held outside, paying positions for part of the year and took domestic employment only during intervals when factories reduced production. Although such women sometimes functioned as domestic servants, they classified themselves as "engaged in housework," which seemed somehow a "more elevated and dignified title than that of 'servant.' "[7] The dignity conferred by a wife's title was apparently self-evident.

Wadlin realized that the separation of housewives from other domestic workers reflected "conventional thought" more than statistical rigor. "Strictly speaking," Wadlin conceded, "housewives are as much in industry as any other women"; their effort required "as much brain and muscle as many other occupations." The work they performed was "surely worth what it would cost to have it done" if they stopped doing

GOOD MEN AND "WORKING GIRLS"

it: "If a housewife were not expected nor required to work, then . . . paid service would have to be substituted," a demand for labor that would outstrip the state's resources. But "it would be contrary to generally entertained opinions to include the home, that is the housewives, under industry." So excluding them from the census of working women was "for conventional and arbitrary reasons."

So arbitrary, indeed, that Wadlin essentially abandoned his defense. "The housewife is as much a member of the army of workers as the clerk or cotton weaver," who usually had uncompensated and statistically ignored "household duties" to perform when her paid day's work was finished. The Bureau itself had added "housewife" to the list of tabulated female occupations in 1875; in the coming census of 1895, Wadlin said, "she should be lifted to her proper position and considered to be as much 'in industry' as those women engaged in any other branch of labor."[8]

Meanwhile, and quite significantly, excluding housewives enabled Wadlin to conclude that very few of the state's married women were "in industry," thereby confirming another tenet of the "conventional thought" of the day. Omitting 373,000 housewives led to the comforting statistic that more than seven of every eight working women were unmarried. (Fewer than a third of men "in industry" were married; only about a quarter of all the state's industrial workers had wed, according to the census.) Even if housewives did not count, however, the absolute number of employed women climbed in the decade after 1875 more rapidly than the female population and more rapidly than the rate for men; in 1875, women constituted less than one quarter of the labor force, a proportion that grew to over one third ten years later. The men at the Bureau knew that popular anxiety rose with escalating female employment. They responded obliquely to this apprehension with detailed tables showing "conclusively that the presence of women in industry has not decreased the number of births or marriages nor increased the number of deaths," thereby documenting the absence of a factual base for fears that paid work endangered health, home, and family.[9]

As the 1889 survey of "Women in Industry" demonstrates, the Bureau simultaneously challenged some stereotypes concerning working women while it exemplified others. It was convention, after all, not logic, that allowed a housewife's marital status, rather than her function, to determine her relevance to the Bureau's tables. Wadlin did not study families for whom women were the major or exclusive source of financial support, circumstances that were presumed to be anomalous in a properly constituted society. In 1884, when Carroll Wright published a detailed survey of "The Working Girls of Boston," he was at pains to contradict prevailing rumors about the lax morality of urban working women, but his prose suggested that he retained other conventional views about appropriate female behavior. (To a contemporary reader, the contrasting titles of the 1884 piece on "Working Girls" and the 1889 research on "Women in Industry" seem striking, but they probably signify little more than nineteenth-century usage.)

The allegation that "shop girls are an immoral class," Wright noted, was often repeated, but ordinarily it was demonstrated not with relevant data but only by assertion that their employment sometimes depended on a "willingness . . . to become the intimate friend of . . . the proprietor or head of a department," or by the observation that "it is largely from their ranks that prostitutes are recruited." Facts, he continued, belied "the vile charge"; economic necessity might result in growing numbers of employed women, but that situation did not threaten society's moral foundation.[10]

That complacent conclusion rested on 1,032 interviews with working women in all of Boston's neighborhoods. Wright calculated that approximately one in five Boston women enumerated in the 1880 census was employed. Of those forty thousand women, about six percent were teachers, artists, musicians, and physicians, together with one lone attorney; these women were not, in this instance, relevant to the Bureau's research. Domestic workers, Wright estimated, made up half of the remainder, and they also were not subjects for this study, which concentrated on the remaining twenty thousand women, most of whom were engaged in trade and manufacturing. The Bureau's staff personally visited a representative sample of these women to construct a statistical profile of Boston's "working girl."

This composite employee was about twenty-three years old, unmarried, born in Massachusetts of foreign-born parents, and in good health. She earned more than six dollars for about sixty hours' weekly work, but occupational interruptions reduced her annual income to less than $270. She lived with parents or other relatives, did her own sewing and laundry, and helped with general housework. In essence, her family subsidized her employment, for those who tried to exist independently found their income barely adequate; families not only provided housing and board but also occasional cash for clothing and amenities.[11]

The fact that most "working girls" continued to reside with their families persuaded Wright that they lived virtuously. Although interviewers had worried about the "delicate" personal interrogations they were assigned, in fact, they reported, their experiences were both "pleasant and profitable." Their informants were cooperative, afforded each researcher a "courteous reception and ladylike treatment," and rarely allowed a "mistaken sense of 'womanly dignity' " to interfere. They were at home in the evening, "busy at some household or personal duty," contributing to the "orderly and artistic arrangement of the household," even when privation made order and art difficult. Their visitors "could not help being struck with the refinement of feeling that existed among them." In their effort to dispel popular myths about the behavior of "working girls," the men who wrote the Bureau's reports chose language that revealed myths of their own.[12]

Preconceptions and omissions also shaped the account of conversations with 170 Boston prostitutes. Although a table charted the previous occupations of these women and implied discussion with each of them, details are scant: no observations about the condition of rooms and surroundings, no comments about taste or style or order, no statistics about income, no information about laundry or mending or cost of living. Inferences were drawn from the data not by the women themselves but by a male police captain, who said that professional streetwalkers were not "working girls" in the usual meaning of the phrase. Wright agreed that clerks, women in the needle trades, and "girls" in other legitimate occupations were "making an heroic, an honest, and a virtuous struggle to earn an honorable livelihood," and only rarely "following a life other than one of integrity." In the exceptional case, he added, men provided the economic temptation and deserved "public condemnation" as much as did "fallen" women. Nor was the economic system that inadequately rewarded diligent, respectable women blameless. "It is easy to be good on a sure and generous income," Wright observed; "it requires the strongest character to . . . be good . . . on an unstable income of five dollars per week."[13]

That insight did not lead to recommendations for legislative policy. Indeed the Bureau's directors apparently believed low wages for women an inevitable and therefore unremediable consequence of the wider economic opportunity that accompanied industrialization. Although a woman's wage was lower than that of a man, and usually insufficient to support a dignified independent existence, Wright seemed comforted that many women were "now earning something where formerly they could earn nothing." Improvement, for which he hoped, must await evolving "industrial and economic conditions," not legislation or even charity.[14]

Wright may not have realized that his conclusion highlighted institutional futility. How useful was a thorough study of Boston's "working girls" that uncovered causes of social and moral problems, when patience was the prescribed remedy? The judgment that neither legislators nor an enlightened public could alter wages sufficiently to help struggling women support themselves and, in the Victorian idiom, defend their virtue may have been consonant with economic orthodoxy in the later nineteenth century. But reaching that conclusion did not require discussion with more than a thousand busy women.

Other recommendations were anticlimactic. The ten-hour law should be observed, not because it was good public policy but because "85+ percent of the working girls of Boston do their own housework and sewing, . . . and this home work must be done in addition to that performed for their employers." Voluntary "kindness" and "thoughtfulness" on the part of employers seemed to the Bureau the most likely avenue of reform. Society should assist benevolent bosses by welcoming "the honest working girl" in churches and social gatherings, rather than "thoughtlessly pass[ing] her by." Institutions providing housing and vocational training for these women should be generously supported and their number increased. But the passive verb left to the imagination precise identification of the public-spirited individuals who might undertake such worthy projects.[15]

In fact, the men who managed the Bureau, like most of their contemporaries, expected husbands, fathers, and an occasional brother or son to support the working women of the Commonwealth. The wages of men ought to meet a family's basic needs; the wages of wives and daughters provided the margin over subsistence that enhanced a small savings account, permitted purchase of a house, or enabled younger, and usually male, members of the family to remain in school. If an unusual woman depended only on her own income to sustain herself

94 and her children, the Bureau assumed, without investigation, that most, whether married or not, retained a link, usually including residence, with relatives.

That situation, as Henry Oliver had noted several years earlier, created competition that depressed wages for all female workers. He thought "the slightest examination" of comparative compensation disclosed "a very great inequity" favoring "the stronger sex."[16] He acknowledged that his data were incomplete and that he lacked analytical tools to account for this disparity; what he called conclusions might more accurately have been listed as beliefs for which he found no contradictory evidence.

Oliver dismissed political inequality, which he thought indefensible, as an explanation for economic injustice. Nor was he persuaded by the frequent claim of employers that support families provided for many female workers reduced their need for compensation. More convincing, he thought, was the notion that a general "expectation" of eventual marriage diminished the career ambitions of young, single women, some of whom regarded employment as temporary and consequently failed to acquire skills that might have enabled promotion and higher wages. In addition to these rationalizations, and probably more important, was a prevailing social "prejudice" that blocked working women from access to better jobs.[17]

Yet the Bureau did not seek out or interview those women who had achieved better jobs or those who supported a family because of a man's death, disability, disappearance, or lack of employment. (Nor did the Bureau remark the evidence that periodic economic crises in the later nineteenth century were more likely to interrupt the income of men than of working women. Layoffs at textile mills or shoe factories ordinarily affected employees without regard to sex, but the predominance of women in domestic service, which was not governed by the same market conditions, made a significant statistical difference.[18]) An effort in 1874 and 1875 to describe "The Condition of Workingmen's Families" in specific, personal terms, for example, began with the proposition that "a man's labor should be worth . . . as much as, with economy and prudence, will comfortably maintain himself and his family." To be sure, the 397 visits the Bureau's staff conducted in the kitchens and corridors of skilled and unskilled, native and immigrant laborers across the Commonwealth demonstrated that male wages did not always suffice.

In those 397 families, only a dozen wives worked outside their homes and their contribution to family income was much smaller than that of 325 children between the ages of ten and seventeen, 85 of whom were girls. The average employed wife earned about $223 annually; a girl, about $260. Wright calculated that children provided nearly a quarter of the aggregate income of these families, while wives earned less than one percent. So small was that fraction that he concluded that "wives, generally speaking, . . . would save more by staying at home than they gain by outside labor." He did not specify the out-of-pocket costs that might be saved.[19]

While the men in the General Court no doubt welcomed Wright's observation, it was also inherent in his choice of those to be interviewed. A more inclusive sample would have revealed that wage-earning wives were more important than this research suggested. A decade later, the Bureau's own data demonstrated that wives, whether they worked inside or outside their homes, made a financial contribution to family income well in excess of one percent.

If the Bureau postulated male domination of families and their re-sources and refused to challenge employers' control of wages, it did gather evidence reformers cited in support of legislation to protect the health of working women. Out of concern for what were delicately termed "functions peculiar to her sex," the agency began early to collect information about ventilation, nutrition, occupational hazards, and re-spites in factory schedules for meals and toilet breaks.[20] By the end of the century, less reticent staff members asked about the effect of indus-trial tasks on menstruation and fertility. Although the Bureau did not conduct the research and only a little of the data pertained to Mas-sachusetts women, the *Annual Report* for 1885 carried a piece demon-strating that higher education did not diminish the vitality of female undergraduates, including their reproductive capacity.[21] Anxiety that unregulated, "strenuous" female activity might reduce the general pop-ulation in both numbers and vigor was perceptible, if not always articu-lated, in much of this material. The relatively broad-minded men of the Bureau certainly sensed, and may have shared, popular fear that "other races," especially French-Canadian and Irish immigrants, might over-whelm and displace "American" traditions and cultural hegemony.

That flawed, ethnocentric definition of "race," of course, is only one illustration of a clouded outlook. However inclusive and sympathetic the Bureau's understanding of the Commonwealth's laboring population may have been, the view was that of men and it was framed by male social assumptions; the reports those men wrote disclose their assumptions as well as a quantified outline of the society they studied. Perhaps their attitudes were not exclusively male but socially pervasive; the Bureau seems to have confronted criticism of its work and noted disagreement with other conclusions, but no dissent, either from women who were temporary members of the Bureau's staff or from the women with whom they spoke, appears in published reports.[22]

The preconceptions of the men who directed the Bureau, however, do not invalidate the evidence they compiled as industrial and social change rapidly transformed the Commonwealth during the later nineteenth century. The irony of the work of Oliver, Wright, and Wadlin, and the object lesson for those who would use their research, is that they did not allow their own evidence to modify their understanding of the way the world ought to work. They documented discriminatory wage rates but were unsure whether the resulting situation was inequitable, inevitable, or a symptom of social disintegration because women ought not to be gainfully employed at all. They worried about the growing number of women in factories but were consoled because most of them were single and presumably would escape to the leisure and security a husband afforded. Marriage differentiated housewives from houseworkers, however objectively similar their tasks.

Yet, whatever the unconscious bounds on the directors' vision, the portrait of Massachusetts labor that emerges from the evidence in the Bureau's reports is credible and extraordinarily detailed. The men responsible for that depiction of women at work in the mills, shops, pantries, and bedrooms of the Commonwealth ought to have examined their own handiwork more closely; it provided a reliable, but unrealized, opportunity to correct assumptions about appropriate roles for women in industrial society.

Notes

1. For an inside account of the founding and earliest years of the Massachusetts Bureau of Statistics of Labor (hereafter MBLS), see MBLS, *Fourth Annual Report* (Boston, 1873), 7–47. The Bureau's annual reports, which continue into the twentieth century, contain an abundance of quantitative and descriptive evidence for the social history of working people and the economic history of the Commonwealth. Initial printings were quite small and soon

exhausted; Greenwood has issued a microfiche edition of volumes through 1900. In *Carroll Wright and Labor Reform: The Origin of Labor Statistics* (Cambridge, Mass.: Harvard University Press, 1960), James Lieby combines a study of the Bureau with a biographical essay on the agency's most prominent director; see also the memorial sketch by Wright's successor, Horace G. Wadlin, in MBLS, *Fortieth Annual Report* (1909), 359–400. For Oliver, see MBLS, *Seventeenth Annual Report* (1886), 3–48, and Henry F. Bedford, "Tenement Houses in Salem: A Report for the Bureau of Statistics of Labor, 1873," in *Essex Institute Historical Collections* 128, no. 1 (January 1992): 3–6.

2. MBLS, *Report* (1871), 197.

3. Although this chapter focuses on the Bureau itself, rather than on the workers the agency studied, the account is informed by the growing scholarly literature about working women. A somewhat arbitrary selection from this impressive bibliography, with an emphasis on Massachusetts, might include, Mary H. Blewett, *Men, Women, and Work: Class, Gender, and Protest in the New England Shoe Industry, 1870–1910* (Urbana: University of Illinois Press, 1988) and her "We are Freeborn American Women," in *Labor in Massachusetts: Selected Essays,* ed. Kenneth Fones-Wolf and Martin Kaufman (Westfield: Institute for Massachusetts Studies, 1990); in that collection, see also Marjorie R. Abel, "Women's Work in the Western Massachusetts Rural Economy." Also, Carol Lasser, "'The World's Dread Laugh': Singlehood and Service in Nineteenth-Century Boston," in *The New England Working Class and the New Labor History,* ed. Herbert G. Gutman and Donald H. Bell (Urbana: University of Illinois Press, 1987); and Renee Toback, "Protective Labor Legislation for Women: The Massachusetts Ten-Hour Law" (Ph.D. diss., University of Massachusetts, 1986), are other recent examples.

4. MBLS, *Third Annual Report* (1872), 114–18.

5. MBLS, *Twentieth Annual Report* (1889), 521–22.

6. MBLS, *Report* (1871), 198, 199; 201–3. In 1871, the Bureau categorized domestic sewing as housework, although much of that labor was probably expended in the production of garments for market; the distinction between domestic sewing and manufacture for sale was eventually drawn more sharply.

7. MBLS, *Twentieth Annual Report* (1889), 578–79.

8. Ibid.

9. Ibid., 598–601.

10. MBLS, *Fifteenth Annual Report* (1884), 118.

11. Ibid., 1–118, passim.

12. Ibid., 4.

13. Ibid., 123–26.

14. Ibid., 129.

15. Ibid., 127, 129, 130.

16. MBLS, *Report* (1871), 224.

17. MBLS, *Third Annual Report* (1872), 114–18.

18. See Alexander Keyssar, *Out of Work: The First Century of Unemployment in Massachusetts* (Cambridge: Cambridge University Press, 1986), 100–108, for a more extended discussion of differential unemployment.

19. MBLS, *Sixth Annual Report* (1875), 193, 360, 363, 369, 384.

20. This sort of data, of course, became the basis for the famous brief of Louis D. Brandeis in *Muller v. Oregon.* Brandeis practiced in Boston, and his published correspondence demonstrates familiarity with the Bureau's research though not specifically with the studies discussed here. See Melvin I. Urofsky and David W. Levy, ed., *Letters of Louis D. Brandeis* (Albany: State University of New York Press, 1971–1978), 1:350.

21. MBLS, *Sixteenth Annual Report* (1885), 473–532.

22. See, for example, MBLS, *Thirteenth Annual Report* (1882), 3ff, for an example of the Bureau's effort to record public criticism.

THE GENDERED FOUNDATIONS OF SOCIAL WORK EDUCATION IN BOSTON, 1904–1930

LINDA M. SHOEMAKER

Social work appeared as a profession in the United States Census for the first time in 1930. To the surprise of no one then in the profession, the government figures revealed social work to be a rigidly sex-segregated and hierarchical profession. Fully 80 percent of social workers were women, and they made up the profession's rank and file as individual and family caseworkers, the lowest-paid and lowest-status positions in social work. Male social workers, despite their smaller numbers, held nearly all administrative, leadership, and policy-making posts and only rarely were counted among the ranks of caseworkers.[1]

This chapter seeks to understand how the creation of social work education contributed to the development of social work as a sex-segregated profession. Using the Boston School for Social Workers (BSSW) as a case study, I argue that social work educators' preconceptions about gender difference led to the construction and institutionalization of separate educational programs for women and men preparing for careers in social work. Graduates entered their field with strictly gendered professional identities, which resulted in the segregated and hierarchical configuration of the profession reflected by the 1930 census.

Historians have devoted little attention to the influence of schools of social work in the process of creating a professional identity, especially in the experimental, formative years of professional social work education prior to World War I.[2] But an examination of the early history of

Women studying at the Simmons College School of Social Work. Courtesy, College Archives, Simmons College.

the Boston School reveals a period of invention and experimentation during which the basis for a gender-divided profession was articulated and institutionalized.

At the turn of the twentieth century, "social work" was a relatively new and imprecise term that encompassed a diverse range of ameliorative, preventive, and reformist approaches to poverty and other social ills. Early social work education leaders, at the Boston School and elsewhere, faced the task of constructing training programs and curricula for the women and men who sought to serve, either as volunteers or paid workers, in a myriad of settings, including relief-giving charities, individual and family casework agencies, public and private correctional and caregiving institutions, neighborhood settlement houses, and also for those who sought to engage in sociological research and advance social reform at the municipal, state, and national levels. So imprecise was the term "social work" that as late as 1909, Jeffrey Brackett, director of the Boston School, observed that the public was at times confused about the differences between social work, sociology, and socialism.[3]

Central to the process of constructing a unified professional identity out of the amorphous category "social work" was the development of what has been termed by historians of social work as a "nuclear skill" or "cognitive core."[4] Roy Lubove, in his classic interpretation of the professionalization of social work, *The Professional Altruist,* argues that schools of social work came to serve the needs and agenda of the country's urban casework agencies and charity organization societies, which had long stressed the individual and pathological causes of poverty and other social ills. In their exclusive emphasis on individual and family casework as a profession-defining "nuclear skill," according to Lubove, schools of social work sacrificed the potentially transformative approaches of broad social science education, sociological research, and social reform, which were rooted in competing ideological traditions and had no easily identifiable "differentiating skill" or transmissible technique. By the 1920s, Lubove argues, schools of social work, for both methodological and ideological reasons, turned out mere "practitioners," rather than the "social administrators, scholars, or theorists" who might have had the potential to use social work as an avenue toward social reform and social justice.[5]

A consideration of gender as a category of analysis in the early history of the Boston School suggests an alternative interpretation of the ascendancy of casework in social work education. The predominance of casework "practitioners" by the 1920s and 1930s is clear in the U.S. Census, but the dearth of scholars and theorists was not solely the result of the victory of the ideology of the charity organization movement, but rather a reflection of professional education's gender-based preparation of social workers. The Boston School did not develop simply as a training facility for the city's charity organization. From its very first year in 1904, the School explicitly sought to transcend the needs of particular institutions and developed instead a broad and inclusive definition of professional social work education. Serving both women and men, the Boston School constructed a cognitive core that included elements of technique, research, and reform. Ultimately, however, that broad definition collapsed under the weight of limiting ideologies about gender-appropriate realms of social work. After 1916, professional social work education in Boston was segregated by sex, leading to the development of separate cognitive cores for women and men and paving the way for the development of a gender-stratified profession. Women were trained in the specialized techniques of individual and family casework while men pursued a more academic curriculum of social science theory and research that prepared them to lead the profession as administrators, policy makers, and social reformers.

In October 1904, Boston's oldest and newest institutions of higher education, Harvard University and Simmons Female College, in cooperation with the city's charity and social welfare leaders, established the Boston School for Social Workers. The School's inauspicious headquarters at 9 Hamilton Place, one tiny office and a single cramped classroom filled with borrowed furniture and the rising sounds of a neighboring tavern, belied the momentousness of the School's early history. As the first school in the nation to offer a year-long, full-time social work program with a university affiliation, the Boston School was a pioneer in the invention of professional social work education.

The leading force behind the creation of the Boston School for Social Workers was Dr. Jeffrey Richardson Brackett.[6] A native of Quincy, Massachusetts, Brackett first rose to national prominence in the 1890s for his leadership of public and private social welfare activities in Baltimore, Maryland, where he was a lecturer in "Public Aid, Charity, and Corrections" at Johns Hopkins University. Building upon an early interest in the charity organization movement, Brackett cultivated an expertise in professional training and education for charitable and philanthropic workers. In 1898, he was a co-founder and lecturer at the pioneering New York Summer School of Applied Philanthropy, a first-of-its-kind, intensive six-week training program designed for active charity workers sponsored by the New York Charity Organization Society. Brackett's experience as a teacher of "applied philanthropy" at both Johns Hopkins and the New York School, and his numerous speeches and publications, gave him the insights and authority to become a leading national spokesman for professional education.[7] By 1903 Brackett had begun to decry the fact that the profession did not have a single school that offered a "sufficiently long term of instruction combined with real training," and for the rest of his career, he devoted himself to the cause of professional education.[8]

At the turn of the century, many voices from the nation's charitable and philanthropic communities argued that social work education needed to move beyond the brief, informal, and narrowly defined apprenticeship-style training practiced in most social welfare settings. Brackett argued that earlier attempts at social work education, even the pioneering New York School, were too limited, both in "the subject of study, [which gave] views from a few points only," and "in the personnel of the class," who were all workers in the same institutions. He emphasized the need for a year-long, full-time program of study rather than a short-term or evening course. Only in such a concentrated setting, Brackett argued, could students give their studies "most of their time and their first thought."[9]

Brackett saw Boston, with its many well-established and nationally prominent social welfare institutions, as an ideal location for a new school. But, having long been away from his native Massachusetts, he needed to secure the interest of local social work leaders in order to launch his plans. In the fall of 1903, Brackett gained the enthusiastic support of Alice Higgins, the recently appointed general secretary of the influential Boston Associated Charities. Higgins used her position to build momentum for the school, and by December she was able to write to Brackett that "there was only one opinion" among Boston's charity leaders: "we want training and we want you."[10]

Because Brackett wanted to build a school that would transcend the narrow training needs of specific charitable or philanthropic institutions, he urged that Harvard University (where he had received his A.B. in 1884) be approached as a potential affiliate of the new school. Harvard was then in the process of developing a Department of Social Ethics chaired by the Reverend Francis Peabody, whose pioneering course, "The Ethics of the Social Questions" (reportedly nicknamed "drink, drains, and divorce" by his more irreverent students), served as the new department's core.[11] Harvard's president Charles Eliot welcomed the opportunity to participate in the development of the Boston School, which served as an extension of the Social Ethics Department. Brackett was appointed Instructor of Charity, Public Aid, and Correction and offered a course of the same name each spring at Harvard. Advanced Harvard students earned credit for two courses toward their social ethics concentration for the completion of the year-long program at the Boston School for Social Workers.[12]

Because Harvard enrolled only male students, Brackett also needed to forge ties with an institution that would channel female students into the Boston School. President Henry Lefavour of the newly incorporated Simmons Female College (1899) had been investigating the possibility of instituting a Department of Social Work at Simmons when he was approached as a co-sponsor. Endowed by Boston garment manufacturer

John Simmons in his 1867 will to teach those "branches of art, science, and industry best calculated to enable the scholars to acquire an independent livelihood," Simmons had a vocational emphasis that was supported by a strong liberal arts foundation, and the college aimed to enable working- and middle-class women to be self-supporting.[13] After a few months of negotiations, a Harvard-Simmons alliance was formed.

The formation of the Harvard-Simmons partnership reveals the breadth of the BSSW founders' definition of social work, which had a place for men and women alike, from the working class to the educated elites. And yet the rhetoric surrounding the alliance also reveals some narrow gender and class assumptions within that seemingly all-embracing definition. Writing to Jeffrey Brackett after the alliance was secure, Alice Higgins anticipated a heady mixture of "the graduate student of first rate ability" from Harvard and "those without college training who would naturally turn to Simmons." Higgins's expressions of enthusiasm for the "union of the democratic spirit from Simmons and the aroma or research from Harvard"[14] foreshadowed the later separation of male and female cognitive cores that would ultimately lead to the dismantling of the Harvard-Simmons alliance.

More apparent at the Boston School's inception, however, was a multifaceted but unified definition of social work. The policy-making Administrative Board included an ideologically diverse group of several of Boston's most prominent social welfare leaders, including Robert A. Woods, the so-called philosopher of the settlement movement and long-time head resident of Boston's first and most prominent settlement, South End House; Joseph Lee, founder of the Massachusetts Civic League and "father of the playground movement"; and Frances Rollins Morse, Simmons College Corporation member, Boston Associated Charities worker, and board member of Boston's Women's Educational and Industrial Union. These men and women, and the others who rounded out the Administrative Board, represented a broad spectrum of philosophical and methodological approaches to education and social welfare.

Brackett's construction of a course of studies further attests to his determination to expose young social workers to the diversity and breadth of social work practice. Lacking precedent or example, however, Brackett found this to be a complicated task. "One difficulty," he recalled thirty years later, "was to know the boundaries of our field of work and so of instruction for it. Other callings feel the same difficulty, but a subject which means the fine art of helpful human relationships seems to take in all of human living!"[15] As Brackett worked to break down "the fine art of helpful human relationships" into an educational program in the Boston School's early years, he incorporated elements of four broad (and often overlapping) categories of social welfare work: individual and family casework, settlement house or community work, social reform, and sociological research, which were woven together in the Boston School's coursework, reading materials, special lectures, and fieldwork assignments.

Coursework at the BSSW was a mixture of lecture and discussion. Brackett lectured twice weekly. His few surviving lecture notes suggest that he emphasized the philosophical and historical underpinnings of social work. One lecture traces the development of "the leading influences by which persons have been led to take up intelligent work for the needy and the offender or by which workers have been led to use better methods."[16] The recollections of Eva Whiting White, the first Simmons College undergraduate to receive a B.S. in social work, who returned to the Simmons College School of Social Work as director in 1922, suggest that this lecture may well have been typical. Nearly fifty years after her graduation from the BSSW, White vividly recalled Brackett's explanation of English Poor Law. "[T]he date 1607," she mused, "will always be illumined in my memory."[17]

Second in command at the Boston School was Assistant Director Zilpha Drew Smith, who coordinated all fieldwork training and met with the students three times a week for intensive "study classes," where students discussed a wide range of historical and contemporary readings. Before joining the BSSW, Smith had served for twenty-four years (1879–1903) as the general secretary of Boston Associated Charities, where she rose to national prominence in the 1890s for her pioneering training classes for BAC staff and volunteers.[18] At the BSSW, Smith's first reading lists reflected her charity organization background. Required reading included Amos Warner's *American Charities* and Mary Richmond's *Friendly Visiting among the Poor;* the latter book was often called the bible of the charity organization movement. Smith's focus was not limited to the tenets of charity organization, however. The scope of her classes broadened each year, as she engaged her students in discussions of "Social Settlements," "Industrial Training and Betterment," and "Government Action Affecting Health."[19] Students were expected to process a daunting amount of material each week. Smith's reading lists on settlement work, for example, were deep and wide-ranging, including titles by national and international settlement leaders Jane Addams, Stanton Coit, Edward Denison, Mary Simkovitch, Graham Taylor, Arnold Toynbee, Robert Woods, and many other lesser-known figures. Discussion topics ranged from the benign, such as "organizations of Debutantes to assist in settlements and other social work," to the more controversial, including "social settlements and the labor question" and "practicable socialism."[20]

Supplementing the ongoing coursework at the Boston School were guest lecturers who spoke to BSSW students on their particular areas of expertise. The list of invited lecturers in the early years of the School reads like an inventory of national social welfare luminaries. Here again, students were exposed to the broad spectrum of social welfare approaches as represented by figures as diverse as Mary Richmond, general secretary of the Society for Organizing Charity in Philadelphia; Lillian Wald, founder and head resident of the Henry Street Nursing Settlement in New York City; Florence Kelley, secretary of the National Consumers League; and Grace Abbott, director of the Chicago Immigrants' Protective League and later director of the U.S. Children's Bureau, among many others.[21] Dozens of local and state social welfare figures served as special lecturers at the School and often opened students' eyes to new worlds of social welfare work. Eva Whiting White remembered vividly the message of one lecturer, who "shocked me into appreciating politics—good or bad—as a governing force in social welfare."[22]

The Boston School's preparation of social workers extended beyond the classroom and into the city's myriad social welfare institutions. Students devoted approximately one-third of their time to fieldwork placements. By 1906, each student was required to do one of two required fieldwork assignments in a charity organization. Zilpha Smith believed that experience in an organization such as Boston Associated Charities was an essential foundation for all social workers, regardless of their intended specializations, because "the training in a good A[ssociated] C[harities] conference gives the best introduction to many kinds of social work."[23]

The foundation of fieldwork in charity organization did not confine students to the casework tradition, however. Many students worked in Boston-area settlement houses as the second component of their fieldwork requirement. Several students worked each year at Robert Woods's South End House, and by 1908 Boston School students were

learning through observation and practice in seven different settle-
ments throughout Boston, including Denison House, Hale House, Lincoln House, and the Elizabeth Peabody House.[24] Several students also worked in settings that properly fall under the rubric of social reform. In 1906, for example, one male student was "watching social legislation at the [Massachusetts] State House" as part of his studies.[25]

Each semester, every student at the Boston School was required to complete an investigative research project, some of which stand out as examples of the kind of innovative and painstaking research increasingly being carried out by young social researchers and sociologists who saw surveys and statistics as basic tools for social improvement and reform. An early sampling of these research projects includes, "Leading Occupations for Working Boys," "Trade Unions for Women," "Evening Schools and the Immigrant," and "Conditions of Work of Waitresses in Restaurants."[26]

In 1907 the Boston School received a seventy-five-hundred-dollar grant from the Russell Sage Foundation to fund studies for the Foundation and to train students in social investigation. The Foundation grant, which was increased to ten thousand dollars in 1908, enabled the Boston School to institute a formal department of research, which aimed to "better some conditions of living and labor" through the collection of social data. The department supported several fellowships for a second year of study and advanced research. Fellows investigated a wide range of social issues, including infant mortality, homeless men, alcohol prohibition and liquor licensing, and the migration of immigrant groups to Boston's suburbs.[27]

The convergence of the casework, settlement, research, and reform traditions at the Boston School is clear. Nevertheless, Jeffrey Brackett's efforts to maintain a broadly conceived cognitive core did not eliminate all strains of ideological or philosophical discord. The balance between the several social welfare traditions was not static, but was contested and renegotiated by various interests within the School.

Brackett and Robert Woods, for example, debated the relative importance of technique, theory, and service in social work education. Woods advocated a strong service orientation, arguing that instilling a broad "perspective of social service" was more important than developing "inner technique." Woods feared that an emphasis on technique would fail to capture the interest of talented students from the most prestigious universities, who, he said, would "be won chiefly by a definite appeal to the positive, constructive imagination."[28] Although Brackett said he "strain[ed] every nerve" to instill a "perspective of social service," he nevertheless emphasized the development of technique. Immersion in the details of practice, he contested, "is . . . as valuable for the social worker as clinical or laboratory work for the physician, or case work for the lawyer."[29]

Expressions of student opinion reveal further ideological differences and played a part in the ongoing evolution and construction of the BSSW curriculum. A 1907 student committee submitted a petition suggesting a "rearrangement of the course" that would address the larger social and economic context of social work. The students argued that the course of instruction was too heavily weighted toward "the problem of relief" and suggested that because relief "is necessarily so bound up with all the problems of the whole course . . . its special treatment . . . might be condensed." The students wanted more time devoted to discussion of the settlement movement and to the "great industrial movements" because, they argued, "the relation between economics and life is so direct."[30]

Debate and disagreement was surely inevitable as an ideologically diverse group of social workers and social work students, all of whom had their own views on the proper balance of approaches to social betterment, sought to reach their often disparate goals. Most striking about the moments of ideological discord, however, was the ongoing commitment to a single, broadly based, coeducational institution. Brackett appears to have been an able and flexible negotiator who energetically attempted to adapt the Boston School's programming to meet the interests of all of its constituents. After the Boston School's first year of operation, Brackett adjusted the curriculum to include "increased stress . . . on the topics under community and voluntary action for improvement of conditions of living and labor."[31] In response to student concerns that their fieldwork experiences in Boston's settlement houses were hampered by a lack of supervision and feedback, Brackett agreed to hire a settlement resident to hold discussions on the settlement house movement with the students twice each week. Because the School's budget was so restricted, Brackett offered to pay for this addition to the staff from his own salary.[32]

Despite the efforts to maintain a unified, broad conceptualization of social work and a cognitive core that encompassed casework, research, community work, and social reform, the alliance of education and social welfare leaders within the BSSW broke down after twelve years. The institutionalization of independent programs at Harvard University and Simmons College does not appear to have been the result of disagreement about social welfare ideology. Rather, the split appears to have been the result of fundamental consensus about gender-appropriate realms of social work. A gender-sensitive reading of the early history of the Boston School for Social Workers suggests that shared ideologies about gender led to the ultimate ascendancy of casework as the cognitive core of professional education for women, who made up the majority of social work students in Boston.

From the start, the Boston School's founders expressed the long-standing nineteenth-century notion that women's participation in social work was a reflection and extension of women's domesticity. Robert Woods wrote that social work was "a perfectly natural extension of the interest and duties of the woman in her own home and in normal neighborhood society." Woods praised women's efforts "to reestablish healthful home conditions and neighborhood relations in communities where these fundamental social units have become disintegrated," which he viewed as "simply . . . new and large adaptations of the specialized capacities she has by nature and training."[33] In practice, the domestic justification of women's participation in social work led to the institutionalization of female-specific functions within the profession. The Boston School's fieldwork assignments, for example, could be rigidly gendered. In 1914, Zilpha Smith declined a request by a Cambridge Associated Charities representative for students to participate in a visiting housekeeping program, in part because "there are only three in our advanced course in organizing charity this year and two of them are men!"[34] In Smith's conceptualization of gender-appropriate activities for social workers, visiting housekeeping was clearly part of a female, domestically oriented domain.

Consistent with the domestic justification of women's participation in social work was the underlying assumption that women would be willing to accept the lowest-paid and lowest-status jobs in the new social work profession. Simmons president Henry Lefavour, during the planning stages of the Boston School, claimed that "there are various inferior grades of work that women will be willing to occupy while men may not."[35] Jeffrey Brackett concurred, asserting that women accepted lower salaries in social work "because many women work with something of a missionary spirit, and are ready to take what can be paid by the organization for which they wish to work." Brackett argued that even though higher pay would probably result in better service from charitable organizations, women should be paid equally to men only if they had the same physical strength. And, according to the meeting minutes, "[Brackett] did not feel sure that a woman can earn as much as a strong man."[36]

The Boston School's justification of women's low salaries was, in part, supported by a commitment to the preservation of and enhancement of nineteenth-century–style voluntarism within professional social work. Zilpha Smith encouraged the School's middle-class women graduates to take volunteer positions in social work agencies after completing their social work education unless their financial status absolutely required them to work for money. When one early female student approached Smith with the exciting news that she had been offered a paid position in a Pennsylvania agency, Smith asked her, "Has your family lost money? Do they need an income from you?" As this was not the case, Smith advised her not to take the job but rather to work as a volunteer, arguing that in becoming a "professional" she would lose influence with "the trustee-director group" and never ascend to the long-range goal of board membership.[37] In fact, fifteen of the twenty-seven students in the first entering class (1904–5) took positions as volunteers. By 1913, a study of the social work positions of BSSW graduates revealed that of the 131 graduates who had attended the School between 1905 and 1913 who responded to the survey, 45 or approximately one-third were working as volunteers.[38]

The construction of a male social worker identity within the Boston School shared little with the low-status, low-paid, and domestically justified conceptualization of social work for women. Robert Woods argued consistently that young men were not interested in work "which centers in the needy family and individual."[39] Harvard president Charles Eliot added that many men were not temperamentally well-suited to work with the "defectives" and the "unattractive mass of human beings" who made up the social worker's usual clientele. Most men, he observed, preferred to work with "the normal human being." Work with defectives, he thought, "requires a missionary spirit," which he, like Brackett, apparently viewed as a female trait.[40]

In constructing a masculine form of social work, Robert Woods, therefore, emphasized public service and leadership rather than help for the needy. Defining social work for men as a form of "unofficial statesmanship," Woods argued that the field "calls upon young men to enter upon a definite and absorbing career of public service at those points where the public need is greatest" and "opens the way in some cases to political action and to public office." Such work, he continued, "brings men into a political activity of that sort which has to do, not only with correcting the technique of government in our cities, but with humanizing them through causing them more largely to meet great collective needs."[41] Jeffrey Brackett hoped his personal example would inspire his male students to aspire to public leadership in social service. After being nominated by Massachusetts Governor Guild to serve on the State Board of Charity, Brackett hoped that his new position would serve as an "example to younger men [at Harvard] of public service in social work."[42]

However, for all the rhetoric about the "statesmanship" and leadership potential for men in professional social work, Brackett could not deny that remuneration for most positions was small, even for men. When he reflected upon social work's low pay, Brackett spoke of social work as a "calling" comparable to the ministry—a "brotherhood," which had "the qualities of heart which make an occupation a calling."[43] Brackett's course at Harvard generally enrolled several students from the Divinity School, but as a group these men did not turn to social work careers in great numbers.

For men who might have regarded social work, even as a form of "unofficial statesmanship," as a low-status career, Woods emphasized that men need not take up social work as a profession, but rather urged them to see how the traditional professions could be used for social betterment and reform with additional training and education in social work: "One social worker is primarily a doctor, another a lawyer, another a teacher, another a clergyman, another an artist, another a musician, another a business man, another a sanitary expert, another a politician."[44]

Although Woods clearly differentiated gender-appropriate spheres within social work, he also argued that the profession fostered "an unmistakably sound and real type of equality between the sexes." The equality Woods envisioned, however, was based not on a gender-neutral sphere but one in which men and women could gain fuller understanding of each other's "distinctive activities" by working together.[45] This kind of "separate but equal" construction of a profession, as Slater and Glazer have suggested in *Unequal Colleagues,* ultimately leads to sex-segregation and gender hierarchy. Slater and Glazer have shown how the founders of the field of psychiatric social work justified women's participation with a domestic and service-oriented rhetoric that succeeded in "defus[ing] male anxieties" but also "set the groundwork for [psychiatric] social work's subordination" to the male-dominated professions of medicine and psychiatry.[46]

The Boston School's institutionalization of gender-appropriate paths for women in social work was reflected in the direction of the School's curriculum and training after Harvard withdrew its affiliation with the School in 1916. The newly independent Simmons College School of Social Work increasingly emphasized a technical, skill-based, and specialized curriculum that clearly established casework skills and technique as its "cognitive core" or "nuclear skill." After World War I, the fast-growing field of psychiatric social work gained prominence in the curriculum and became a second-year specialization during the 1920s.[47] By 1923, all the last vestiges of the original broad definition of social work were dismantled when the School broke its curriculum into departmental specializations. Students were trained in the "art and science of adjusting personal relationships" in either Children's Work, Family Welfare, Community Work, Medical Social Service, or Psychiatric Social Work.[48] The School's research or "social inquiry" component was reduced, and "most of the money was diverted to an advanced program of one year in specialized casework."[49]

The School's early determination that social work education should not be specialized, but instead broadly encompass the diverse approaches to social welfare of the early twentieth century, had been abandoned. By 1930, and in the decades to follow, the School focused its efforts on training medical and psychiatric social caseworkers. According to one observer, students concentrated increasingly on "acquiring knowledge about the causation and intricacies of human behavior, in mastering the details of [their casework specialization] . . . and especially in developing skills in individual relationships."[50]

Harvard's rationale for withdrawing from the Boston School for Social Workers is not clear in the record, but the University did continue to offer its students preparation for careers in professional social work through its expanding Social Ethics Department. Harvard students followed a course of studies that was in keeping with the "masculine" version of social work articulated by Robert Woods. The social ethics curriculum reveals a "cognitive core" for men that was substantially different from that institutionalized at the Simmons College School of Social Work. Building on the social ethics core course, "Social Problems and Social Policy," students studied "Immigration and Race Problems," "Social Amelioration in Europe," "Labor Legislation," and "Recent Theories of Social Reform," and a wide range of courses in the social sciences.[51] Harvard's Social Ethics Department was preparing male social workers for careers in social research, social reform, and government, not careers in casework.

In 1920, Richard C. Cabot, a leader in the creation of the field of medical social work, took over the chairmanship of the department. Cabot reintroduced casework technique into the curriculum, but with an "emphasis upon social theory and the theory of values." Cabot's explicit goal in teaching professional technique and methods was to "train men to become *executives* in public or private agencies of social welfare." Graduates of the program, he proudly wrote, were "doing distinguished work in social service administration, and the books and articles which they have produced in recent years demonstrate the value of comprehensive training in the backgrounds of social service, as well as the actual technique required of professional students."[52]

During the 1920s, Harvard's preparation of men for careers in social service continued to evolve. The Social Ethics Department was merged with the Department of Sociology and then abandoned altogether in 1931. As the Simmons College School of Social Work increasingly emphasized casework practice and technique, Harvard's Sociology Department, based on the academic foundations of social science theory and research, provided its male students with the academic background and skills they needed to advance to administrative and policy-making positions in the field.[53]

Historians and social workers alike have long recognized the sex segregation of professional social work. Women social workers began systematically to attack the gender inequality in their profession in the 1960s, and although women have made significant advances, the struggle continues to the present day.[54] The construction and institutionalization of gender-specific social work identities was an exceedingly complex process that certainly cannot be reduced to a single causal force. But this study of the early history of social work education in Boston suggests that the development of gendered educational practices during the profession's formative years played an important part in the sex segregation of the field.

For twelve years, a broad coalition of Boston's education and social welfare leaders managed at times to transcend intense ideological and methodological differences in the effort to invent and institutionalize a broad definition of social work education. This unprecedented alliance, founded with the hope of creating a new kind of social worker in a setting that brought together the "democratic spirit" of Simmons College and the "aroma of research" from Harvard University, collapsed under the weight of gender ideology. Unable to transcend their era's prevailing ideologies about gender difference, the Boston School's founders institutionalized professional social work education on strictly gendered foundations that continue to reverberate through the profession today.

Notes

1. See Daniel Walkowitz, "The Making of a Feminized Professional Identity: Social Work in the 1920s," *American Historical Review* 95 (October 1990): 1051–75; Clarke Chambers, "Women in the Creation of the Profession of Social Work," *Social Service Review* (March 1986): 1–33; Alice Kessler-Harris, *Out To Work: A History of Wage-Earning Women in the United States* (New York: Oxford University Press, 1982), 116–17; Esther Brown, *Social Work as a Profession* (New York: Arno Press, 1976), 142–43, 178–80.

2. One notable exception is Penina Migdal Glazer and Miriam Slater's *Unequal Colleagues: The Entrance of Women into the Professions* (New Brunswick, N.J.: Rutgers University Press, 1987). In their chapter "The Creation of Psychiatric Social Work," Glazer and Slater examine the gendered creation of psychiatric social work education at the Smith College School of Social Work. But this was not until after World War I, at which time the segregation of the profession was well underway.

3. Jeffrey Brackett, "Social Work," 1909. Jeffrey Richardson Brackett Papers (MS 8), Simmons College Archives (hereafter SCA), Boston.

4. The term "cognitive core" is used by Glazer and Slater in their discussion of the development of psychiatric social work at the Smith College School of Social Work in *Unequal Colleagues,* 172. Roy Lubove used the idea of a "nuclear skill" to explain the ascendancy of casework in professional social work by the 1920s in *The Professional Altruist: The Emergence of Social Work as a Career, 1880–1930* (Cambridge, Mass.: Harvard University Press, 1965), 137–56. I chose to retain Glazer and Slater's concept of "cognitive core" because it suggests

questions not only about core skills or techniques but also about the broader intellectual basis of the profession.

5. Lubove, *The Professional Altruist*, 118–56; quotes: 119, 188, 144.

6. For a concise biographical summary, see John David Smith, "Brackett, Jeffrey Richardson," in *Biographical Dictionary of Social Welfare in America*, ed. Walter Trattner (Westport, Conn.: Greenwood Press, 1986), 117–19. The only full biography was compiled by Brackett's second wife and two former colleagues: Katherine D. Hardwick, Rose Weston Bull, and Louisa Bacot Brackett, *Jeffrey Richardson Brackett: "Everyday Puritan"* (Boston: Privately printed, 1956).

7. See especially his 1901 National Congress of Charities and Corrections (NCCC) address, "Present Opportunities for Training in Charitable Work"; his 1903 book, *Supervision and Education in Charity* (New York: Macmillan, 1903); and his 1904 NCCC presidential address, "The Worker: Purpose and Preparation" (MS 8), SCA.

8. Alice Channing, "The Early Years of a Pioneering School," *Social Service Review* (December 1954): 430; Brackett, *Supervision and Education in Charity*.

9. Jeffrey Brackett, "The First Statement," June 1, 1904. Brackett Papers (MS 8), SCA.

10. Letter from Alice Higgins to Jeffrey Brackett, December 23, 1903. Brackett Papers (MS 8), SCA.

11. David B. Potts, "Social Ethics at Harvard, 1881–1931: A Study in Academic Activism," in *Social Sciences at Harvard, 1860–1920: From Inculcation to the Open Mind*, ed. Paul Buck (Cambridge, Mass.: Harvard University Press, 1965), 91–128; Samuel Eliot Morison, *Three Centuries of Harvard, 1636–1936* (Cambridge, Mass.: Harvard University Press, 1946), 368–77; James Ford, "Social Ethics, 1905–1929," in *The Development of Harvard University since the Inauguration of President Eliot, 1869–1929*, ed. Samuel Eliot Morison (Cambridge, Mass.: Harvard University Press, 1930), 223–30. (Quote: Morison, *Three Centuries*, 377.)

12. Harvard University, Harvard University Catalog, 1905–6, 401.

13. Kenneth L. Mark, *Delayed by Fire, Being the Early History of Simmons College* (Concord, N.H.: Rumford Press, 1945), 25.

14. Letter from Alice Higgins to Jeffrey Brackett, December 23, 1903. Brackett Papers (MS 8), SCA.

15. Letter from Jeffrey Brackett to Eleanor L. Dodge, February 13, 1934. Brackett Papers (MS 8), SCA.

16. Jeffrey Brackett, "Supervisory and Educational Movements," Lecture Notes, n.d. Brackett Papers (MS 8), SCA.

17. Eva Whiting White, "Fiftieth Anniversary, Simmons College School of Social Work," April 21, 1954, p. 2. School of Social Work Records (RG 24), SCA.

18. On Zilpha Smith see Jeffrey Brackett, "Zilpha Drew Smith (1852–1926)," c. 1926, Brackett Papers (MS 8) SCA; and Nancy G. Isenberg, "Zilpha Drew

Smith," in Trattner, *Biographical Dictionary of Social Welfare in America*, 682–83; Lubove, *The Professional Altruist*, 138.

19. Study Class Reading Lists, 1906 and 1910. Zilpha Drew Smith Papers (MS 9), SCA.

20. Study Class Reading List, "Social Settlements," December 20, 1909. Smith Papers (MS 9), SCA.

21. Report from Jeffrey Brackett to Charles W. Eliot, Fall 1904. Charles W. Eliot Papers (UA I.5.150), Harvard University Archives (hereafter HUA); Simmons College, School of Social Work Course Catalogs, 1904–1908; Boston School for Social Workers Administrative Board Meeting Minutes, April 25, 1913. School of Social Work Records, SCA.

22. White, "Fiftieth Anniversary," 3.

23. Zilpha Smith, Report on Assignments to Field Work, January 21, 1914. Smith Papers (MS 9) SCA.

24. Social Work Catalogs, 1906–1908.

25. Boston School for Social Workers Administrative Board Meeting Minutes, April 30, 1906. School of Social Work Records, SCA.

26. Some less-inspired (and more representative) early examples include: "Charity and Public Aid in Milton," "Charity and Public Aid in Brookline," "Neighborhood Improvement in the Country," and "Possibilities in Local Associated Charities Conferences." Boston School for Social Workers Administrative Board Meeting Minutes, April 17, 1905. Jeffrey Brackett, 1906 Director's Report, October 15, 1906. Eliot Papers (UA I.5.150), HUA.

27. Letter from Jeffrey Brackett to Charles W. Eliot, August 13, 1907, Eliot Papers (UA I.5.150), HUA; *School of Social Work Bulletin*, 1908, 7; Channing, "Early Years of a Pioneering School," 438.

28. Letter from Robert Woods to Jeffrey Brackett, April 15, 1904. Brackett Papers (MS 8), SCA.

29. Letter from Jeffrey Brackett to Robert Woods, April 18, 1904. Brackett Papers, SCA.

30. Report of the Student Committee, 1907, 1–2. School of Social Work Records, SCA.

31. Boston School for Social Workers Administrative Board Meeting Minutes, April 17, 1905. School of Social Work Records, SCA.

32. Boston School for Social Workers Administrative Board Meeting Minutes, March 1905. School of Social Work Records, SCA.

33. Robert A. Woods, "Social Work: A New Profession" (1905). Reprinted in Woods, ed. *The Neighborhood in Nation-Building* (New York: Arno Press, 1970), 88–104.

34. Letter from Zilpha D. Smith to Susan Hinckley, February 5, 1914, Smith Papers (MS 9), SCA.

35. Henry Lefavour, quoted in Channing, "Early Years of a Pioneering School," 432.

36. Boston School for Social Workers Administrative Board Meeting Minutes, January 20, 1908. School of Social Work Records, SCA.

37. This story is told in slightly different versions. See Dorothy Lindsay, "A Quarter Century," *The Social Worker* (June 1930): 38–39; Lotta Stetson Rand, "The First Class," *The Social Worker* (August 1945): 6; Channing, "Early Years of a Pioneering School," 434.

38. Channing, "Early Years of a Pioneering School," 432.

39. Boston School for Social Workers Administrative Board Meeting Minutes, April 30, 1906. School of Social Work Records, SCA.

40. Boston School for Social Workers Administrative Board Meeting Minutes, April 30, 1906. School of Social Work Records, SCA.

41. Woods, "Social Work: A New Profession," 96.

42. Letter from Jeffrey Brackett to Charles Eliot, June 12, 1906. Eliot Papers, (UA I.5.150), HUA; Channing, "Early Years of a Pioneering School," 437.

43. Jeffrey Brackett, "Social Work as a Calling," (1906). Brackett Papers (MS 8), SCA.

44. Woods, "Social Work: A New Profession," 97.

45. Woods, "Social Work: A New Profession," 99–100.

46. Glazer and Slater, *Unequal Colleagues,* 202.

47. The BSSW added a second year to its program in 1912.

48. *School of Social Work Bulletin* (February 1922): 4; *School of Social Work Bulletin* (March 1923): 8; "Log of an Eventful Half Century: Two Former Directors Highlight the School History, 1904–1954," *Simmons College Bulletin of Social Work,* Alumni Bulletin, April 1954.

49. Channing, "Early Years of a Pioneering School," 438.

50. Channing, "Early Years of a Pioneering School," 440.

51. Harvard University course catalogs, 1904–1917.

52. Ford, "Social Ethics, 1905–1929," 223–30 (emphasis added).

53. Ford, "Social Ethics," 1905–1929," 228.

54. Chambers, "Women in the Creation of the Profession of Social Work," 2–4.

PART TWO

SOCIAL REFORM AND
POLITICAL ACTIVISM

CAROLINE HEALEY DALL

Her Creation and Reform Career

NANCY BOWMAN

There is no modern reform that we take so little interest in as the movement in regard to the rights of women . . . , we never for a moment supposed that the court-room, the council-hall, or the caucus was a proper place for us. . . . The business of our country and our age, it has been most truly said, is to organize the rights of man. One of the holiest of his rights is to find woman in her proper place. It is *he* who is robbed by a wrong condition of things.

—Caroline Healey Dall, 1838

Whatever may be your personal opinion on the question of Universal Suffrage, I think you will allow [that] no such barrier [in the wording of the Fourteenth amendment] should be created at this late hour. When we have overcome the difficulties in our respective States, we shall not be likely to pause before such an obstacle in the Constitution itself.

—Caroline Healey Dall, 1866

These excerpts illuminate two extremes in nineteenth-century thought on the issue of women's rights. The first represents the contemporary status quo, characterized by sharply defined and separate spheres of activity and rights for men and women. The second speaks to the determination and purpose of participants in the growing movement for women's rights. The contents and motives of the two passages are contradictory and full of tension. They suggest the difficulty faced by women generally—and their author, Caroline Dall, in particular—in identifying and claiming their proper role in society.[1]

Caroline Healey Dall. Courtesy, Massachusetts Historical Society.

Born in Boston, Massachusetts, in 1822, Caroline Healey Dall held an anomalous position within the movement she spoke for in 1866, and she wrestled with the contradictions inherent in society's construction of woman. Within a few years of her early denunciation of the movement for women's rights, she was in the thick of the fray. Over a long life she corresponded with the leading liberal, or even radical, figures of the mid-nineteenth century—Charles Sumner, Elizabeth Cady Stanton, Susan B. Anthony, Theodore Parker, William Lloyd Garrison—and played important roles in two of the major reform movements of the time: antislavery and women's rights. Yet Dall became active in political reform very reluctantly, always—even while writing about "woman's proper place" and the "rights of man"—a champion of women's intellectual and economic rights, but not initially convinced of the importance of woman suffrage and never completely abandoning the conservative sentiments that informed her opinions on the roles of women.[2]

Dall's most active participation in the women's movement spanned a

SOCIAL REFORM AND POLITICAL ACTIVISM

relatively brief period in her long life, just over ten years in the 1850s and 1860s, but her period of activism was characterized by an efficiency and intensity that bordered on drivenness. She abruptly withdrew from activist participation in 1867 for reasons both personal and political. Having entered the movement somewhat reluctantly to begin with, Dall was temperamentally ill suited to cooperative endeavor, never fully in step with the national leaders of the movement and certain of their goals, and most content following her own agenda after disassociating herself from the formal women's organizations. This personal agenda included writing, some lecturing, extensive work as a founding member of the American Social Science Association (ASSA), and teaching by example. In 1877 Alfred University (in Alfred, New York) made her at fifty-five the first woman "in modern history" to earn the degree of L.L.D., a step toward the fulfillment of her adolescent hope that she would see the time "when a finished education shall be every woman's birthright; when the respect of the other sex shall be her legitimate inheritance; when the woman of any rank will be able to obtain a livelihood for herself or her children without overtasking the generosity of man; when she shall no longer find herself, even for a moment, a tool or a plaything."[3]

Obviously an accomplished woman, prominent in her time and of critical importance to the women's movement of New England, Dall has been the subject of remarkably little study and none that explains her character and participation in reform. Barbara Welter, the only historian to consider her at any length, asserted in her 1969 essay "The Merchant's Daughter: A Tale from Life" that Dall fully accepted the parameters set upon a woman's life by the "cult of true womanhood," largely passing over Dall's career as a reformer and downplaying her remarkable independence and strength of mind outside that arena.[4]

Welter, with Carroll Smith-Rosenberg, Nancy Cott, and others, contributed to the basic framework in which women's history has been studied for the past twenty-five years. Through a study of contemporary women's magazines, domestic manuals, and so forth, Welter identified the "cult of true womanhood" as the dominant social construct for middle-class women of the nineteenth century. Emerging in the midst of economic changes early in the century, the "cult" demanded piety, purity, submissiveness, and domesticity of the "true" woman. The fact that production was moving outside the home and the new premium placed on domesticity and its usual circumstances—marriage and motherhood—effectively limited women to the domestic realm unless the church or family necessity demanded that she bring her womanly qualities to bear in society.

Cott and Smith-Rosenberg enlarged upon Welter's work and took a more positive view of the separation of male and female spheres of activity.[5] They defined a female culture and a sisterhood arising from women's extended contact with other women and their limited interaction with men. A network of female kin formed the core of this sisterhood as daughters worked alongside mothers, learning the responsibilities of the home and gradually assuming certain of those responsibilities. The sisterhood then extended outward as new acquaintances were made. As women empathized with other women, some gradually moved beyond their intimate sisterhood to correct perceived evils in the behavior or treatment of all women.[6] In any event this female culture exerted a powerful force in women's emotional lives as their social identification rested in other women.

I contend, however, that Caroline Dall's life—particularly with respect to her reform activities—cannot be adequately explained by reference to social strictures, as Welter would have it in "The Merchant's Daughter," or to family relationships, as the paradigms of Cott and Smith-Rosenberg suggest. While not as radical in her demands for women and for social reform as Elizabeth Cady Stanton or Victoria Woodhull, for example, Dall's actions and words implied a conscious, if incomplete, rejection of the "cult of true womanhood." Further, her means of social identification were not those of most women. Though raised in a house full of women (she had five sisters and two brothers), her primary relationship, as a child and even into adulthood, was with her father.

Dall did not exemplify strict adherence to the dictates of the "cult" but, rather, an adaptation of those principles that subverted the original intent—a situation that Welter earlier said obtained as the contradictions within the ideal became clear.[7] Dall certainly was not unique in adjusting ideals to reality; it was virtually a given that most women could not, in fact, live up to *all* of the demands of the "cult." She was, however, perhaps more self-conscious than many of her contemporaries in her adjustments and must be seen as both a product of her times and a creation of her own strong will.[8] Self-consciously, through rigorous intellectual application, religious study, and ceaseless introspection,

Caroline Dall formed her ideas of who she was, what she should do, and how she should be perceived.[9] She created herself as, variously, an intellectual wunderkind, a slave to duty, a prop of tradition, and a righteous if reluctant reformer. Unfortunately, in day-to-day relations, others did not always perceive Dall as she might have wished, and she frequently proved unpopular. Susan B. Anthony noted her "self-conceit" and found her difficult to work with, and another reformer, Fanny Ames, "supposed" that Dall knew there were "a great many people" who did not like her. Dall apparently did not realize that introspection gave way at some point to self-absorption and that she played a part in creating unfavorable impressions. Rather she created herself anew as a victim of misunderstanding and a woman alone.[10]

Caroline Dall's self-definition had, of course, profound implications for her relationships both within and without her family. The nature of various relationships in turn influenced her reform activities. Three connections—and her interpretation of related events and interaction—are of particular importance in understanding the course of Dall's reform career and will be examined below. In the earliest stages of her development, Dall's father encouraged her intellectual growth and self-confidence; his eventual financial debacle pushed her even further toward autonomy. Her intellectual encounter with Margaret Fuller in late adolescence brought Dall greater awareness of women's power. Finally, her marriage to Charles Dall—and particularly the failure of that marriage—radicalized Caroline Dall and moved her into woman's rights activism.

The bond between Caroline Dall and her father was by far the most important and complex of her family relationships. Dall never underestimated the importance of that father-daughter relationship in her development. At twenty-one, in correspondence with her future husband, she wrote, "Until you know many other things you cannot know how near my father is to me. Our hearts have grown together; we have no divided thoughts."[11]

This strong bond resulted from the fact that Caroline was the oldest child in a family that for several years consisted only of girls. Mark Healey wanted a son and, according to Caroline, "decided that I should supply the place of one."[12] The education that would have been given a male child was hers. Healey envisioned a literary career in his daughter's future and saw her educated in the classics and half a dozen foreign languages in her teens; she also took an active interest in the natural sciences. In the course of this education, Caroline made a commitment to her father and to self-cultivation, but she made few friends.

Caroline was unquestionably devoted to her father, but as she matured she found herself increasingly frustrated by his contradictory demands as he first encouraged her study, thoughtfulness, and opinions, and then denied the validity of those opinions; she complained, even in childhood, that he "refused to accede to many of the philosophical positions which I assumed."[13]

Mark Healey not only urged his daughter in two directions emotionally and intellectually but also forced her, at the age of eleven, into the domestic role of housekeeper after numerous pregnancies (successful and unsuccessful) left his wife an invalid. Caroline herself complained of chronic poor health and depression from the time of her early teens. Yet while she felt "overworked in body and mind," her "strong sense of duty" nonetheless forced her to keep busy from dawn to dusk, overseeing the household staff, sewing, caring for the children, and studying.[14] As the children grew she took an active role in their education, tutoring them on occasion and making suggestions to her father as to the course of their studies. Years later, as she re-created her childhood and their relationship in reconstructed journals, responding no doubt (whether she realized it or not) to the pressure that she as well as her father placed on her, Dall claimed that he, in fact, "never allowed [her] to be a child" and that he and his love did much "to embitter [her] life."[15]

Father and daughter clashed not just over intellectual opinion and domestic duty but also over her commitments within the church. She had, from a very early age, been a member of the West Parish congregation of the Boston Unitarian Church to which her parents belonged and, after a brief period of skepticism, exhibited a remarkable zeal in her attendance and activity. In the 1830s this church became more liberal, encouraging the conversion of the whole person, heart and mind, and likewise encouraging the benevolence of its members.[16] By the time she was fifteen, Caroline had begun visiting among the poor of Pitts Street Parish in Boston. At sixteen she taught Sunday School for the West Boston Parish. Both projects met with resistance from her father. He described her Pitts Street friends as "low and vulgar" and, after her late return from a Sunday School teachers' meeting one evening, threatened

to forbid her continued participation in the school. As was her wont,
Caroline vented her feelings, most eloquently and dramatically, on paper. She admonished her father to set a suitable example for his children if he expected them to bend to his will.[17] Defending her Pitts Street friends, Caroline said she did not pay her "respects to broadcloth [implying that her parents did] but to benevolence." She further claimed that her Pitts Street friends offered her the love and sympathy that her parents did not.[18] In the end, Caroline continued to work on Pitts Street and in the Sunday School.

Despite its peaks and valleys, Caroline's relationship with her father was not only the most important but also the most successful of any she maintained with a family member. Though increasingly at odds over her actions and opinions, Caroline and Mark Healey always reconciled. With the rest of her family there was little closeness. Only with her brother Charlie, the family "treasure," did Caroline have a deep, affectionate attachment, and he died before his fifth birthday, when Caroline was roughly eighteen.[19] The active role that she played at her father's behest in the care and education of her other siblings shifted toward an often grating relationship. She later wrote: "The position is unnatural. Gratitude might be expected, but envy is more often felt."[20]

Having soured relations with her sisters early in life, Caroline never grew close to any of them. Despite the remarkable breadth of her papers, there are very few letters, extant or recorded in letterbooks, that indicate any sort of family intimacy.

Some of the letters that do survive between Caroline and her mother are remarkable for their bitterness and distance. Caroline's mother opposed her daughter's intense education and her writing and did her best to repress Caroline's intellectual urges. She, in fact, attempted to force Caroline into the traditional mold for women. She tried to impress upon her daughter the uselessness of her writing since "all that you will ever write . . . will be thrown away" and the importance of becoming "a beautiful seamstress if [you] never kn[o]w anything else." Caroline thought she understood her mother's attitude—attributing it to her mother's own intellectual repression growing up—but at the age of sixteen Caroline considered herself "born for a better purpose."[21]

However, at times, she was ready to do almost anything to gain the mother's love that she felt she had missed. At the age of eighteen, she asked if there "is anything I can do to please you? I will make any sacrifice and I will give up—dearly as I love them—my books and my pen. I will promise never to read or write another line if you will give me the love a mother owes her child."[22]

These feelings of alienation were particularly strong in adolescence and they persisted into adulthood. When Caroline left home at the age of twenty, she still desired, but did not expect, a rapprochement. She insisted again that she would do much to "win this love, to which the world can see I have a right," but as late as 1849, years after Caroline left home, married, and became a mother herself, the relationship was still unsteady, with unresolved problems.[23]

Other contemporary female reformers experienced developmental strains similar to Dall's. Elizabeth Cady Stanton felt alienated from her mother and identified with her father in her intellectual and reform pursuits. Sarah Grimké experienced a similar distance from her mother and a strong inclination toward academic pursuits. Catharine Beecher had a complicated relationship with a father whom she held responsible for both her intellectual growth and her ultimate repression in a world dominated by men. Margaret Fuller possessed the same "New England drive for self-culture almost to the point of mania."[24] There were also parallels for her spiritual experience among her contemporaries. Membership in liberal organizations such as the Society of Friends or the Unitarian Church was a common stepping-stone for those women who made the leap from benevolence and reform, accepted in woman's sphere, to women's rights. Transcendentalism, with its broad humanism that emphasized the freedom, dignity, and worth of every human being, male or female, also helped to bridge the gap.[25]

As Caroline approached adulthood, she began to move slowly but with certainty across and then beyond the traditionally accepted spectrum of female activities. The church encouraged her benevolent activity and pious nature. Her charitable visits to Pitts Street, while opposed by her parents, met with little resistance in society at large. Other incidents led Caroline a little further afield. The plight of a poor Irish washerwoman of Caroline's acquaintance, legally stripped of her wages by her husband, "was the first to call [her] attention to the . . . unequal legislation" on the subject of a woman's rights to her earnings, when she was fifteen.[26] His wife's opposition notwithstanding, Mark Healey encouraged his daughter's continued education and independent thinking, and this experience gave her confidence and certitude. In late adolescence, Caroline stated that "I have never known what it was to be

SOCIAL REFORM AND POLITICAL ACTIVISM

without an opinion of my own." Demanding, intellectually assertive, and highly critical of herself and others, she had clearly shed the "most feminine virtue"—that of submissiveness.[27]

Contact with Margaret Fuller when she was eighteen only strengthened Caroline's commitment to women's elevation and convinced her of woman's power to bring about this change. Margaret Fuller was among the first to enunciate the need and right that women had to be heard, respected, and empowered. At the time of their meeting, Fuller was one of the most prominent members of the (mostly male) Transcendental-ist circle and had just been selected by that group as editor of their new publication, *The Dial.* She was passionately devoted to truth, self-culture, and the notion that society must eventually realize that the "growth of man is two-fold, masculine and feminine," each deserving of the respect and rights then granted only to men.[28] Twenty years later, while touting women's rights before the law, in the marketplace, and in the world of academics, Caroline Dall paid her respects to Fuller, credit-ing her with presenting "the first clear, uncompromising, scholarly de-mand for the civil rights of her sex."[29] Fuller's "respect for a woman's individual identity . . . and her awareness that together women shared a problem rooted in the structure of society" marked her as a protofemi-nist, and at least one historian has credited her with having "influenced virtually all advocates of women's rights in this country."[30]

The social and intellectual exchange between Fuller and Caroline was limited to one short season, but it had a profound impact on Caroline. Fuller's "conversations" began in Boston in the winter of 1839 and con-tinued every winter for roughly the next five years. Those "conversa-tions" initially included only women and were intended to offer them a forum for thought and self-expression that was all too frequently stifled in whatever other social and intellectual circles they might have moved. In the winter of 1841, however, they included men as well as the female charter members, and in that year Elizabeth Peabody invited Caroline to attend. Caroline later remembered the "conversations" and the inter-action with Fuller as invaluable. She remembered enjoying absolute intellectual freedom and for the first time encountering a number of persons with the same interests as she.[31]

While Caroline enjoyed the meeting of the minds, however, she was an outsider in the "conversations." Her strong opinions and her in-ordinate confidence in their correctness alienated many in the company. Elizabeth Peabody wrote Caroline a note in the course of one of the meetings asking her not to speak unless spoken to. Caroline self-righteously claimed a right to speak but later noted that even her beloved Margaret "had doubtless been repelled by my positiveness and my self-esteem, while she had not known me long enough to value my truthfulness." This admission came in a letter written years after the fact, and again we see Dall going back to re-create herself as she wanted to be remembered.[32]

Whether Fuller would have invited Caroline to participate in the "conversations" of the following winter is unknown. Caroline, in any event, was unable to attend. The economic depression of the early 1840s ruined her father's business in 1842, and she left home in the fall of that year to aid in supporting her family by becoming a teacher.

Her father's economic failure proved a pivotal event in Caroline's life. The necessity of finding a job pushed her toward greater autonomy. The lack of suitable teaching positions in Massachusetts led her south, to Miss Lydia English's Seminary in the Georgetown section of Washington, D.C. There she witnessed slavery first-hand and also renewed her acquaintance with another New England native, Charles A. Dall. She subsequently married Dall and participated in the antislavery movement.

Caroline knew little of slavery and less of abolitionism when she moved south. Within a short time, though, she learned to dislike both the "peculiar institution" and its setting. Life in the South required adjustments on Caroline's part that she was not altogether willing to make. She initially spoke openly about freedom, education, and service to God with the slaves on the school grounds. She also spoke with her students and colleagues about her religious beliefs. But she found herself treated as an "infidel," and her principal, Miss English, quickly suggested the wisdom of acquainting herself with her environs before making her "peculiar sentiments" public.[33] Caroline acquiesced slightly; she wrote her old sewing circle in Boston that she had discovered that "self-control and a quiet tongue are an excellent thing in a woman" in the South, and she hoped "for a distant but ultimate return to the North."[34]

Caroline remained in the South, however, until 1845. Miss English's admonitions aside, Caroline made a census of the free blacks in the District of Columbia, with the hopes of organizing them into free schools, and taught those free blacks in her vicinity who were willing to learn. By her account, she achieved some success in teaching them about

God and reading.[35] Her immediate attempts to aid the slaves and free
blacks ended temporarily when she left Miss English's school to marry
Charles Dall in 1844.

Marriage was, of course, another crucial event in Caroline Dall's life—
in the development of her character generally and of her commitment
to reform particularly. The Reverend Charles Dall was a missionary
engaged in community outreach under the auspices of the Unitarian
church in Baltimore when the couple first married. His occupation
subjected the family to frequent moves but it also fed Caroline's pious
nature, and its informal structure permitted her to share in his work.
One might even say that the marriage was founded on that work;
Caroline herself wrote during their courtship that "your mission helps
your cause [of marriage]," suggesting a certain absence of passion on her
part but a great respect for his position and the possibility that a connection of this sort was a necessary part of her self-fulfillment.[36] The marriage also seemed to founder somewhat on his work; his departure for
the mission in India in 1855 signaled the beginning of years of separation. In the face of her husband's departure, however, Caroline Dall's
public commitment to the cause of woman's rights strengthened and
crystallized.

In fact, with her husband's blessing and encouragement, Dall participated in reform projects from the beginning of her marriage, balancing
traditional benevolence with her increasing interest in current reforms.
Her experiences in Georgetown and Baltimore had converted her to
abolitionism, and in 1848 she began contributing to *The Liberator*, William Lloyd Garrison's antislavery newspaper. In 1850 she started writing for Maria Chapman's antislavery annual, *The Liberty Bell*. She had
"opened her heart to the cause of freedom" and, when her husband's
calling took the family to Toronto in 1851, she became a little more
personally involved, serving as a contact for fugitive slaves until the
family moved again in 1854.[37]

The antislavery movement soon brought her into the movement for
women's rights. Membership in the two movements overlapped considerably, and Dall was invited to attend and address conventions on
women's rights. Her initial opposition to the demand for woman suffrage, however, evidently led some to doubt her position on woman's
rights. Wendell Phillips, for example, extended an invitation in 1849 "to
attend and take part in the women's convention at Worcester . . . I hope

you sympathise with its purpose."[38] Dall did "sympathise" with the purpose of the convention but was absent due to the birth of her daughter. The pleasures and demands of wife- and motherhood kept her from women's conventions until 1855, and reform activities were for her a secondary occupation, for she entered marriage in 1844 with many conventional expectations and opinions and held those opinions even when she later embarked on her formal crusade for women's rights. "You will find," she said at an 1855 convention, "that they [reformers such as Elizabeth Stanton, Ernestine Rose, and Paulina Wright Davis, all in attendance] did not become reformers until they had shown themselves good housekeepers and good wives, above all, perhaps, good mothers." Dall attended to these "higher duties" before actively entering the field of reform, bearing a son in 1845 and a daughter in 1849.[39]

In the meantime, however, she was not completely absent from the field but combined her interest in public reform and her commitment to elements of the domestic ideal in work as an essayist. The alternative to being a physical presence in the movement was to be an intellectual support and "keep up the discussion," and writing was a means of participation particularly suited to Dall's independent nature.[40] She had long said that she did "not believe that woman is inferior to man in any respect, nor that her nature essentially differs from or is superior to his." Her crusade in *The Liberator* and other publications was not so much for woman's rights as for human rights, for, she wrote, "I know of no one who loses so much as man by what he withholds from woman." Dall became a well-known figure in the woman's movement on the basis of her independent writing alone, with virtual strangers writing to tell her that what she had said "harmonized with [their] own views."[41] Paulina Wright Davis solicited Dall's contributions for *The Una* when it went into circulation in 1853 even though Dall was in Toronto at the time; she wrote for the paper from the beginning and eventually co-edited the publication.

The Una remained in circulation for only three years but was important as the first paper devoted to the cause of woman suffrage. Dall's contributions, however, did not usually address this political issue. She wrote moralistic tales or, more importantly, the stories of historic female figures—artists, authors, queens, and physicians. Her primary duties on the paper consisted of "ransacking the records of the past, and supplying biographical matter to these pages," so that readers might see what women were capable of accomplishing.[42] What she sought for women—

equality of educational and employment opportunities—did not seem in the beginning to require the suffrage but first and foremost the respect of men and the willingness of women to break out of the mold into which society had forced them. "Women have been too well, and too long satisfied with Ladies Books . . . and Miscellanies," wrote Dall, "[and] it is time that they should have [and demand] stronger nourishment."[43] Returning to the teachings of Margaret Fuller on the capacity of women to help themselves, Dall provided historical examples and then called in her articles for "eloquent livers, by every hearth stone in America," to work to gain the respect of men, for it was "upon such women, even more than . . . reformers, [that] the national progress [will] depend."[44] In this excerpt Dall was clearly urging that women comply with precepts of the "cult of domesticity" in form so that they might subvert it in fact and thereby gain public standing and respect; the claims of Welter, Cott, and other recent commentators that the "cult of womanhood" sowed the seeds of its own destruction could not have been more deftly illustrated.[45]

Dall's own domestic life, however, did not proceed according to hers or any other plan. Marriage did not meet her expectations (her husband's encouragement and evident admiration for her commitment to reform notwithstanding), and her disillusionment coincided with a reconsideration of reform goals—now to include woman suffrage. The deterioration of the marriage is evident in the course of events more than anything else since Dall's papers contain few references to her marriage in general or her husband in particular.[46] Apparently the marriage was never ideal. In 1845, while the couple was living and working in a Baltimore parish, Charles Dall's health collapsed, prompting them to return to Boston. Dall welcomed that move, but her husband's calling repeatedly uprooted the family as they moved from Boston to New Hampshire, to Needham, Massachusetts, and then to Toronto in 1851. Charles Dall's failing health continued to trouble the marriage, sapping his strength for work and necessitating Caroline's cooperation in meeting the obligations of his office as minister. Dall welcomed the opportunities to work in the church, whether alongside her husband or in his stead, but she did not relish the financial hardships that his illnesses visited upon the family.

Letters to family and friends reflected Dall's growing concern over the family finances within five years of her marriage. By 1849, she sought to earn money from her reform writings. A letter from Wendell Phillips, informing her that the leading reform periodicals did not pay and that her best chance on that count would be to "arrange with some of the little monthlies, *Ladies Reformatory* and such like," indicated that this was no easy task.[47] Even her father, at odds with her reform efforts and considering abolitionists in general to be "traitors to their country," felt obliged to offer financial aid. Still devoted to her father in spite of the never-ending cycle of love, estrangement, reproach, and reconciliation that marked their adult relationship, Dall was reluctant to borrow. All she wished for was "$800 in a year without improper dependence on anybody."[48]

The virtual disintegration of the marriage in the early 1850s exacerbated Dall's financial troubles and awakened her to the necessity of women gaining full political, as well as economic and educational, rights. In 1855 Charles Dall departed (alone) to assume the responsibilities of a missionary in India, and as she assumed the traditionally male role of economic provider, Caroline Dall gained an intimate acquaintance with the difficulties faced by a woman trying to support a family on her own. This enforced autonomy and responsibility, greater than she had hitherto experienced, propelled her toward active, political involvement in the movement for women's rights in that same year. Shortly after her husband left, Dall cooperated with Paulina Wright Davis in organizing a Massachusetts convention on women's rights. She delivered an exhaustive report on women's legal status in Massachusetts and for the first time spoke before an audience on the subject of women's rights, including suffrage. As she explained later, she cared "very little for politics as such but . . . [sought] the right of suffrage because . . . without it, [women] can never rest secure in any other right, whether educational or industrial."[49] This marked the beginning of her most active and political involvement in the women's movement, and in 1857 she reluctantly conceded herself a "woman's rights woman."[50]

Lectures, conventions, and petition drives filled her time, and Dall came into contact with the leaders of the movement—for good or ill—and came to occupy a position of some responsibility within the movement at large and especially in her native Massachusetts. And, of course, writing continued to be a prime focus of her energies on the public stage. But she did not enjoy the new role in all its parts. Though Dall now supported the notion of woman suffrage, it was a means to an end for her rather than an end in itself; her particular crusade—now directly connected to her own circumstances as mother *and* breadwinner—was, as always, for women's economic rights and security.[51]

She began to lecture locally (in Massachusetts) in 1856 and embarked on her most famous series of public lectures in 1859 in various cities across the country. This method of supporting the cause was, like writing, well suited to her nature since it allowed her to work more or less on her own terms. Furthermore Dall inferred a triumph from every invitation to lecture; it was a "mark of that respect" that every woman deserved as an "equal though differing human creature."[52] Her lectures followed the formula of her best-known articles on woman's place in the "College, the Marketplace, and the Court." They included the exhaustively researched history of women's efforts virtually worldwide to change exclusionary practices that prohibited them from full participation in the market and professions. She sounded the same note in her convention addresses during those years. She called and organized the New England conventions of 1859 and 1860 and delivered reports on the progress of the movement, which she described as rapid, but made it clear that women should help themselves; men must eventually recognize that women could contribute to society outside the home, but women must want to change the facts of their oppression by demanding and showing themselves worthy of respect, employment, and equal pay.[53]

The Civil War virtually silenced the demands of the women's movement for the suffrage, and Dall retreated with the rest. In fact, she returned to her conventional roots, arguing that the "thinking woman [had] a higher duty" than that of agitator. It became woman's duty to "nurse the halting faith of the nation" as men died to free the slaves. The linkage between the antislavery and women's rights movements, always present, nearly overwhelmed the women's movement during the war, but the movement, and Dall with it, staged a comeback immediately after war's end.

The early years of Reconstruction marked Dall's greatest cooperative efforts within the women's movement and her most difficult efforts as she worked closely with and for other people instead of as an organizer or independent lecturer. Between 1865 and 1867 she worked closely with the leadership of the movement, especially Susan B. Anthony. Strident and politically engaged, Dall evidently agreed with Anthony that the movement had "too long held women's claims in abeyance to the Negroe's" and worked for universal suffrage and equal rights in the new constitutional amendments.[54] She circulated petitions on behalf of the women's movement and the Equal Rights Association, founded in 1866, returning to the theme of human rights from the 1850s.

The period of cooperation between Caroline Dall and the movement's organizational structures was very brief. Her certitude and sensitivity made her difficult to work with, despite her obvious contributions to the movement and the trust placed in her by women such as Stanton and Anthony. Anthony, in particular, had to deal with Dall's concern for reputation and recognition and her insistence that her lengthy reports not be edited. "Yes," Anthony wrote, "the report is to go down to history as *yours* not anybody's else," but she and Stanton hoped that Dall would permit some changes to "render it more acceptable."[55] For her part, Dall found fault with the petitions being forwarded to Congress from women in various sections of the country, stating that "[t]hey do not suit my taste, nor are they, in my opinion, adapted to the emergency at hand." Under her direction a simpler form would be circulated in Boston. But she was not working alone in Boston, and either the change in form that she initiated or (more likely) a clash of temperaments between her and co-worker Caroline Severance produced a delay in communicating the petition to Congress.[56]

While the women's movement enjoyed some success in the years after the Civil War, the more radical aims of Stanton's branch and its increasingly bureaucratic structure overall made it difficult for Dall to cooperate. New clubs formed in Boston and conventions continued to be called, but after 1867 Caroline Dall ceased to occupy any part of the limelight in the organized women's movement.

Quick to take offense and slow to forgive, even in the name of women's rights, Caroline Dall was ill suited temperamentally for continued association, and she abruptly withdrew her affiliation with the organized movement after a disagreement with Caroline Severance and Julia Ward Howe, directors of the New England Women's Club in Boston. She felt that a "willingness to work for women" should be the only requirement for membership in the new club and it was one she easily met; Severance had "unfairly excluded" her. Attributing her own prejudices to these women, Dall was certain that they disliked her. For that reason among others, she refused to participate in the 1868 women's convention that Caroline Severance was organizing, declining "to serve *under her* until matters are made clear."[57]

Dall's entry into political reform had been halting, and her with-

drawal suggested her continued preference for other means of action.
In 1855 she had pronounced conventions unwieldy, "masculine imple-
ments" and urged women to find alternatives to such means of organization, for "what have men accomplished by them in politics or reform?" More than ten years later, she still held that opinion, writing in
response to an invitation to a convention that so far "such *organization,*
witness Mrs. Stanton and Miss Anthony [had] been the bitterest en-
emy" of the women's cause.[58]

This disassociation left her hovering between two camps, those of
tradition and reform. Despite an unsuccessful marriage, she continued
to fashion herself in some ways as a prop of domesticity and was thus
too moderate for the increasingly radical efforts of Anthony and Stanton, with whom she had worked most closely. She maintained her belief
in marriage as a sacred and eminently desirable end (though she believed in the necessity of loosening divorce laws to encompass certain
circumstances—perhaps her own) and thought of motherhood as naturally desired by every woman.[59] On the other hand, by her early forties
she stood far outside the traditional role for women impressed upon her
in youth and, in fact, berated women who clung to the teachings of the
ladies' books and magazines and kept their hands white and affected "a
general air of uselessness." She encouraged women to work and move in
the world, abandon their submissive attitudes, and teach men to respect
and admire them, to treat them as equals, and not assume that every
woman's place is only in the home.[60] Dall herself did not, of course,
retreat into the home after her withdrawal from the women's organizations; her quarrel with the movement was one of personalities and
politics, not purpose. For the remainder of her life she was an illustration of what women might do and achieve in the world.

After leaving the formal women's movement, Dall not only demonstrated what all women might do, she also satisfied her own desire to
project several discrete public identities. She served variously as social
critic, social prop, problem solver, and, of course, intellectual leader.
Dall's interests were always wide ranging, and women's advancement,
though a continuing concern, was bound up with broader issues. One
organization in particular filled her time, provided a forum for address-
ing those broad social concerns, and allowed her to fill those roles in
which she cast herself: the American Social Science Association (ASSA),
of which she was a founding member. This association addressed "pub-

138   lic questions" and problems and set about finding solutions to those problems.[61] During Dall's fifty-odd years of affiliation, which began in the 1850s, she worked to solve the most stubborn social problems—poverty, crime, and the need for increased revenue to deal with them—and brought pet projects of her own to the attention of the ASSA—including public education, the expansion of public library systems and holdings, and, of course, women's issues—economic, educational, health, and otherwise.[62]

Dall's membership in the women's rights movement and the ASSA overlapped for a period of several years in the 1860s. As early as 1859 she was involved in a movement to establish social science as a respected academic discipline and as a valid resource for policymakers. At roughly the same time she struggled to make women's issues a concern of the Association and the "Woman Question" a topic of discussion within that organization.[63] Dall won the respect of her male peers in the Association early on and over the years served numerous terms on its board as librarian, director, and vice president. The organization's acceptance of women's issues and other female board members was slower in coming, though, due to the fear of certain prominent male members that taking up the "Woman Question" or accepting female professionals on the board would prejudice the public against the ASSA as a tool of the "woman party." Dall was, in fact, for many years the only woman prominent in the organization (although others certainly participated in conferences and made occasional contributions to the Association's journal).[64] Dall succeeded in becoming the conscience of the ASSA on women's issues, framing important discussions on a variety of topics. She spoke out, for example, against abortion as "unmotherly" and unnatural—hardly a surprising stand in her day, but she also took a more controversial stand when she addressed the spread of syphilis. In this matter she lobbied physicians to recognize the danger and error of treating syphilis—a disease that contributed so much to the problems that physicians and social scientists wished to solve—"as if it originated in and was perpetuated by women only." This assumption, she felt, perpetuated a double standard that allowed men to act without restraint and culpability and endangered the population by permitting the disease to spread. She also continued to push for women's economic and educational advancement and earned a law degree herself from Alfred University of New York in 1877.[65]

Dall was devoted not just to the educational advancement of women;

SOCIAL REFORM AND POLITICAL ACTIVISM

she evinced a long-standing commitment to public education in general. Both before and after her withdrawal from the women's movement,
Dall aided the cause of education and increased public access to information, both as a member of the ASSA and as a private citizen. She
helped develop and implement learning strategies in public libraries
and, over the years, contributed books, tracts, and pamphlets to various
institutions from her own sizable collection of materials.[66] Through
such contributions she guided public thought on the issues dearest to
her heart by making available those materials she deemed important. As
in so much of her public activity throughout her life, she served both
personal and public needs through those gifts by making herself and her
assistance available on her own terms.

In the end, Dall's ambiguous position in society did not hinder her
effectiveness as an agitator for women's rights. After she withdrew from
the formal women's movement, she continued to press for women's
advancement through various means and at various levels. On the one
hand, through her pursuit of education at Alfred University, her writings, and simply her continued independence, Caroline Dall re-created
herself for the general public as one of her own "eloquent livers" and
contributed to the creation of the "New Woman" that so shocked bour-
geois males and matrons of the late nineteenth and early twentieth
centuries.[67] On the other hand, the ASSA allowed her to address a more
elite audience and assume the role of intellectual leader so dear to her
sense of self. In a report to the ASSA Dall outlined her understanding of
the Association's purpose and the distinctions between that organization
and the various reform organizations from which she would soon dis-
associate herself: "it is not a Reform society, but the *inspirer* of such a
society. . . . In a reform Meeting you inveigh against evils, you summon
all the power of rhetoric to paint and impress upon the minds of an
audience. . . . But the people who come together in Social Science
Associations are supposed to know the evils—to be fully impressed with
the need of reform—*and they are to stimulate, not passions and prejudice,
but intellectual insight, cool and calm inquiry.*"[68]
Dall took this statement of purpose as a blueprint not just for ASSA
activity but for her own continued public efforts on behalf of society
generally and women particularly. And both in her work with the ASSA
and in her independent writing—in other words, in the identities she
presented to both the general public and the professional social science

community—Dall succeeded in completing the creation of a lifetime. So reluctant to enter active reform earlier, and so ill suited to close cooperative efforts, she was, after 1868, an important, independent voice outside the reform bureaucracy, and yet she helped set the tone and pace for such activity. She pointed the way but removed herself from the fray as halting progress was made toward universal suffrage and equality.

Regrettably, Dall's life and her significant contributions as a scholar and reformer have long been ignored. As a reform activist she was effective (if difficult to work with) and contributed much to the women's movement of the mid-nineteenth century. Independent of the reform movements through which she had established herself on the public stage, she nonetheless succeeded in placing important issues before the public eye and advancing her ideas in intellectual and policymaking circles. Further, whether one dwells on her association with various reform organizations or not, her life linked the nineteenth with the twentieth century, the traditional with the "New" woman, and the romantic with Progressive reformers.[69]

Finally, Dall's life offers an opportunity to explore the ever-present linkage between the personal and political. Clearly Caroline Dall's activism was spurred, though not completely driven, by the circumstances of her own life and by her own personality. The drive for women's economic and academic opportunity clearly reflected her personal situation, although it is not clear whether Dall was aware of the degree to which she was reacting to events in her own life as she pursued those reforms. Her efforts on behalf of antislavery and the professionalization of social science, for example, were less derivative of her own life but rather indicative of her wide-ranging interests and social concerns. Certainly, though, Dall (and other individual activists) cannot be understood without studying all facets of their activity and the numerous ways in which the personal and political overlap. The connection is not always obvious, but it is always important.

Notes

1. Caroline Wells Healey Dall, *Essays and Sketches* (Boston: S. G. Simkins, 1849), 83; and Caroline Dall to Charles Sumner, January 8, 1866, Caroline Healey Dall Papers, Massachusetts Historical Society, hereafter referred to as Dall Papers.

2. At sixteen, while writing of "woman's proper place" and "the rights of man," Caroline Dall nonetheless expressed her longing "for the time when a finished education shall be every woman's birthright; when the respect of the other sex shall be her legitimate inheritance; when the woman of any rank will be able to obtain a livelihood for herself or her children without overtasking the generosity of man; when she shall no longer find herself, even for a moment, a tool or a plaything." Dall, *Essays and Sketches*, 84.

3. Dall, *Essays and Sketches*, 84.

4. Barbara Welter, "The Merchant's Daughter: A Tale from Life," *New England Quarterly* 42 (March 1969): 3–23.

5. See Nancy Cott, *The Bonds of Womanhood* (New Haven: Yale University Press, 1977); and Carroll Smith-Rosenberg, "The Female World of Love and Ritual," in *Disorderly Conduct: Visions of Gender in Victorian America* (New York: Knopf, 1985), 53–76.

6. Among the earliest reforms of the nineteenth century were those undertaken by women for women, as the pressures of poverty dragged females of the working classes down, frequently toward licentious behavior. Barbara Berg investigated the involvement of urban middle- and upper-class women in reform movements to aid working-class women. Her thesis stated that a genuine affection and sisterhood developed even between women of these disparate classes. She further maintained that these early reforms for women, organized in the early years of the nineteenth century, provided the seeds for feminism as women recognized a double standard in the prescribed behavior for women and men, and then recognized women's obvious deprivations. Barbara Berg, *The Remembered Gate: Origins of American Feminism* (New York: Oxford University Press, 1978).

7. Barbara Welter, "The Cult of True Womanhood, 1820–1860," *American Quarterly* 18 (Summer 1966): 173–74.

8. Helen Horowitz looked at a woman's "creation" of her identity in a different context and by a different means in "Nous Autres: Reading, Passion, and the Creation of M. Carey Thomas," *Journal of American History* 79 (June 1992): 68–95. Though the circumstances and motives of the women differed, the notion of Caroline Dall's self-creation as a means of (partially) explaining her activities in life crystallized for me after I read Horowitz's article.

9. When Caroline was eighteen, she wrote a long autobiographical letter to the Reverend Theodore Parker that went far in illuminating her personality. At the age of nine she was in torment over questions of God and religion. "Did you ever hear of skeptic child? I was such a child," she told Parker. Her skepticism was short lived but her introspection was not; she searched for a rationale for her beliefs and "connected "Moral Force with my idea of the Absolute Intellect, and became convinced of my own accountability and immortality." Her accountability drove her to be conscientious and scrupulous to a fault. Caroline Healey to Theodore Parker, November 30, 1841, Dall Papers.

10. Susan B. Anthony to Elizabeth Cady Stanton, November 28, 1860, Stanton Papers, Library of Congress, quoted in Robert Riegel, *American Feminists* (Lawrence: University Press of Kansas, 1963), 161; notes from reconstructed journals, 1870 and December 5, 1879, Caroline Dall Papers. These "reconstructed" journals are the products of Dall's editing and rewriting in the 1870s and again in the 1890s. She had a passion for setting the record straight, and in addition to revising her journals she also sifted through her letters, destroying or partially destroying those that did not seem to her to be pertinent to history's understanding of her life. Fortunately she did save many of her original journals, in addition to leaving behind the "reconstructed" versions, but the Massachusetts Historical Society (to whom Dall promised her papers in 1873) was no doubt disappointed in this activity on the part of a woman who had written that she believed her papers would "have the same value a century hence, that the papers of John Wheelwright or Anne Hutchinson would have today" (Dall to Massachusetts Historical Society, October 26, 1873, Dall Papers).

11. Caroline Healey to Charles Dall, February 2, 1843, Dall Papers.

12. Caroline Healey to Charles Dall, February 22, 1843, as quoted in Welter, "The Merchant's Daughter," 5.

13. Caroline Healey to Charles Dall, February 2, 1843, Dall Papers.

14. Reconstructed journal for December 1837 and January 1838, Dall Papers.

15. Notes from 1870 and 1896 prefacing reconstructed journal, Dall Papers. This negative reassessment of her father's influence perhaps also reflected the values and expectations of Dall the reformer and woman's rights activist.

16. Anne C. Rose, *Transcendentalism as a Social Movement, 1830–1850* (New Haven: Yale University Press, 1981), chapter 1 ("Boston Unitarianism").

17. Caroline Healey to Mark Healey, December 10, 1840, Dall Papers.

18. Journal, December 9, 1840, Dall Papers.

19. Dall wrote briefly of Charlie in Caroline Dall, *Alongside* (Boston: Thomas Todd, 1900), 84. The relatively few letters exchanged with her siblings—especially her sisters—offered glimpses of distant and troubled, if not bitter and acrimonious, relationships among the children of Mark and Caroline Foster Healey. See, for example, Caroline Healey Dall to Fannie Healey, April 18, 1872; Caroline Healey Dall to Ellen Healey Childe, December 12, 1873; Carline Healey Dall to Emily Healey, April 5, 1876, Dall Papers.

20. Caroline Dall, *The College, the Market, and the Court* (Concord, N.H.: Rumford Press, 1914), 89. Caroline Dall first presented these lectures (on women's position in history and contemporary society) in 1858 and 1859. This assessment of sibling relationships is found in Dall's account of the life of Mary Wollstonecraft. She may as well have been describing her own familial relations. Since I found a tendency in much of her work to personalize things, I have here assumed that she was in part referring to the quasi-parental role she took on vis-à-vis her younger siblings as "unnatural." She was, after all, but a youth herself, and her parents still lived.

SOCIAL REFORM AND POLITICAL ACTIVISM

21. Reconstructed journal from January 1838 and original journal, April 17, 1838, Dall Papers.

22. Caroline Healey to Caroline Foster Healey (mother), April 9, 1840, Dall Papers.

23. Journal, August 6, 1842, Dall Papers; Caroline Foster Healey to Caroline Dall, January 20, 1849, Dall Papers.

24. See Lois Banner, *Elizabeth Cady Stanton: A Radical for Woman's Rights* (Boston: Little, Brown, 1980), chapter 1; Gerda Lerner, *The Grimke Sisters of South Carolina* (Boston: Houghton Mifflin, 1967), chapter 2; Kathryn Kish Sklar, *Catharine Beecher: A Study in American Domesticity* (New Haven: Yale University Press, 1973); Welter, "The Merchant's Daughter," 10.

25. Nancy Cott suggests a link between feminism and a rejection of the evangelical faiths. "Quakerism, Unitarianism, radical sectarianism, or 'deconversion' often led the way" across the boundaries between woman's sphere and woman's rights. Cott, *The Bonds of Womanhood*, 204. Anne Rose asserts a relationship between the feminist movement and the liberal theories of Transcendentalism and the new Unitarianism (Rose, *Transcendentalism as a Social Movement*, 42, 56–60).

26. *The Una: A Newspaper for the Elevation of Women* (Providence, R.I.), October 15, 1855.

27. She was also self-absorbed, oversensitive, and nearly humorless. A letter to a close friend demonstrated certain of these qualities and reflected an unusual consciousness and conscientiousness in the seventeen-year-old girl. Well aware of responsibilities in the household, Caroline wrote, "I am tempted to wish that such a thing as duty had never been invented, but . . . I am sure that I am precisely the sort of person that could not live without it." On the other hand, she evidently could or did live without laughter. Going on in the letter, she struck an almost pathetic note, recounting a story and closing with the comment, "I believe I should have laughed . . . Martha, if you had been here to laugh with me . . . but I never laugh alone." Caroline Healey to Martha Choate, July 5, 1839, Dall Papers.

28. Margaret Fuller, *Woman in the Nineteenth Century* (1845; reprint, New York: W. W. Norton, 1971), 169.

29. Caroline Dall, *Historical Pictures Retouched* (Boston: Walker, Wise, and Company, 1860), p. 261.

30. Rose, *Transcendentalism as a Social Movement*, 184; Keith Melder, *Beginnings of Sisterhood: The American Woman's Rights Movement, 1800–1850* (New York: Schocken Books, 1977), 134–35.

31. Caroline Dall to Anna Parsons, March 16, 1852, Dall Papers. Caroline's letter reveals her sense of gratitude toward Margaret Fuller but also an urgent desire to identify with her. Considering their brief acquaintance (Caroline only knew Fuller that one winter), the evident depth of her affection for Fuller and her insistence on knowledge of Fuller's life and character are surprising. Be that

as it may, Caroline drew numerous parallels between their lives and no doubt took a certain comfort from the idea that she followed in the footsteps of one so admired.

32. Caroline Healey Dall to Anna Parsons, March 16, 1852, Dall Papers.

33. Journal, September 11, 1842, Dall Papers.

34. Caroline Healey to Sewing Circle, West Boston Parish, September 16, 1842, Dall Papers.

35. A. P. Putnam, preface to Dall, *The College, the Market, and the Court*, xvi; Caroline Healey to the teachers of the West Parish School, September 1842, Dall Papers.

36. Caroline Healey to Charles Dall, February 15, 1843, Dall Papers.

37. Caroline Dall to William Lloyd Garrison, May 24, 1850, and Samuel May to Caroline Dall, June 10, 1854, Dall Papers.

38. Wendell Phillips to Caroline Dall, May 8, 1849, Dall Papers.

39. *The Una*, October 15, 1855.

40. Paulina Wright Davis to Caroline Dall, June 8, 1851, Dall Papers.

41. Caroline Healey to Sarah Balch, April 24, 1841, Dall Papers; *The Una*, October 15, 1855; Caroline Dall to Catharine Sedgwick, October 4, 1857; Harriet Farley to Caroline Dall, September 18, 1850, Dall Papers.

42. *The Una*, January 15, 1855.

43. *The Una*, January 15, 1853.

44. *The Una*, August 15, 1854; October 15, 1855.

45. See note 7 above and the final chapters of Cott, *Bonds of Womanhood*.

46. In fact, Dall, in the course of reviewing her papers in the 1870s and 1890s, edited or eliminated parts of her journals and parts of letters to and from her husband. There remain only a handful of letters from forty years of marriage. There are, however, surviving references to evidently happy day-to-day experiences with the children.

47. Wendell Phillips to Caroline Dall, November 11, 1849, Dall Papers.

48. Caroline Foster Healey to Caroline Dall, July 3, 1851; Caroline Dall to Mark Healey, June 22, 1850, Dall Papers.

49. Caroline Dall to the Reverend F. D. Huntington, October 20, 1858, Dall Papers.

50. Caroline Dall to Catharine Sedgwick, October 4, 1857, Dall Papers.

51. Historian Mary Kelley wrote of "literary domestics" whose circumstances mirrored those of Caroline Dall. In their work, these women tried to accommodate their desire to be heard to their domestic roles. Dall, too, was trying to maintain one identity as she formulated another for herself. See Mary Kelley, *Private Woman, Public Stage: Literary Domesticity in Nineteenth-Century America* (New York: Oxford University Press, 1984), esp. chapter 6.

52. Caroline Dall to (editor of the *Christian Union*), November 29, 1859, Dall Papers.

53. Caroline Dall, *The College, the Market, and the Court*; Elizabeth Cady

Stanton, Susan B. Anthony, Matilda Jocelyn Gage, eds., *History of Woman Suffrage,* 4 vols. (Rochester, N.Y.: Charles Mann, 1889), 1:265–70.

54. Susan B. Anthony to Caroline Dall, January 30, 1866, Dall Papers. The movement once again met with considerable resistance after its dormant years during the war; some evidently believed that the hiatus indicated a lack of will and, in fact, a "general expression" that women did not want the vote. Caroline defended the move for universal suffrage and once again noted the necessity of men's respect for women: "Women will never express a 'general desire' for suffrage until men have ceased to ridicule and despise them for it; until the representatives of men have been taught to treat their petitions with respect. There would be no difficulty in obtaining this right if it depended on a property qualification. It is consistent democracy which bars our way." Caroline Dall in *The Nation,* January 20, 1866, quoted in Stanton, Anthony, and Gage, *History of Woman Suffrage,* 3:102.

55. Susan B. Anthony to Caroline Dall, May 30, 1866; Elizabeth Cady Stanton to Caroline Dall, April 30, 1866, Dall Papers.

56. Caroline Dall to Charles Sumner, January 8, 1866; Susan B. Anthony to Caroline Dall, January 30, 1866, Dall Papers.

57. Caroline Dall to Louisa Hall, June 4, 1868; Caroline Dall to Samuel Sewall, August 14, 1868, Dall Papers. A typewritten copy of part of her 1869 journal (February–May) details the course of Caroline Dall's relationships with Caroline Severance and Julia Howe—as she interpreted events, of course. See also a letter, copied over in a letterbook for posterity's sake but evidently unsent, to a Mrs. Tolman, January 20, 18?? [n.d.].

58. Caroline Dall to Samuel Sewall, August 14, 1868, Dall Papers.

59. Although Caroline and Charles Dall never divorced, it is not clear—thanks to Caroline's censorship of her marital correspondence—whether divorce was ever considered or desired by either party. By 1859, however, Caroline was willing to admit the occasional necessity of divorce in a letter to William Channing, a man with serious marital troubles of his own. And by 1861, her husband gone for six years in India, Caroline wrote to one of Charles's friends that she was broken-hearted in spirit and had "given up every hope [she] ever had of seeing [Charles] again." And, in fact, she saw little of her husband before his death in 1886; he returned to America only a handful of times for brief visits. Indeed, Susan B. Anthony could not refrain from observing in a letter of condolence that she had never seen Charles and thus found it "difficult to associate [Caroline] with a husband." Dall to William Channing, January 18, 1859; Dall to Thomas Whitridge, October 19, 1861; Susan B. Anthony to Caroline Dall, December 20, 1886, Dall Papers.

60. Caroline Dall, "Something about Women," *Putnam's Magazine* 1, no. 6 (June 1868): 695–703.

61. Carl Kelsey (secretary of the American Academy of Political and Social Sciences) to Caroline Dall, October 18, 1906; Report of Caroline Dall to the ASSA, December 15, 1865, Dall Papers.

62. These latter concerns—particularly education and the position of women in society—are also quite popular with policy makers today ("hot-button" issues, so to speak), but Dall was instrumental in bringing and keeping those topics to the fore of scholarly and public attention in the late nineteenth century.

63. Dall to Edward Caper (Boston Public Library), March 19, 1859; Dall to trustees of Boston Public Library, March 25, 1859, Dall Papers.

64. Dall to Franklin Sanborn, September 24, 1865; (partial) ASSA journal of Caroline Dall, September 21, 1865, Dall Papers. Dall indeed faced some stiff opposition within the ASSA, as in 1870 when E. L. Godkin, an influential member, well-known reformer, and editor of *The Nation,* attempted to "raise the level of discussion" within the organization and thought this could best be done by restricting membership and limiting the role of women within it. Fortunately for Dall and other women, and no doubt for the ASSA itself, Franklin Sanborn, the central figure in the Association, opposed the move to limit membership and remove women from the governing board. For more on the ASSA, see Thomas Haskell, *The Emergence of Professional Social Science: The American Social Science Association and the Nineteenth-Century Crisis of Authority* (Urbana: University of Illinois Press, 1977).

65. Dall to H. B. Storer, June 5, 1866; Dall to a Dr. Eliot, February 23, 1876, Dall Papers. Dall also addressed herself to the problems of children and the poor, serving on numerous committees that visited such places as Bellevue hospital, the almshouse and workhouse on Blackwell's Island, and the Deaf and Dumb Asylum of New York—all in New York City. November 21–22, 1867, typewritten journal; also, part and parcel of concern expressed by Dall and the ASSA for the welfare and health of children, the Report of the Milk Committee, n.d., Dall Papers.

66. Dall to the editor of *The Nation,* January 5, 1907; Sarah Clarke to Caroline Dall, November 18, 1886; Henry Van Dyke to Caroline Dall, October 13, 1906, Dall Papers.

67. See Smith-Rosenberg, "The New Woman as Androgyne," in *Disorderly Conduct,* 245–96. These "New Women" essentially enlarged upon the demands and progress made by such women as Caroline Dall and asserted that women's education, exercise, and careers, far from weakening "the race" as male physicians predicted, would strengthen women's bodies and minds, whether they eventually took up a career in society or remained at home.

68. Report of Caroline Dall to the ASSA, December 15, 1865, Dall Papers. Emphasis mine.

69. As Thomas Haskell pointed out, the ASSA—which occupied so much of Dall's time and attention both before and after she withdrew from the women's movement and explored so many modern issues in the 1870s and 1880s—offers the scholar the opportunity to draw "a valid, if thin, line of continuity linking the romantic reformers of the antebellum era . . . to . . . Progressive reformers" (Haskell, *The Emergence of Professional Social Science,* 203).

SOCIAL REFORM AND POLITICAL ACTIVISM

JOSEPHINE ST. PIERRE RUFFIN

A Nineteenth-Century Journalist of
Boston's Black Elite Class

RODGER STREITMATTER

As a presence and a force in the history of American journalism, women of African descent have remained largely invisible. The standard history of American journalism describes only one black woman, Ida B. Wells-Barnett, compressing her life and work into eight lines.[1] The standard history of the African-American press summarizes the contributions of all women journalists of the last two centuries in four paragraphs.[2] Histories of women journalists gradually have become more inclusive of African-American women, with several anthologies finding room for either one chapter or one representative of the race;[3] at the same time, however, scholars of women journalists repeatedly have called for additional work in this under-researched field.[4]

This chapter responds to that call by illuminating the life and work of Josephine St. Pierre Ruffin, a nineteenth-century journalist from Boston's black aristocracy. In 1890, Ruffin founded and edited this country's first newspaper published both by and for African-American women, the *Woman's Era*. The Boston-based monthly carried news articles and opinion pieces to middle- and upper-class black women across the country. The *Woman's Era* was closely connected with the African-American women's club movement, and Ruffin became a driving force in that movement.[5] In 1893, she founded the Woman's Era Club in Boston, one of the first black women's clubs in the country. Two years later, she called for, organized, and led the first national meeting of

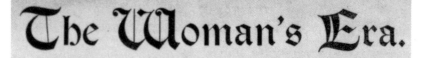

The Woman's Era.

VOL. II. NO. 1.   BOSTON, MASS., APRIL, 1895   PRICE 10 CENTS.

JOSEPHINE ST. P. RUFFIN.
(By permission of Boston Journal.)

FLORIDA RUFFIN RIDLEY.

NOTES AND COMMENTS.

Mrs. Abby Morton Diaz gave the first in her series of talks on the " Science of Human Beings " before the Era Club Tuesday evening, March 28, at the Charles St. Church vestry. At a time and in a community where people are talked to, and at, and about until they are more inclined to run from rather than to lectures, it is gratifying to note that, so novel in scheme and so inspiring in result was this talk, that the enthusiasm created by it is likely to run and spread and create a wide interest to hear the remainder of the course. These lectures are given at the Club's expense and are free to the public. The next one will be given April 11.

Mrs. Fannie Barrier Williams, editor of the Illinois department of the WOMAN'S ERA and secretary of the Illinois Woman's Alliance, is expected to deliver a series of lectures in New England in April.

The March literary meeting of the Woman's Era Club was in charge of the Committee on Manners and Morals, Miss Eliza Gardner, chairman.

Two well prepared papers were read, one by Mrs. Agnes Adams on " Our Needs," and the other by Mrs. Alice Casneau on " Morals and Manners." As a result of suggestions made by Mrs. Casneau, the following resolution was adopted by the Club :

WHEREAS, The Woman's Era Club having had their attention called to the very common practice of putting tickets in the hands of children to be sold for the benefit of different objects, do herewith

RESOLVE, That inasmuch as the custom of permitting young girls to solicit men to buy tickets from them is damaging to modesty and a menace to morality, we do set the seal of our condemnation upon it, and call upon the church people especially to help us abolish the custom.

The Club then listened to an interesting narration by its president, who went as a delegate to the Triennial Council of Women at Washington, and then farther south on a visit to Women clubs in that section. The president reported that she had returned with health and enthusiasm in and for our women but more brightly than ever. Her stay was short, long enough to show her that the women of the south-land are as active in trying to " help make the world bet-

Mrs. N. A. Ridley
Mar 22 1930

The Woman's Era (vol. 2, no. 1, April 1895). Courtesy, Trustees of the Boston Public Library. Illustration located by Kate Larson.

SOCIAL REFORM AND POLITICAL ACTIVISM

black women, which led to the creation of the National Federation of Afro-American Women. In 1900, Ruffin received nationwide news coverage for her attempt to desegregate the General Federation of Women's Clubs, the national organization of middle- and upper-class white women.[6]

Ruffin used her newspaper to document the achievements and showcase the abilities of African-American women. In a *Woman's Era* editorial, Ruffin explained that, "The stumbling block in the way of even the most cultured colored woman is the narrowness of her environment. . . . It is to help strengthen this class and a better understanding between all classes that this little venture is sent out on its mission."[7]

As the individual who financed and published the *Woman's Era* during its seven-year lifespan, Ruffin was in a position to promote, through her newspaper, themes that she valued. Analysis of the editorial content reveals that Ruffin was a committed feminist who urged her readers to expand beyond their traditional sphere, through both their occupations and their knowledge about the public issues that defined the day. Ruffin also was a militant racial reformer who encouraged African-American women to fight racial injustice and demand increased rights for their race. Ruffin was an integrationist who believed that blacks would benefit from increased interaction with white America, and she used her position as a newspaper editor and her status as a member of upper-class society to promote interracial activities.

Josephine St. Pierre was born in Boston, August 31, 1842. Her mother, Eliza Matilda Menhenick, was a white woman from Cornwall, England; her father, John St. Pierre, was the dark-skinned son of a Frenchman from Martinique. Josephine's father secured wealth and prominence as a clothes dealer and as a founder of a Boston Zion church.[8]

The St. Pierres saw to it that Josephine received the proper education for a young woman of her station. They initially enrolled their light-skinned daughter in a private grammar school in Boston. After six months, when her racial background was discovered, Josephine was forced to leave the school. The St. Pierres then enrolled her in the integrated schools of nearby Salem. She later graduated from a Boston finishing school and completed two years of private tutoring in New York.

At the age of fifteen, Josephine married George Lewis Ruffin, a member of another of the city's leading black families. The Ruffins purchased a home on Charles Street, and she bore five children, the youngest of whom died in infancy.[9]

In 1869, George Lewis Ruffin became the first American of African descent to graduate from the Harvard Law School. He later served in the Massachusetts State Legislature and on the Boston Common Council. Ruffin received national attention in 1883 when Governor Benjamin Butler appointed him as judge of the municipal court of Charlestown, making Ruffin the first African-American judge in the North.[10]

As the career of George Lewis Ruffin advanced, Josephine St. Pierre Ruffin emerged as an individual of talent and resources. During the Civil War, she worked with the United States Sanitary Commission, precursor of the American Red Cross. After the war, she founded the Kansas Relief Association, convincing wealthy Bostonians to send money and clothing to former slaves who had migrated west. After Massachusetts women won the right to vote in school board elections, Ruffin became a charter member of the Massachusetts School Suffrage Association, which encouraged and prepared women to exercise their new right.[11]

As Ruffin's organizational abilities evolved through her benevolent efforts, she was catapulted into relationships with the most renowned New Englanders of the day. She and abolitionist William Lloyd Garrison, who also lived in Boston, collaborated on relief work in Kansas.[12] Ruffin also worked with antislavery orators Wendell Phillips and Charles Sumner.[13] Among the African-American men with whom she worked on various projects were Frederick Douglass and T. Thomas Fortune, who both came to Boston for the historic meeting of black women that Ruffin organized in 1895.[14] The Ruffins became close friends of the Booker T. Washington family as well, and Josephine Ruffin spent winters with the Washingtons in Tuskegee, Alabama.[15]

But it was after George Ruffin's sudden death in 1886 that Josephine Ruffin made her most important contributions. As a forty-four-year-old widow with grown children, financial security, and a national reputation for organizational ability and social reform endeavors, Ruffin was poised to make a major contribution to her gender and her race. As her vehicle, she chose journalism.[16]

Ruffin began her most important journalistic work in 1890, personally financing the creation and operation, from her home, of the first newspaper in history aimed specifically toward African-American women.

Ruffin handled all editing and publishing responsibilities for the *Woman's Era*—editing copy, laying out pages, and selling advertise-

ments. She wrote an editorial page for each issue and occasionally wrote 151
news items, but she left most of the news writing to the upper-class
women from around the country whom she had recruited as unpaid
correspondents.[17]

The *Woman's Era* carried items from local black women's clubs, and
when the National Federation of Afro-American Women was formed in
1895, the *Woman's Era* became the Federation's official publication. Likewise, when the Federation emerged as the National Association of Colored Women a year later, it, too, chose the *Woman's Era* as its official
voice.[18]

Like other newspapers, the *Woman's Era* discussed current subjects
relevant to its readership. A typical article, based on interviews with
Boston police and hospital officials, exposed the fact that a sixteen-year-
old black girl had been held in slavery for four years. Another stated that
a prominent black woman, Fannie Barrier Williams, had been rejected
from membership in the Woman's Club of Chicago. Ruffin's subjective
journalistic style, which was typical of journalism of the time, allowed
her to add editorial comments as she saw fit. At the end of the article about Williams's rejection, Ruffin stated: "The modicum of negro
blood in her veins outweighed her eminent fitness, and club principle
made a weak surrender to personal prejudice."[19]

Ruffin boasted that all items in the *Woman's Era* were written specifically for it rather than reprinted from other publications, as was the
custom with most newspapers of the period. The *Woman's Era* measured
nine by twelve inches, and the issues ranged from sixteen to twenty-
eight pages. Early issues carried two pages of advertisements, later issues
ten. Each issue included at least one photograph, some as many as
fifteen. An annual subscription cost one dollar.[20]

In 1891, Ruffin also became editor of the *Boston Courant,* an African-
American weekly. After producing both the *Woman's Era* and the *Courant* for two years, however, she became ill from overwork. Ruffin then
continued to edit *Woman's Era* but reduced her work for the *Courant* to
writing an occasional article.[21]

Publishing the *Woman's Era* was a highly demanding job because the
newspaper, like others published for African Americans, had difficulty
attracting an advertising base.[22] Ruffin had hoped that the *Woman's Era*
would become self-supporting, but her journalistic enterprise faced for-
midable obstacles. Most significant were a scarcity of black-owned businesses and the reluctance of white-owned businesses to advertise to

152   black readers. The national scope of the *Woman's Era* added to the challenge; American newspapers had not yet evolved into national enterprises with national advertisers. Ultimately, the *Woman's Era* failed to attract an advertising base outside of Boston, and most local advertisers were owners of small businesses—a dressmaker, wallpaper hanger, baker—who could only afford small advertisements. By 1896, the *Woman's Era* had become a bimonthly, and the final issue appeared in January 1897.

The *Woman's Era* was a feminist publication whose contents Ruffin selected to advance the status of African-American women. Ruffin was very direct in asserting her feminist position, saying of the *Woman's Era:* "Being a woman's movement, it is bound to succeed." She reiterated her feminist convictions through statements about black women, such as: "Our indignation should know no limit. We as women have been too unobtrusive, too little known."[23]

One specifically feminist theme threaded through the newspaper was that women should not limit themselves to the narrow identity of wife and mother, to which most nineteenth-century women had been confined. Ruffin cautioned the African-American woman not to become "a mere machine to one's children," and she insisted that "advice given to women about their staying at home is wrong altogether." Ruffin's strongest endorsement of an expanded role for black women was a frank declaration that may have been a personal statement as well: "Not all women are intended for mothers. Some of us have not the temperament for family life."[24]

The feminist editor fostered expansion of the woman's sphere by sprinkling the pages of her newspaper with stories about African-American women who had broken new ground, ranging from the first named to the District of Columbia school board to the first to operate her own gold mine. Ruffin's article "Women in Business" concluded with the statement: "Women should indulge and pursue special bent or cultivate a peculiar power as do the men."[25]

Ruffin recognized the power of politics, and she encouraged readers to fight for national suffrage for women. She highlighted the ways in which women had benefited from having the vote in Colorado and Kentucky, asserting that "the finer virtues of women" as voters could further the country's noble mission.[26] Another feminist measure that Ruffin promoted was legislation to penalize the physical abuse of women.[27]

SOCIAL REFORM AND POLITICAL ACTIVISM

Although a committed feminist, Ruffin did not advocate women working in isolation from men. She wrote: "If women wish to advance any worthy cause by organizing, that cause would be better advanced by the co-operation of men and women than by their separatism."[28]

Ruffin exhorted American women of African descent to become more educated about public affairs. She said they should "read and think in order that they may not sit like idiots" while men talked. Consequently, she printed articles about a full range of political, social, and economic issues, such as Hawaiian independence, temperance, and, as the 1896 presidential election approached, the free coinage of silver.[29]

The issue that Ruffin most wanted her readers to influence was racial reform. Like other African-American women before and after her, Ruffin felt the pain of racial prejudice even more acutely than the pain of sexual prejudice. This priority is fully understandable when framed by such events as slavery and lynchings, which were prominent in Ruffin's consciousness.[30]

When writing about racial injustice, in the advocacy tradition of the black press, Ruffin sacrificed journalistic objectivity. When Boston realtors denied wealthy African-Americans the right to buy homes in affluent sections of the city, Ruffin demanded that they change their policy, writing: "The position is absurd. No other class of vendors may say who shall and shall not buy their wares." Her haughty tone clearly communicated that realtors were a working-class segment of the population who served the monied class—regardless of color.[31]

Ruffin's editorial voice grew most strident in its opposition to the legalization of segregation. When the United States Supreme Court upheld segregated travel by train, Ruffin went so far as to advocate breaking the law. "If laws are unjust," she wrote, "they must be continually broken until they are killed or altered. The thing to do is to force the recognition of manhood by any and all means. . . . It is evident that the only way now to get what we want is to take it, even if we have to break laws in getting it."[32]

Ruffin's commitment to reducing racial injustice also elicited harsh words for middle-class white women. Ruffin chastised them for contributing to job discrimination. She wrote: "The exclusion of colored women and girls from nearly all places of respectable employment is due mostly to the meanness of white women."[33]

Despite Ruffin's criticism of some white women, she worked to increase the interaction between black and white women of her own class. Ruffin invited several white women into the Woman's Era Club, and she routinely arranged integrated social activities, such as lectures, receptions, and musical performances.[34]

Ruffin cultivated interracial activities because she was concerned that the refined African-American woman's cultural outlets were too limited. In a *Woman's Era* editorial, she wrote of the African-American woman: "The impossibility of mingling freely with people of culture and learning, and so carrying on the mental growth begun in schools, shuts her out of physical touch with the great world of art, science and letters which is open to all other ambitious women."[35] By organizing interracial social events, Ruffin expanded the cultural contacts of her black sisters.

Light-skinned Josephine St. Pierre, the offspring of an interracial marriage, had begun her own interaction with Boston's white elite during her early education in the city's private schools. Her parents' wealth and prestige had ushered her into the finest social circles, and her husband's Harvard education and political prominence further enhanced her social position.

Ruffin's closest friends included several prominent white women. Ednah Dow Cheney entertained Ruffin in her home each Monday afternoon for tea. Julia Ward Howe, Abby W. May, Lucy Stone, and Mabel Loomis Todd were also in Ruffin's circle of friends. The women socialized in each others' homes while working together with their various social and reform-oriented organizations.[36]

These socially progressive women accorded Ruffin fully equal status. They welcomed her into their homes for meetings and social events. And during luncheons, dinner parties, and banquets, the Victorian-era women seated her at their table—a courtesy rarely extended to black women of the nineteenth century.[37]

The most significant of the organizations in which the Boston women participated was the venerable New England Women's Club, which Cheney, Howe, and May helped to found in 1868 and which Ruffin integrated in the mid-1890s. The women's other mutual affiliations included the Massachusetts Moral Education Association, Massachusetts School Suffrage Association, Massachusetts and New England Woman Suffrage Associations, and New England Women's Press Association.[38]

Ruffin's commitment to the woman's suffrage movement extended

SOCIAL REFORM AND POLITICAL ACTIVISM

her white friendships beyond Boston. Susan B. Anthony and Elizabeth Cady Stanton were among the women's rights activists who worked with Ruffin.[39]

The women demonstrated their respect for Ruffin by electing her to office in white-dominated organizations. After Ruffin desegregated the Massachusetts State Federation of Women's Clubs in 1895, members elected her to the Federation's executive board, asked her to join them in founding the Northeastern Federation of Women's Clubs, and supported her attempt to desegregate the National Federation. The women also elected Ruffin to the board of directors of the Massachusetts Moral Education Association.[40]

That Ruffin socialized with wealthy white women demonstrated how class similarities could transcend racial distinctions in late nineteenth-century New England. Her friendships with these prominent women reformers were mutually beneficial. When the women sought the support of the African-American elite, Ruffin served as their liaison. In 1890, for example, Cheney organized a fair to raise money for the New England Hospital for Women and Children, which she served as president. Seeking to tap into the financial strength of the city's African-American elite, she asked Ruffin to help. Ruffin agreed, promising: "You can depend upon my club to make a good showing at the fair."[41]

In reciprocation for such support, Ruffin called upon her white friends to attend integrated activities hosted by members of the black aristocracy. In 1890, for example, Ruffin organized a lecture in Boston for Fannie Barrier Williams, a leading black clubwoman from Chicago. Cheney and Howe agreed to serve as sponsors, allowing Ruffin to use their names on circulars promoting the lecture and the reception that followed it. When Williams returned to Boston for another lecture in 1896, Ruffin went a step further by asking the president of each women's club in the Massachusetts Federation not only to attend the lecture but also to sell tickets to it.[42]

Ruffin also used her journalistic position as a tool for integration. When she published an "Eminent Women's Series," the biographical articles featured both white and black women. In an early instance of journalistic integration, tributes to Lucy Stone and Harriet Beecher Stowe alternated with those to Harriet Tubman and Sojourner Truth.[43]

Although Ruffin created the *Woman's Era* as a vehicle to showcase the work of African-American women, she was happy to expand her editorial bounds to foster integration. She wrote: "The *Era* is not 'colored.'

It is a paper whose managers and editors are colored, but the paper is open to all. . . . We do not believe in accentuating race lines."[44] The majority of articles were written by black women, but Ruffin made exceptions for her white friends. Cheney wrote an article, for instance, to promote the New England Hospital for Women and Children.[45]

After Ruffin ceased publication of the *Woman's Era* in 1897, she increased her activities as an orator by lecturing, most frequently on the importance of moral courage, to audiences throughout Massachusetts and in other states. She also helped found the American Mount Coffee School Association, which operated a school for Liberian children, and she served as vice president of the association under Edward Everett Hale's presidency.

During the next quarter century, Ruffin's organizational skills and national prominence benefited both the African-American women's club movement and a number of civic organizations. She helped found the Boston branch of the NAACP and the Association for the Promotion of Child Training in the South, which supported a school for black children in Atlanta. She also continued to serve on the executive board of the Massachusetts Federation of Women's Clubs.

Ruffin died of a disease of the kidneys at her Charles Street home on March 13, 1924, at the age of eighty-one. Her body lay in state at the League of Women for Community Service Building in Boston. Funeral services were held at Trinity Episcopal Church on Copley Square, and she was buried in Cambridge.[46]

Josephine St. Pierre Ruffin, with other nineteenth-century women such as Lucy Stone and Ida B. Wells-Barnett, employed the vehicle of journalism to promote the larger goal of racial equality. As the editorial force behind the first newspaper created by American women of African descent, Ruffin wielded considerable power in influencing how black women would perceive themselves as well as how they would be portrayed in the larger and often hostile society. Like Wells-Barnett, she saw a crusading black press as an important venue in which black women could demonstrate their strength and their refusal to be the victims of subjugation. Personal empowerment and responsibility played an important role in Ruffin's own self-definition as a resourceful woman fully capable of uplifting her gender and her race.

As was true for Ednah Dow Cheney and many other prominent nineteenth-century women, Ruffin's most productive years were in midlife, after her husband died and her children were grown. Although

Ruffin had been active as a social reformer throughout her life, she embarked on her distinctive work as a journalist and publishing entrepreneur only after she became a widow. Freedom from the duties of marriage and motherhood provided Ruffin with the opportunity to demonstrate the full dimensions of her vast talents and abilities.

Yet Ruffin was not content merely to break new journalistic ground; rather, she employed publishing as a means rather than an end. After achieving success at building a national network of African-American women writers to support the themes she promoted through the *Woman's Era*, Ruffin created a smaller-scale network of prominent Boston women to further her efforts on behalf of integration. What was truly extraordinary about that second network was that it crossed racial lines. During an era when a huge gulf separated white America from black America, Ruffin was at the center of an interracial social circle based on shared values, shared wealth, and shared social prestige. The correspondence between Ruffin and the white women in her social circle reveals no trace of the distance and the strain that continue to characterize race relations in this country today. Because of her class and her well-honed skills as an organizer, Josephine St. Pierre Ruffin was, more than a century ago, able to forge a unique class, gender, and racial alliance that succeeded in overcoming prejudice and racial bigotry to further her ultimate goal of achieving equality for her black sisters.

Notes

1. Michael Emery and Edwin Emery, *The Press and America: An Interpretive History of the Mass Media,* 7th ed. (Englewood Cliffs, N.J.: Prentice-Hall, 1992), 228. Mildred I. Thompson, *Ida B. Wells-Barnett: An Exploratory Study of an American Black Woman, 1893–1930* (Brooklyn, N.Y.: Carlson Publishing, 1990). Emery and Emery mentions half a dozen other African-American women journalists but devote no more than one line to any of them (see pp. 181, 429–31, 497, 499–500). The other standard history of the American mass media, Jean Folkerts and Dwight Teeter, *Voices of a Nation: A History of the Media in the United States,* 2d ed. (New York: Macmillan, 1994), mentions no black women journalists. Nor were any mentioned in earlier journalism histories, such as James Melvin Lee, *History of American Journalism* (New York: Garden City Publishing, 1917), and Frank Luther Mott, *American Journalism* (New York: Macmillan, 1941, 1950, 1960).

2. Roland E. Wolseley, *The Black Press, U.S.A.,* 2d ed. (Ames: Iowa State University Press, 1990), 38–40. In 1992, a second history of the black press was

158   published. Clint C. Wilson II, *Black Journalists in Paradox: Historical Per-spectives and Current Dilemmas* (New York: Greenwood Press, 1992), confines its material on African-American women journalists to four pages (pp. 46–49, 74–75). The material on women in two earlier histories of the African-American press consists of positivist biographies with few specific details. See I. Garland Penn, *The Afro-American Press and Its Editors* (Springfield, Mass.: Wiley, 1891), 366–427, and Martin E. Dann, *The Black Press 1827–1890: The Quest for National Identity* (New York: Putnam, 1971), 61–67.

3. The first history of women journalists, Ishbel Ross, *Ladies of the Press* (New York: Harper, 1936), mentioned no African-Americans. The next, Marion Marzolf, *Up from the Footnote: A History of Women Journalists* (New York: Hastings House, 1977), devoted seven pages to black women (see pp. 25–26, 90–92, 192–93). Maurine H. Beasley and Sheila Silver, *Women in Media: Documentary Source Book* (Washington, D.C.: Women's Institute for Freedom of the Press, 1977), included a reprint of an 1889 article on black women journalists (see pp. 38–44). Madelon Golden Schilpp and Sharon M. Murphy, *Great Women of the Press* (Carbondale: Southern Illinois University Press, 1983), included a chapter on Ida B. Wells-Barnett (see pp. 121–33). Kay Mills, *A Place in the News: From the Women's Pages to the Front Page* (1988; reprint, New York: Columbia University Press, 1991), included a chapter on women of color (see pp. 174–96).

4. See Beasley and Silver, *Women in Media,* viii; Paula Matabane, "Strategies on Studying Women of Color in Mass Communication," in *Women in Mass Communication: Challenging Gender Values,* ed. Pamela J. Creedon (Newbury Park, Calif.: Sage Publications, 1989), 117–22; Mills, *A Place in the News,* 176.

5. The black women's club movement, which involved some fifty thousand women in one thousand local clubs, provided a vehicle through which members were able to expand beyond the limited sphere of nineteenth-century domesticity, allowing them to acquire a greater sense of independence. For the women who led the movement, club work also provided a new level of personal fulfillment as the privileged women helped meet the needs of their less fortunate sisters through educational and philanthropic activities. On the African-American women's club movement, see Angela Y. Davis, *Women, Culture, and Politics* (New York: Random House, 1989), 3–15; Willard B. Gatewood, *Aristo-crats of Color: The Black Elite, 1880–1920* (Bloomington: Indiana University Press, 1990), 210–46; Paula Giddings, *When and Where I Enter: The Impact of Black Women on Race and Sex in America* (New York: William Morrow, 1984), 95–117, 135–42; Elizabeth Kolmer, "Nineteenth Century Woman's Rights Movement: Black and White," *Negro History Bulletin* 35 (December 1972): 178–80; Gerda Lerner, ed., *Black Women in White America: A Documentary History* (New York: Random House, 1972), 433–58; Gerda Lerner, "Early Community Work of Black Club Women," *Journal of Negro History* 59 (April 1973): 158–67; Jeanne L. Noble, *Beautiful, Also, Are the Souls of My Black Sisters: A*

History of the Black Woman in America (Englewood Cliffs, N.J.: Prentice-Hall, 1978), 129–43; Charles H. Wesley, *The History of the National Association of Colored Women's Clubs: A Legacy of Service* (Washington, D.C.: National Association of Colored Women's Clubs, 1984).

6. During the 1900 convention of the General Federation of Women's Clubs in Milwaukee, Ruffin was seated as a delegate of the Massachusetts Federation of Women's Clubs and the New England Women's Press Association, thereby desegregating the national organization. She was not accepted as a delegate of the Women's Era Club, however, as the club was barred from the federation. See "Club Women's Last Day," *Boston Evening Transcript,* June 8, 1900, p. 5; "What the Woman's Federation Did," *Chicago Tribune,* June 10, 1900, p. 36; "Colored Club Is Barred out by Directors," *Milwaukee Sentinel,* June 5, 1900, p. 1; "Federated Clubs in Session," *St. Louis Globe-Democrat,* June 5, 1900, p. 5.

7. Josephine St. Pierre Ruffin, "Editorial," *Woman's Era,* March 24, 1894, p. 8.

8. The St. Pierre family tree is in the Ruffin Family Papers, Amistad Research Center, Tulane University, New Orleans. Profiles of Ruffin, stressing her club work, include Floris Barnett Cash, "Josephine St. Pierre Ruffin," in *Notable Black American Women,* ed. Jessie Carney Smith (Detroit: Gale Research, 1992), 961–65; Julia Ward Howe, ed., *Representative Women of New England* (Boston: New England Historical Publishing Company, 1904), 335–39; Edward T. James, ed., *Notable American Women 1607–1950: A Biographical Dictionary* (Cambridge, Mass.: Belknap Press of Harvard University Press, 1971), 3:206–8; John William Leonard, ed., *Woman's Who's Who of America: A Biographical Dictionary of Contemporary Women of the United States and Canada* (New York: American Commonwealth, 1915), 706; Lerner, *Black Women in White America,* 440–41; Rayford W. Logan and Michael R. Winston, eds., *Dictionary of American Negro Biography* (New York: W. W. Norton, 1982), 535–36; G. F. Richings, *Evidences of Progress among Colored People* (Philadelphia: George S. Ferguson, 1897), 371–72; L. A. Scruggs, *Women of Distinction: Remarkable in Works and Invincible in Character* (Raleigh, N.C., Privately published, 1893), pp. 144–48.

9. The Ruffins were married June 30, 1858, in Twelfth Baptist Church in Boston. Their marriage certificate is preserved in the Ruffin Family Papers, Amistad Research Center. The four Ruffin children who lived to adulthood all achieved success. Hubert Ruffin practiced law and served on the Boston Common Council and in the Massachusetts State Legislature. Florida Ruffin Ridley taught in Boston public schools. Stanley Ruffin was an inventor and manager of a Boston manufacturing company. George Lewis Ruffin Jr. was organist at St. Augustine's Church in Boston and a music instructor. See Hallie Q. Brown, *Homespun Heroines and Other Women of Distinction* (Freeport, N.Y.: Books for Libraries Press, 1971), 151; Howe, *Representative Women of New England,* 336–37.

10. Sylvia G. L. Dannett, *Profiles of Negro Womanhood*, vol. 1, 1619–1900 (New York: M. W. Lads, 1964), 309; Elizabeth Lindsay Davis, *Lifting as They Climb* (Washington, D.C.: National Association of Colored Women, 1933), 237; Howe, *Representative Women of New England*, 337.

11. Massachusetts women won the right to vote in elections of school board members in 1879. The Massachusetts School Suffrage Association was founded a year later.

12. Letters written by Ruffin to Garrison, January 13, 1875 and April 19, 1879, Department of Rare Books and Manuscripts, Boston Public Library.

13. Letter written by Ruffin to Garrison, January 13, 1875, Department of Rare Books and Manuscripts, Boston Public Library.

14. Logan and Winston, *Dictionary of American Negro Biography*, 535. Frederick Douglass was the most prominent African-American leader of the nineteenth century. T. Thomas Fortune rose to national prominence as editor in the 1880s of the black weeklies the *New York Globe* and *New York Age*. When he joined the editorial staff of the *New York Evening Sun* in the early 1880s, he became the first African-American to work for a mainstream newspaper. Heralded as the "dean of black journalism," Fortune was read by Theodore Roosevelt and other political leaders.

15. Letter written by Booker T. Washington to Francis Jackson Garrison, February 22, 1904, Booker T. Washington Papers, Library of Congress, Washington, D.C.

16. George Lewis Ruffin died of kidney disease at the age of fifty-two. See "Death of George L. Ruffin," *New York Freeman*, November 27, 1886, p. 1; unidentified and undated obituaries in folder 26 of the George Lewis Ruffin Papers, Moorland-Spingarn Research Center, Howard University Library, Washington, D.C.

17. Several historians (Brown, *Homespun Heroines*, 152; Penelope L. Bullock, *The Afro-American Periodical Press: 1838–1909* [Baton Rouge: Louisiana State University Press, 1981], 169; Dorothy Sterling, ed., *We Are Your Sisters: Black Women in the Nineteenth Century* [New York: Norton, 1984], 441) have stated that *Woman's Era* was founded in March 1894, the date of the earliest extant copy. Ruffin correspondence preserved in the Boston Public Library, however, shows that *Woman's Era* began in 1890. Two letters that Ruffin wrote to Ednah Dow Cheney, May 19 and 22, 1890, carry the printed letterhead: "The Woman's Era." Both letters are in the Ednah Dow Cheney Papers. In the May 22 letter, Ruffin specifically mentions the "May *Era*." The fact that *Woman's Era* predated the Woman's Era Club, which Ruffin founded in 1894, is verified by two 1902 magazine articles that state that the club took its name from a newspaper called *Woman's Era*. See Pauline E. Hopkins, "Famous Women of the Negro Race," *Colored American Magazine* 5 (August 1902): 273; and Helen Porter Utterback, "Mrs. Ruffin and the Woman's Era Club of Boston," *Los Angeles Herald Illustrated Magazine*, p. 7. (This undated article is preserved in

Contents of the article indicate it was written in 1902.) Ruffin initially may have begun by distributing *Woman's Era* only in Boston but then expanded to national distribution in 1894.

18. Bullock, *The Afro-American Periodical Press*, 191; Giddings, *When and Where I Enter*, 93.

19. "Slavery Case in Boston," *Woman's Era*, September 1894, p. 14. Ruffin, "The Chicago Woman's Club Reject [*sic*] Mrs. Williams," *Woman's Era*, December 1894, p. 20.

20. All twenty-two extant issues of *Woman's Era* are preserved in the Rare Books and Manuscripts Department, Boston Public Library. The July 1896 issue also is preserved in the Moorland-Spingarn Research Center, Howard University Library, Washington, D.C.

21. Statement by Florida Ruffin Ridley, Schomburg Center for Research in Black Culture Clipping File, New York Public Library, "George Lewis Ruffin" entry, p. 4; Scruggs, *Women of Distinction*, 147–48; letter from Ruffin, *St. Paul* (Minnesota) *Appeal*, November 14, 1891, p. 3; Ruffin to Garrison, January 13, 1895, Boston Public Library. The *Boston Courant* was founded in 1890, but the earliest extant copies are dated 1900, according to *Newspapers in Microfilm: United States* (Washington, D.C.: Library of Congress, 1984).

22. For discussion of the financial difficulties of the black press, see Armistead Scott Pride, "Negro Newspapers: Yesterday, Today and Tomorrow," *Journalism Quarterly* 28 (Spring 1951): 179–82.

23. Ruffin, "Why You Should Subscribe for the *Woman's Era*," *Woman's Era*, May 1, 1894, p. 15; "New York," *Woman's Era*, July 1895, p. 3.

24. Ruffin, *Woman's Era*, "We Decline to Name This Child," November 1895, p. 10; "Women in Politics," November 1894, p. 12.

25. *Woman's Era*, "Washington," May 1895, p. 3; "Bonita Gold and Silver Mining Co.," January 1896, p. 17; Ruffin, "Women in Business," March 24, 1894, p. 13.

26. *Woman's Era*, "What Equal Suffrage Has Done for Colorado," November 1894, p. 12; "Colored Women and Suffrage," November 1895, p. 11; "Women in Politics," November 1894, p. 12.

27. Gertrude Bustill Mossell, "The Open Court," *Woman's Era*, May 1895, p. 19.

28. Ruffin, "Editorial," *Woman's Era*, May 1895, p. 10.

29. *Woman's Era*, "Club Gossip," March 24, 1894, p. 15; "The Drink Traffic vs. Labor," June 1, 1894, p. 2; "A Danger and a Duty," August/September 1896, p. 8.

30. For discussion of race as a more salient force than gender in the lives of black women, see bell hooks, *Feminist Theory: From Margin to Center* (Boston: South End Press, 1984); Gloria Joseph and Jill Lewis, *Common Differences: Conflicts in Black and White Feminist Perspectives* (New York: Avon, 1981);

162   Diane K. Lewis, "A Response to Inequality: Black Women, Racism, and Sexism," *Signs* 3 (Winter 1977): 339–61.

    31. Ruffin, "Editorial," *Woman's Era,* December 1894, p. 10.

    32. Ruffin, "Separate Car Law," *Woman's Era,* February 1896, p. 9.

    33. Ruffin, "Editorial," *Woman's Era,* March 24, 1894, p. 4.

    34. Howe, *Representative Women of New England,* 337; "Colored Club Is Barred out by Directors," *Milwaukee Sentinel,* June 5, 1900, p. 1.

    35. Ruffin, "Editorial Greeting," *Woman's Era,* March 24, 1894, p. 8.

    36. Ruffin letters to Cheney, May 19 and 22, 1890, Ednah Dow Cheney Papers, Department of Rare Books and Manuscripts, Boston Public Library. Brown, *Homespun Heroines,* 152–53; Bullock, *The Afro-American Periodical Press,* 189; Logan and Winston, *Dictionary of American Negro Biography,* 536; Scruggs, *Women of Distinction,* 147. Ednah Dow Cheney was a Bostonian philanthropist and social reformer who worked for abolition and woman's suffrage. Julia Ward Howe was committed to various reforms including abolition, woman's suffrage, prison reform, and the cause of peace. Abby W. May was a Boston reformer who first worked with Ruffin on the U.S. Sanitary Commission. Lucy Stone was a pioneer in the women's rights movement. Mabel Loomis Todd was director of the Massachusetts State Federation of Women's Clubs.

    37. "Club Women's Last Day," *Boston Evening Transcript,* June 8, 1900, p. 5; "Colored Club Is Barred out by Directors," *Milwaukee Sentinel,* June 5, 1900, p. 1.

    38. On the New England Woman's Club, see Karen J. Blair, *The Clubwoman as Feminist: True Womanhood Redefined, 1868–1914* (New York: Holmes & Meier, 1980), 31–38; Julia A. Sprague, *History of the New England Women's Club from 1868 to 1893* (Boston: Lee and Shepard, 1894).

    39. Bullock, *The Afro-American Periodical Press,* 189; Howe, *Representative Women of New England,* 337; James, *Notable American Women,* 207; Margaret Murray Washington, "Club Work among Negro Women," in *Progress of a Race,* ed. J. L. Nichols and William H. Crogman (Naperville, Ill.: Nichols, 1929), 178. Susan B. Anthony and Elizabeth Cady Stanton organized and led the National Woman's Suffrage Association.

    40. Howe, *Representative Women of New England,* 337; James, *Notable American Women,* 207; "Color Question May Come up in a New Form," *Milwaukee Sentinel,* June 4, 1900, p. 1; Scruggs, *Women of Distinction,* 147.

    41. Ruffin letter to Cheney, May 22, 1890, Cheney Papers. Cheney was president of the New England Hospital for Women and Children from 1887 to 1902.

    42. Ruffin letters to Cheney, May 19 and 22, 1890, March 24, 1896, Cheney Papers.

    43. See, for example, *Woman's Era,* "Lucy Stone," March 24, 1894, p. 1; "Harriet Beecher Stowe," June 1896, p. 1.

44. Ruffin, "Notice to Subscribers," *Woman's Era,* April 1895, p. 12.

45. Ednah Dow Cheney, "New England Hospital for Women and Children," *Woman's Era,* June 1, 1894, p. 1.

46. "Deaths," *Boston Evening Transcript,* March 15, 1924, p. 9; Monroe N. Work, *Negro Year Book, 1925–1926* (Tuskegee Institute, Ala.: Negro Year Book Publishing, 1925), 422.

JULIA HARRINGTON DUFF AND THE POLITICAL AWAKENING OF IRISH-AMERICAN WOMEN IN BOSTON, 1888–1905

POLLY WELTS KAUFMAN

In December 1900 Julia Harrington Duff, a mother from Charlestown, became the first woman from the Irish-American community to be elected to the Boston School Committee. Although she was a graduate of Boston Normal School and a former teacher in the Boston public schools, her election was rather unexpected. It was unexpected, that is, by the *Woman's Journal,* the organ of the American Woman Suffrage Association published in Boston, because Duff was unknown to them. A few days before the election, the *Journal* editors, who earlier had warmly endorsed the two other women candidates, noted that the Democrats had nominated a woman and weakly said they "would be glad to see all three of the ladies elected." At first it seemed as if Duff had lost her election bid, but, demonstrating a characteristic toughness, she demanded a recount and won.[1]

The election of Julia Duff to the Boston School Committee was the culmination of the political awakening of young Irish-American teachers and working women in turn-of-the-century Boston. It demonstrated how late nineteenth-century Boston women were able to extend their roles as teachers and mothers into public participation in school politics. Except for the world of the public school, where their traditional roles gave them both legitimacy and a sense of urgency, political boundaries kept women out of direct participation in state and municipal politics. Duff's School Committee service also revealed the cultural bound-

Julia Harrington Duff, Boston School Committee, 1901–1905. Courtesy, Dr. John Duff.

Emily Porter Fifield, Boston School Committee, 1883–1902. Courtesy Unitarian Universalist Women's Federation.

aries separating groups of women from each other. As Boston's ethnic communities increasingly influenced city politics, disparate groups of women were stimulated to use their newly won power in school politics to define and protect their differing cultural identities.

Although it is not commonly known, women were elected quite regularly to seats on the Boston School Committee in the last quarter of the nineteenth century. What is more, all women in Massachusetts won the right to vote for School Committee members in 1879, forty years before they gained full suffrage. When Abby May, a pioneering and well-respected School Committee woman who had been elected by men in 1875, was defeated for reelection in 1878, there was such an outcry that women and their supporters convinced the Massachusetts State Legislature to grant women school suffrage. Among other actions, Abby May had led the drive to open a Latin school for girls in Boston.

Between 1875 and 1905 women generally held from two to four positions on the twenty-four-member Boston School Committee, all elected at large. But for nearly fifty years after 1905, when the School

Committee was reduced to five members, women served singly half the time and not at all half of the time. It was not until the modern crisis of school desegregation coincided with the second wave of feminism that it became the norm for women to run for and be elected to the Boston School Committee.

Even though women could vote for the Boston School Committee, at first the vote was small, hovering around one thousand, and it reflected liberal Yankee women only, despite the efforts of the women's Massachusetts School Suffrage Association to get out the women's vote. It was a school crisis in 1888 that finally caused the women's vote to jump in just one year to nearly twenty thousand, one-quarter of the total vote.

A major part of the increase came from Irish Catholic women who, for the first time, registered to vote in numbers because they believed their cultural values were in jeopardy. The school crisis had been set off by a backlash to a protest from male Catholic Boston School Committee members. Charles Travis, a teacher at English High School, had defined an indulgence as "permission to commit sin . . . sometimes bought with money." When the School Committee censured Travis and dropped the textbook he cited, anti-Catholic organizations, led by the British-American Association and several evangelical Protestant ministers, feared an imminent Catholic takeover of the school system. Yankee Protestant women split into two main groups. The evangelical anti-Catholic Independent Women Voters, led by Eliza Trask Hill from Charlestown, broke away from the Massachusetts School Suffrage Association and campaigned against Catholic School Committee members. The remaining moderate women, who reflected the values of liberal Protestantism, formed the Citizens' Public School Union to support the censure and try to subdue the crisis.[2]

The majority of the new Irish Catholic women voters were single native-born working women in their early thirties. Some were among the first Irish-American women to become teachers in the Boston schools. Not only were they incensed by the campaign of the anti-Catholic voters, especially by that of the Independent Women Voters, but they also feared that Catholic women would lose the opportunity to teach in the Boston schools.

The Irish Catholic women rallied during the last week of voter registration, jamming the City Hall corridors. The competition between evangelical Protestant and Catholic women voters rose to a peak on the last day of registration. When the Protestant women appeared with little American flags in their buttonholes, the Catholic women responded with larger red, white, and blue rosettes.[3]

One of the young Irish Catholic women teachers who voted in 1888 was Julia Harrington Duff, who had been a pioneer among the young Irish-American women who became Boston public school teachers. When she graduated from the Boston Normal School in 1878, she had been one of only nine Irish-American women in a class of fifty-eight. She was immediately appointed to a school in Charlestown, where she taught for fourteen years before her marriage to Dr. John Duff. By 1900 it appeared to Julia Duff that Boston Normal School graduates were no longer assured teaching positions in Boston. She believed that the Yankee administration preferred Protestant women as teachers and would go great distances to find them: to Nova Scotia, Vermont, Maine, and western Massachusetts. Duff was determined to protect the jobs of young Irish-American women teachers from Boston. To secure her goal, she undertook a two-fold mission: to keep Boston Normal School in the control of the city and to protect the futures of its graduates by assuring them the teaching positions to which she believed they were entitled. She served as president of her normal school class for fifteen years and chaired a committee organized to oppose transferring control of the school from the city to the state. When her younger brother, Arthur Harrington, a recent Harvard graduate, entered politics, Julia Duff saw the opportunity to carry her campaign to the Boston School Committee as an elected member.[4]

A lifelong resident of Charlestown, which was long the center of sectarian rivalry and also the home of Eliza Trask Hill, the leader of the anti-Catholic Independent Women Voters, Julia Harrington Duff possessed a reservoir of resentment over the Protestant Yankee control of the Boston schools that had been so much a part of her life. Her father was born in Ireland, but her mother was a fourth-generation American. The Duff and Harrington families saw themselves as contributing members of the broader society and deserving of its acceptance. Julia's husband was a highly respected doctor. Another of her brothers, Louis, was a priest, and a third, Walter, a teacher.[5] When the issue of who would teach in the Boston schools was raised, no arguments on behalf of hiring experienced teachers from outside of Boston could begin to satisfy Julia Duff. The issue tapped her store of resentment and aroused her sense of justice.

SOCIAL REFORM AND POLITICAL ACTIVISM

By 1901, when Julia Duff took her seat on the Boston School Committee, the inevitable had happened. Young women with Irish last names accounted for more than half of that year's Boston Normal School's graduating class, and they expected traditional job assurances. Duff was also a parent of three Boston schoolchildren. She did not see the schools as a vehicle to improve society by reforming other people's children, as did many of her predecessors. For Duff Boston schools were the place where her own children were being educated, and she wanted to make sure their teachers gave them all the respect she believed the Harringtons and Duffs deserved.[6]

Three Protestant women held seats early in 1901, including Emily Fifield, who, after nearly twenty years in office, was the grand Protestant lady of the Boston School Committee. Her power base was the Public School Association, called the PSA. Although she was twenty years younger, Julia Duff's connection with the Boston public schools was virtually lifelong, and she was ready to confront the authority of Emily Fifield and the PSA.

In city politics generally, opposing forces reflecting a similar division continued to build strength. On the surface, the popular business-minded mayor, Patrick Collins, an Irish-American Democrat, would soon unite Boston, but underneath lay a still suppressed power struggle. The Democratic Irish-American ward bosses were anxious to run the city without consideration for the Yankee Democrats because the goals of the ward bosses were to meet the needs of their own people in the struggle to earn a living and gain public respectability. Yankee political leaders from both the Republican and Democratic parties in turn would unite in 1903 to form the Good Government Association. They were certain that nonpartisan reform conducted according to the principles of sound administration would not only stabilize the city as it became increasingly divided by ethnic interests but also keep the "best men" (like themselves and Collins) in control. Paternalism was essentially the Good Government approach, in contrast to self-actualization, the drive that motivated the Irish Bostonians.[7]

When Julia Duff and Emily Fifield faced each other as two elected Boston School Committee members, on the individual level they represented the same opposing points of view. Yet each woman brought an earnestness to her actions that rose from her personal, intense belief in the moral righteousness of her cause. Each considered herself independent of partisan politics and, needless to say, above them. Each was the wife of a family doctor, used to deference from residents of one of Boston's neighborhoods. The differences between the two women, defined by their individual cultural and religious values, added to the depth of their feelings and made confrontation almost inevitable.

Although Julia Duff and Emily Fifield brought long years of experience in the Boston schools to their School Committee positions, their perspectives about school affairs were entirely different. As one of the young Irish Catholic women who conscientiously prepared her home lessons year after year under Yankee Protestant women teachers in order to become a Boston teacher herself, Julia Duff was determined to protect the claims of the new young Boston women, particularly young Irish-American women, to opportunities for careers in the school system.

Emily Fifield was active in the Unitarian Church and had come from the small town of Weymouth, but she had moved to the Dorchester neighborhood of Boston after her marriage. Accustomed to acting by established principles, she took an approach that was essentially paternalistic; she tended to see people in categories and to want to determine what was best for them without consultation. She made a distinction, for example, between the Boston Latin School and the new Mechanic Arts High School. The former school would continue to appeal to boys who came from "families where wealth and culture have been an inheritance for generations," while the latter offered "golden opportunities," including a higher appreciation of the dignity of labor, to the "vast number of equally worthy boys."[8]

Duff's first public disagreement with Fifield arose when the question of the appointment of Duff's sister-in-law, Ellen L. Duff, to principal of the schools of cookery came before the full board. Fifield asked that Ellen Duff's appointment be reconsidered because it was "inexpedient" to fill the position "at the present time." After Fifield's motion lost, Ellen Duff's appointment was approved by the entire board, with only Fifield and a PSA leader dissenting.

The *Boston Globe* described the debate between Fifield and Duff in full. Noting that Duff had made her first speech as a school board member, the *Globe* said she "showed herself to be a very capable debator, the equal of Mrs. Fifield, who is one of the best talkers on the school board." Fifield denied the need for a principal of cooking "while admitting the fitness of the appointee." Duff told of her visits to all the cooking classes and of finding that all the teachers wanted a "head, to bring system to the classes and encourage cooking in schools where it was neglected." The discussion had "just a tinge of sharpness," the *Globe* reported, "but on the whole it was very good natured." Duff had noted that the former principal of cooking had come from England. "Think of it," she remarked, "it being necessary to go out of the country to obtain a teacher of cooking." Fifield's true reason for opposing the appointment was made clear when, in reply to a question about the proceedings of the subcommittee, she said, "the subject was the exemplification of the spoils system."[9]

The next controversy followed a month later. Elizabeth Keller, chair of the textbook committee, recommended that no more copies of the Franklin readers, in use for thirty-seven years, or the Warren geographies, in use for forty-six years, be purchased. In their place, the majority of the committee, including Duff, proposed Supervisor Sarah Louise Arnold's new series, *Stepping Stones to Literature,* as one of two choices, as well as three new geographies. Fifield and one other member filed a minority report opposing the new texts on the basis of limited finances. That Fifield's real reason was undoubtedly again her view of "the spoils system" was soon evident. Within minutes of the dissenting report, a letter of resignation from Arnold was read.

Duff and Keller worked together to try to convince the entire board to accept their textbook choices and to retain Arnold. Within a month they presented a supporting letter from the Board of Supervisors signed by the superintendent. In a School Committee meeting a few weeks later Duff announced Sarah Arnold's decision to withdraw her resignation, and Keller asserted that there was enough money for Arnold's textbooks. The old readers had been in the schools "so long," she argued, and the teachers had grown "so familiar" with them that "a wrong word would startle them into wakefulness." Duff described "the scramble among publishers to get their books into the schools." She related that the representative for the publisher of the Franklin readers had told her they would "fight to keep the old readers." When she replied, "Don't you care about the children?" his response was that he "was after the money." Duff ended the debate by triumphantly calling for the yeas and neas on each of the seven votes, all clear majorities, required to reject the old texts and accept the new ones, including Arnold's readers.[10]

The disputes over Ellen Duff's appointment and Sarah Arnold's readers were only the preliminaries for Julia Duff's major confrontation with Emily Fifield early the next year. By then Duff's adversaries had increased in both quantity and quality, a fact that acted on her more as a spur than a deterrent. By backing candidates acceptable to the Democrats, the PSA survived the Democratic sweep in December 1901 that brought Patrick Collins into the mayor's office. Seven of the ten new school board members held a PSA endorsement. Among them was James Jackson Storrow, son of a prominent Yankee family. For Storrow, a graduate of Harvard Law School and new to the PSA, Boston School Committee service would be an eye opener to municipal politics. It would convince him to lead the drive to reform the structure of municipal government, beginning with the School Committee.[11]

Fifield could not have helped believing the December PSA victory was a vindication of her point of view. When she presided over the dedication of the new Dorchester High School, her pride in Dorchester and the Boston schools was evident in her opening address. She reminded the audience that Dorchester had established "the first free school" in the country and that the new high school would "carry on the work of the fathers" of making "unselfish, honest, upright citizens." Perhaps unconsciously, Fifield set herself apart as she extended a welcome "to those who have lately come to live among us."[12]

But Fifield's pride was matched, if not superseded, by that of the Duffs. Julia Duff was escorted to nearly every school board meeting by her husband, Dr. John Duff, conspicuous in his white hat. As the family story goes, Julia's father, who was known as Harrington the Hatter, was left with an unsold white hat because none of his customers dared to wear it. Believing that his new son-in-law had "courage enough for anything," Harrington offered it to him. John Duff had studied mining engineering at the Massachusetts Institute of Technology (MIT) and practiced it in the West before entering Harvard Medical School. He had been the center on MIT's first football team and captain of the tug-of-war team. The Duff family's style was influenced by its love for athletics and the theater and by their idealization of women. Their sons and grandsons became specialists in sports medicine. The children all studied elocution, and one of their sons remembers being taken to the theater to see Sarah Bernhardt. Julia and John Duff enjoyed both the sport and the drama of politics and worked as a team. There is no doubt that Julia was earnest in her purpose, or that she wrote and read all the lines and selected the issues that she would contend, but if she ever felt lacking in courage, support was only as far away as the public seating.[13]

When the Boston School Committee convened in January 1902, the new PSA majority dropped Julia Duff from the textbook committee but retained Emily Fifield. At the next meeting Duff demanded the right to tell the board why she was not returned to the textbook committee. The chair had informed her, she said, that the reason was her "differences with Mrs. Fifield." Stating that she did indeed have such differences, Duff proceeded to outline them in a prepared speech, a copy of which she made available to the newspapers.

Duff carefully built her case. First she explained that she refused to vote for books that were "educationally detrimental to the children . . . simply because they were published by certain companies favored by this person." A representative of the American Book Company, she said, "took" her "to task" for opposing the Franklin readers and the Warren geographies. After her surprise at finding he was conversant with the private minutes of the textbook committee, Duff found that the minutes were not with the secretary of the School Committee but at Fifield's home. Then, with obvious relish, Duff revealed newly found information. If Fifield were "conscientiously honest," Duff said, she would not remain on the textbook committee while her daughter held "a high-salaried position in one of the large publishing houses to which the city of Boston was paying thousands of dollars every year."

Emily Fifield made only an oblique response to Duff's charges that night. "All this is very amusing and interesting," she said. "It has certainly served one expedient purpose. It has demonstrated, once and for all, why the Public School Association, the republican and the democratic parties find it is difficult to secure a self-respecting woman for the school committee." In reply to a question about resigning, Fifield answered, "Why, I haven't thought of such a thing. I haven't been worrying over the matter at all."[14]

Several newspapers said that Fifield should either explain herself or resign. The Democratic *Post* thought the PSA should tell Fifield "as politely as possible, that her usefulness in that position is ended. If she remained, it would be embarrassing to that element which looks for reform." After stating that Fifield "may be as honest as any others are, and may intend to act as honestly as any others can," the Republican *Herald* said, "That is not the point." By continuing on the textbook committee, she provided "an example which the corrupt may plead when they desire opportunity to promote selfish interests." The *Pilot* commended Duff, saying she had "begun a good work . . . in exposing the grip on the schools of the great school book companies."

Emily Fifield decided not to run for School Committee when her term ended the following December. During the peak of the controversy, Fifield gave as her reason for not replying to Duff's charges: "The people of the city know what I have done and what my work has been."[15] She did not appreciate the fickleness of the body politic, who seemed to forget so quickly her nearly twenty years of devotion to the Boston public schools. In the end, however, it was both her complacency and self-righteousness that made her a perfect target for Julia Duff.

The issue that engaged Duff's greatest attention, however, was not textbooks but Boston Normal School. The PSA bloc presented such a solid wall of opposition to her proposals that she decided to take on the whole organization at the polls, with a great deal of initial success. The essence of the conflict in Duff's view was opportunity for young Boston women. Teaching offered the best chance for careers for young educated women. Convinced that Boston Normal School graduates were losing their chances to become Boston teachers to women graduates of private colleges, Duff raised her cry, "Boston Schools for Boston Girls."[16]

In order to help Boston women who could not afford private colleges to be competitive with the new college graduates, Duff asked the school committee to petition the state legislature for permission to replace the Normal School with a teachers' college that could grant degrees. Unlike the Normal School, it would also be open to men. Although it was "common custom to criticize young teachers as narrow and limited in experience," Duff stated, it was "unjust to the teachers, unless Boston provides opportunity for broader education."[17]

Duff's proposal for a teachers' college was eventually defeated by the PSA bloc, despite support from the supervisors and superintendent, who admired the model of New York's Teachers College. In her final argument, Duff noted, "It is only the children of the wealthy who can afford to attend the universities." She demanded that the city "provide similar instruction for others as well." Eventually Boston Normal School did become Boston Teachers' College, but it was not until the opening of the University of Massachusetts in Boston in 1965 that Duff's demand for a public university in Boston was realized.[18]

Her frustration with PSA opposition to her proposal for a public teachers' college and the positive reaction to her stand on textbooks combined to give Duff both the courage and confidence to carry her fight against the PSA into the Democratic City Committee in the 1902 December election. When the City Committee continued to accept PSA endorsement of three of their regular candidates, despite Duff's objection, she organized an independent party called the Democratic Citizens. The *Post* reported that sixty people from all over the city met at the Duffs' home to pick up nomination papers and plan the campaign. For every PSA candidate endorsed by the Democrats, the Democratic Citizens placed one of its own candidates in the field.

Duff surprised not only the PSA but the Democratic City Committee with the success of her organization. Except for the Boston School Committee president, who came in last, the only PSA candidates elected were the three with Democratic endorsement. The three candidates with only the Democratic Citizen endorsement not only won but they polled an average of twenty thousand votes each, two-thirds of the total received by candidates with both Democratic and Democratic Citizen endorsement.[19]

Part of the reason for Duff's success was that she got out the Catholic women's vote. The *Woman's Journal* reported that Duff's movement for registering Democratic women was so successful that she "astounded Democratic leaders." The total increase in the registration of women was three thousand. Although Charlestown showed the highest rise at 250 percent, Duff's campaign brought increased women's registration in Democratic wards in South Boston and other parts of the city.[20]

The election of 1902 brought to the Boston School Committee a second Democratic woman who became an ally of Julia Duff. Mary A. Dierkes was a proud young woman from the German-American Catholic community chosen, according to the *Post,* in "recognition of the German voters." Like Duff, Mary Dierkes was born in Boston. Closely associated with the German-American community centered at Holy Trinity Church in the South End, her family also expected to be fully accepted by the broader society. Mary's father, Auguste, who owned and ran the Hotel Dierkes, known for its restaurant, was described as a "well-known German gentleman." As a young woman, Mary Dierkes was given unusual advantages. After she graduated from the Franklin Grammar School, she studied music with William Whitney in Boston before traveling and studying in Europe for seven years. She graduated from the Conservatory at Leipzig, Germany, where she prepared to become an opera singer. She returned to Boston around 1895 upon the final illness of her father. After her mother's death in 1900, Dierkes was left in charge of the family affairs, including a younger brother.[21]

It was unusual enough for a Catholic woman to run for public office, or even to vote, but it was even more so in the German-American community. An article published not long after her service on the school committee in the Holy Trinity parish newspaper, the *Monatsbote,* opposed woman suffrage, saying, "The dignity and character of woman would be degraded . . . if she engaged in the turmoil of our corrupted politics." Yet, when Mary Dierkes decided to run for school committee, the *Monatsbote* was proud of her candidacy. Mary Dierkes had such special standing in her community that even though women were not expected to exercise their school suffrage, the men of her parish were urged to vote for her. She was described as "in education and ability at least the quality of the other . . . women candidates," and "beyond this," the editors proudly stated, "she is also a German."[22]

Dierkes's decision to run for Boston School Committee can perhaps be explained by where she lived after she returned from Europe. By then the family had moved from the South End to a large house in the small Harrison Square community in Dorchester where Emily Fifield had lived since her marriage. Considering that Dierkes was elected directly after Fifield's retirement, it can be conjectured that she ran for office in competition with a Yankee woman. Julia Duff must have given her the Democratic Citizen endorsement with particular enthusiasm.

Julia Duff herself came up for reelection in December 1903. She warned the Democratic City Committee that she would set up her own organization again if they endorsed PSA candidates. Although the *Post* said that there were "none who openly champion her cause, her powerful personality dominated the entire proceedings." Successful with her arguments, Duff maintained that it was not she but "the principle" that won.

Duff stumped the city, making over one thousand speeches largely to women. Her appeal was to "mothers, sisters and daughters, and through them, reach the fathers, brothers, and sons." She was careful to preserve her womanly image: illustrated articles in the *Post* and the *Globe* described her home life in traditional and elegant terms. The women's vote rose to a high of nearly fourteen thousand. Duff topped the entire ticket, and no new PSA members were elected. At last she became chair of the Normal School committee.[23] It was now Julia Duff who was riding high, a dangerous place for any political figure in an era of shifting political fortunes, particularly for a woman with a mind of her own.

When Julia Duff, with the help of her ally Mary Dierkes, decided to oppose James Jackson Storrow's special project, she met her match. During his School Committee term, Storrow developed five evening centers in school buildings. They attracted twenty-five hundred people for courses in dressmaking, bookkeeping, carpentry, and music, besides providing gymnasiums and reading rooms.[24]

Apparently believing that the centers were being promoted to build Storrow's reputation at the expense of the fourteen regular evening schools that taught academic subjects, Duff and Dierkes decided to oppose them. Despite his "careful and calm . . . rejoinders," Storrow refused to run for reelection in December 1904. Instead he began a campaign to bring professional administration to the schools by centralizing power in a small, appointed board.[25]

Duff, with her feet firmly in the community, supported decentralization. One of her early proposals was to increase the supervisors to nine and place them in divisions as superintendents so they would be "more closely in touch" with parents, teachers, and schools.[26] Julia Duff's strong belief in keeping the power of school governance in the community was in direct opposition to the members of the Good Government Association, who would muster all their strength to centralize control of the school system in 1905 and, four years later, reform city government. Her independence also put her in conflict with the Irish-American ward bosses, who became engaged in a power struggle among themselves when Mayor Collins died in 1905, near the end of his term. Neither group would have tolerated Julia Duff much longer. She had succeeded in dramatizing the gulf between the confident Yankee businessman, so anxious to professionalize city government, and the second-generation Irish politician, so eager to guide his own destiny.

But Julia Duff lost her power more swiftly and dramatically than anyone would have expected. In September 1904 her brother Walter Harrington became master of the Washington School in the West End, a predominantly Jewish community devoted to its evening center. In the fall of 1905, a member of the West End community brought charges against Harrington, supported by 140 signatures, and demanded his dismissal. The school board voted to remove Harrington from his position in December 1905. It is not certain precisely what the charges against Harrington were, although the newspapers mentioned his padding payrolls by certifying absent teachers as present and pocketing the difference, passing bad checks, and smoking in front of pupils. Pleading for her brother in a speech that lasted more than two hours, Julia Duff asked that Harrington be suspended without pay "until such time as the present condition of the public subsides." She placed the blame on her position, declaring that her brother was being sacrificed for her, saying dramatically, "I am the prisoner. I have been condemned in the person of my brother." It was to be her last school board meeting.[27]

In 1905, after several contentious hearings, the Massachusetts State Legislature, after a campaign led by Storrow, reduced the Boston School Committee from twenty-four to five members elected at large. Although the reduction would have the effect of curtailing women's opportunity for direct participation in school politics, women suffragists viewed the final vote with relief. The issue on which they were forced to focus their energies was the question of an appointed or elected board. The *Woman's Journal* kept its readers aware of the threat to Boston women's only suffrage. They had heard "asserted publicly and without contradiction" that a major purpose of the bill was "to exclude the women of Boston from all voice in choosing the Boston school board." Julia Duff led the opposition for the Democratic women. Storrow's bill "originated in pique and disappointed ambition," she declared. If the "book [publishing] concerns were able to control nine members of the present school board," she contended, they would "own a board of five." Duff ran for reelection in November 1905, under the new rules. She revived the Democratic Citizens Party and ran on nomination papers. Although she was defeated, her nearly thirty-four thousand votes constituted a respectable showing.[28]

Julia Duff and Mary Dierkes were the only Catholic women to hold seats on the Boston School Committee until 1950. Between 1905 and 1950 three women served singly for a total of twenty-one years, and no women served at all in twenty-three years. Yet from 1875 to 1905, the terms of fourteen women added up to seventy-seven years. Apart from the reduction in the size of the Boston School Committee, why did the participation of women in school politics decline?[29]

From the point of view of Democratic and Republican men, women had proved to be a disruptive force in Boston politics. In their commitment to improve the life chances of Boston children, they voted for costly new programs. In their desire to preserve cultural values, they brought Boston's cultural conflicts to the surface and called for a continuation of community control. Their vote in school elections rose and fell according to how deeply they cared about the issues. In their impatience with men whose ambitions they believed took precedence over

the needs of the schools, committeewomen hindered the personal careers and programs of individual men and groups of men.

Still, Julia Duff's refusal to accommodate to Yankee political leaders
and goals foreshadowed imminent actions of other Boston-born members of the Irish-American community. In 1905, after the sudden death
of Patrick Collins, John Fitzgerald became the first Democratic ward
boss to be elected mayor. In 1909, although the Good Government
Association's proposed city charter passed and James Jackson Storrow
became a candidate for the first four-year mayoralty, it was all over for
the "expert." Fitzgerald won the election. When James Michael Curley
became the next mayor, the Irish-American Democrats' control of Boston city government was virtually complete.[30]

When the reduction in the size of the Boston School Committee
made positions on the board politically desirable, there was no longer
room for more than an occasional token woman. For more than twenty-
five years, however, women's traditional roles had been extended to
include elected positions on the Boston School Committee. The participation of women in Boston school politics would lie dormant for
nearly fifty years until a revived women's movement, combined with
another school crisis created by cultural conflicts—this time beginning with the demands of the African-American community for a role
in determining the cultural values of the schools—would again galva-
nize women into assuming public roles. Once again the expansion of
women's traditional roles into school politics would become socially
acceptable.[31]

Notes

1. *Woman's Journal,* December 1, 1900, p. 381; *Boston Globe,* December 12,
1900, p. 9.

2. See Polly Welts Kaufman, *Boston Women and City School Politics, 1872–
1905* (New York: Garland, 1994), 94–99, 139–58; and Lois Bannister Merk,
"Boston's Historic Public School Crisis," *New England Quarterly* 31 (June
1958): 172–99.

3. *Boston Globe,* October 2, 1888, p. 6; Boston *Pilot,* September 29, 1888, p. 4;
Donahoe's Magazine, November 1988, pp. 423–24. Julia Duff, who was twenty-
nine and a single woman teacher at the time, undoubtedly voted in 1888. She
was born in 1859 and died in 1932. Thanks to Paul Faler and his students Mary
McDonald and Diane Shephard for their work in 1988 of finding and analyz-
ing the Boston women's voter registration records for 1888 in two sample Irish
Catholic wards, 13 and 16.

4. *Boston Post,* November 27, 1900, p. 4, excerpted in *Woman's Journal,* December 1, 1900, p. 381; "How Mrs. Duff Compelled the Machine to Oppose the PSA," *Boston Sunday Post,* November 29, 1903, p. 16; City of Boston, *Boston Public School Documents,* 1878, no. 25, p. 54; City of Boston, *Boston School Committee Report,* 1898, p. 215.

5. Interview with Dr. Paul Duff, son of Julia Duff, February 23, 1976, Peabody, Massachusetts.

6. *Boston School Committee Report,* 1898, p. 215. For a discussion of why Boston Catholics preferred public education over parochial education, see James W. Sanders, "Boston Catholics and the School Question, 1825–1907," in *From Common School to Magnet School,* ed. James W. Fraser, Henry L. Allen, and Sam Barnes (Boston: Boston Public Library, 1979), 43–75.

7. See Geoffrey Blodgett, "Yankee Leadership in a Divided City: Boston, 1860–1910," *Journal of Urban History* 8 (August 1982): 371–96; Geoffrey Blodgett, *The Gentle Reformers: Massachusetts Democrats in the Cleveland Era* (Cambridge, Mass.: Harvard University Press, 1966), 261, 278–83.

8. "Emily A. Fifield," *Boston Transcript,* April 13, 1913, p. 12, and September 10, 1896, p. 5; *Boston School Documents,* 1894, no. 16, pp. 16–17. Emily Fifield (1838–1913) was the first recording secretary of the National Alliance of Unitarian Women, serving from 1891 to 1913.

9. City of Boston, *Boston School Committee Proceedings,* 1901, pp. 112, 123–25; *Boston Globe,* April 10, 1901, pp. 1–2.

10. *Boston School Committee Proceedings,* 1901, pp. 176–84, 213–14, 258–62; *Boston Globe,* 1901: May 15, p. 1; June 26, p. 6.

11. Henry Greenleaf Pearson, *Son of New England, James Jackson Storrow, 1864–1926* (Boston: Thomas Todd Co., 1932), 43–49; Public School Association Leaflets, 1900, and Candidates, 1901 [Leaflets, Boston Public Library].

12. *Boston School Committee Report,* 1901, pp. 359–405.

13. Interview with Dr. Paul Duff, February 23 and March 1, 1976. Duff family scrapbook clippings: *Boston Traveler,* September 19 and 22, 1924; *Boston Post,* September 20, 1924; *Boston Telegraph,* September 20, 1924.

14. *Boston School Committee Proceedings,* 1902, pp. 4–5, 15–17, 38; *Boston Globe,* 1902: January 17, p. 14; January 29, p. 5; *Boston Post,* 1902: January 29, pp. 1, 10; January 30, pp. 1, 8; *Boston Transcript,* January 30, 1902, p. 4; *Boston Herald,* January 20, 1902, p. 1.

15. *Boston Post,* 1902: January 30, p. 4; January 31, p. 6. Boston *Pilot,* 1902: February 8, p. 4; February 15, p. 4. The *Herald* was quoted in the *Pilot.*

16. The PSA campaign leaflets of 1900 and 1901 indicate that the successful PSA candidates included five bankers and four lawyers. Professor Frank Vogel and Mark Mulvey, a Catholic and a labor representative, eventually sided with Duff. Public School Association Leaflets, 1900 and 1901 [Leaflets, Boston Public Library]. For the importance of teaching as a career for second-generation Irish-American women, see Hasia R. Diner, *Erin's Daughters in America: Irish*

Immigrant Women in the Nineteenth Century (Baltimore: Johns Hopkins University Press, 1983), 96–99.

17. *Boston School Committee Proceedings*, 1903, pp. 117, 266; 1901, pp. 422, 453–56, 459–61; *Boston Globe*, November 30, 1901, p. 7.

18. *Boston School Committee Proceedings*, 1902, pp. 16, 31–36, 115–26; *Boston Globe*, January 17, 1902, p. 14. Boston Normal School became Boston Teachers' College in 1922 but still belonged to the city. It became part of the state college system in 1952. Until the opening of the University of Massachusetts in Boston in 1965, Boston State, as it came to be called, did indeed serve as the only "people's university" in the city of Boston. It merged with the University of Massachusetts in Boston in 1982. For an overview of the statewide opposition to public higher education in Massachusetts, see Robert T. Brown, *The Rise and Fall of the People's Colleges: The Westfield Normal School, 1839–1914* (Westfield, Mass.: Institute for Massachusetts Studies, 1988).

19. *Boston Post*, November 21, 1902, pp. 5–6; December 11, 1902, p. 1; *Boston Globe*, December 11, 1902, p. 1.

20. City of Boston, *Boston Municipal Register*, 1903, pp. 291–93; *Woman's Journal*, 1902: November 22, p. 372; November 29, p. 380. Although he leaves out Julia Duff's role in encouraging Boston Catholic women to vote, the following article sets the question of Catholic attitudes toward woman suffrage in perspective: James J. Kenneally, "Catholicism and Woman Suffrage in Massachusetts," *Catholic Historical Review* 53 (April 1967): 43–57.

21. *Boston Post*, November 21, 1902, p. 6; *Boston School Documents*, 1886, p. 209; Dierkes file, the Morgue, Boston University School of Public Communications; *Woman's Journal*, December 13, 1902, p. 393; *Boston City Directory*, 1880, 1885, 1896–1916. Until 1914, Mary Dierkes's entry was "vocalist." Telephone interviews with Mrs. Joseph Reiss, Dedham, Mass., May 10, 1976, and Martha C. Engler, Dorchester, Mass., May 25, 1976. Dierkes was born in 1871 and died in 1950.

22. *Monatsbote* 7 (November 1906): 9; 9 (January 1908): 11; 10 (January 1909): 21. Translation by Martha Engler and Fr. Burckhart of the *Monatsbote* (Messenger) at the Holy Trinity Church, Shawmut Avenue, Boston. Mary Dierkes received the highest vote of any candidate in Ward 9. *Boston Municipal Register*, 1903, p. 291.

23. *Boston Post*, 1903: November 20, p. 16; November 29, p. 16; *Boston Globe*, November 22, 1903, p. 44; *Municipal Register*, 1904, pp. 277–79; *Boston School Committee Proceedings*, 1904, p. 30.

24. *Boston School Documents*, 1903, no. 9.

25. Pearson, *Son of New England*, pp. 44–50; *Boston School Committee Proceedings*, 1904, pp. 130, 145–46, 176, 184, 401–2, 429–31. With a touch of irony, Dierkes tried twice alone and twice with Duff's help to require pupils taking "Indian Bead Work and Basketry" in the centers to pay for their own materials.

26. *Boston School Committee Proceedings*, 1902, p. 500; 1904, pp. 140–44,

172–73, 290, 302; George A. O. Ernst, "The Movement for School Reform in Boston," *Educational Review* 28 (December 1904): 433–43. Julia Duff's plan for decentralization was implemented in Boston in the 1960s.

27. *Boston School Committee Proceedings*, 1905, pp. 337–38, 380–81, 445–47; *Boston Advocate*, September 29, 1905, pp. 1–2; *Boston Globe*, 1905: October 25, pp. 1, 9; December 17, p. 1; "Knows Schools from A to Z," *Practical Politics*, February 7, 1905.

28. *Boston Transcript*, March 8, 1905, p. 2; *Boston Globe*, 1905; March 7, p. 1; March 8, p. 1; *Boston Post*, April 29, 1905; p. 5; *Woman's Journal*, 1905: January 7, p. 1; March 4, p. 33; March 11, p. 37; March 18, p. 41; Commonwealth of Massachusetts, *Massachusetts Acts*, 1905, ch. 350; *Shall the Boston School Committee be Reorganized?* (Boston, February–March 1905) [Leaflet, Boston Public Library]. No women's names appear on Storrow's petition. The best discussion of how laypeople and teachers lost their influence in governing public schools in this period is David Tyack, *The One Best System* (Cambridge, Mass.: Harvard University Press, 1974).

29. The African-American community also lost its representation on the Boston School Committee when it was reduced in size. Dr. Samuel Courtney, who served from 1897 to 1900, was the last black School Committee member until John O'Bryant took his seat in January 1978. In 1983 Boston increased the size of the School Committee to four members at large and nine from individual districts, in order to allow for broader representation. In 1991 a referendum passed to change the Boston School Committee to a board of seven members appointed by the mayor beginning in 1992.

30. See Blodgett, "Yankee Leadership in a Divided City," 390–93.

31. For a discussion of the way traditional definitions of women's roles reflect issues of power, see Linda Kerber, "Separate Spheres, Female Worlds, Woman's Place: The Rhetoric of Women's History," *Journal of American History* 75 (June 1988): 9–39.

"THE SIMPLEST OF NEW ENGLAND SPINSTERS"

Becoming Emily Greene Balch, 1867–1961

PATRICIA A. PALMIERI

In 1919, while attending the Women's International League for Peace and Freedom (WILPF) Zurich peace conference, Emily Greene Balch received word that she would not be reappointed as professor of economics at Wellesley College. While the news did not come as a complete surprise, she noted it was a shock. In response she "celebrated the occasion by smoking a cigarette. . . . At Wellesley, at that time, smoking was strictly taboo and I felt that for members of the faculty to smoke, certainly for them to smoke clandestinely at the college, was 'not the thing.'" (She added, "However, I found that I did not like smoking and did not continue the habit.")[1]

It is characteristic of Emily Greene Balch to have celebrated her termination from Wellesley College with a smoke: having observed two taboos while teaching at Wellesley by not advocating pacifism and not smoking, she could finally engage in both acts freely. Such a response inscribes her for us: at fifty-two she was not too old to want to partake of the habits of the young—indeed in pacifist circles she was known for her capacity to act in concert with younger socialist radicals and pacifists like Crystal Eastman, a stance that someone like Lillian Wald found difficult. Smoking was a very small emblem of Balch's radicalism and of her taste for unconventionality. Balch recorded having wanted to flaunt tradition even more at times, wishing, for example, to advocate dress reform, but she noted that she held so many unconventional political

Emily Greene Balch at Bryn Mawr College. Papers of Emily Greene Balch, Swarthmore College Peace Collection.

mean to celebrate being fired?

Well into middle age, Emily Greene Balch was without a job after having taught at Wellesley College for more than twenty years. In being prematurely terminated, she lost her claim on the Carnegie pension. While from a middle-class family, Balch lived on her salary. She eventually depleted the funds she inherited from her father by giving money away. In the second half of her life, she became dependent for income on the charity of friends for the rest of her life. Balch wrote that the trustees' decision "left me at fifty-two with my professional life cut short and no particular prospects," and that her pacifist stance not easily taken entailed "many different kinds of cost, experienced at the time as well as foreseen for the future."[3]

Without deprecating the feelings that Emily Green Balch had in 1919 and later about the price she paid for her pacifism, nor dismissing the seriousness of this setback, it is important to consider the meaning of her celebrating being cast out of Wellesley. What sort of victory could this be?

While this bitter event cut short her academic career, it also catapulted Balch into the larger arena of international relations. By allying herself with the radical peace movement of World War I, Emily Balch courted, if only subconsciously, a much-sought-after destiny she had dreamed of since adolescence—to "serve in a dome more vast." Eventually in 1946, after three decades of working with WILPF, serving as international secretary, organizing countless peace and disarmament conferences, and writing proposals for the termination of international hostilities, she won the Nobel Prize for peace.[4]

It is ironic that an external event, the First World War and the patriotic zealousness that it unleashed on Wellesley's campus and throughout the nation, allowed the outlet for what Balch termed her inner light; the war enabled her to demonstrate the radical intellectual, social, and political self that she had been constructing since childhood. The pacifist cause was just the right kind of vehicle for Balch—it permitted her to practice many aspects of her complex personal, familial, religious and Progressive Era generational social creed.

A highly educated woman in late Victorian America, Emily Greene Balch exemplified in her life many of the conflicts that beset the women of her generation. For example, like Jane Addams, Vida Scudder, M. Carey Thomas, and others, she felt keenly the demands of the family

186   claim, the unfocused social obligation to repay society for one's education in service, the experience of drift after college, the "cruel choice"
between marriage and career.[5] In attempting to explain how this generation of women coped with these conflicting demands, historians
have offered a variety of interpretations. Some note that many women
suffered illness and succumbed. This was surely the case for two of
Balch's sisters. More positively, they note that some creative women
channeled their intellectual energies into service, thereby building on
the traditional female nurturing role. Other scholars have argued that
some educated women seized on science and modeled themselves after
men, renouncing the stereotypical road to achievement through social
motherhood.[6]

Interestingly, Emily Greene Balch's life represents a pursuit in some
degree of all of these paths but also the rejection of each. Her search for
a different "theoretical model on which a woman's life can be constructed" is therefore significant. As a New Englander who respected her
Puritan ancestors, as a late Victorian woman schooled in the Unitarian
conscience, she sought a "consecrated life."[7] Yet she sought fame and
glory as well. These emotions, toward ambition and recognition, troubled, perplexed, angered, and even frightened her. They are certainly
traits less attributed to her in the extant biographical literature and, for
that matter, are ones with which women are less identified generally.
This chapter focuses on these conflicts and attempts to make sense of
the turmoil Balch experienced as a result. It argues that Emily Balch's
inner tensions found their reconciliation in the larger World War I
conflagration. By 1920, Balch's self-described "inner dragons"—the
troubling pangs of selfishness, vanity, ambition, and ego (feelings which
often led her to feel guilty, isolated, and alone)—found release in her
unconventional and isolated stance in the peace crusade. Hence while it
is extremely important to study Balch's political philosophy of pacifism
and her religious worldview, it is also necessary to understand her drive
toward acclaim and the passion for ambition and achievement that
sustained her, even while she sought to tame and eliminate it.

Many women of Balch's social and educational group, having been
raised on high expectations, felt a strong urge to accomplish something
worthwhile—as Emily Balch expressed it, the need "to be somebody."
For Emily Greene Balch, this propensity, felt intensely in adolescence,
was never lost, even while it was at times obscured or deferred. This
essay seeks to explain what propelled Emily Greene Balch amid great

doubt, drift, and at times despair, to meet her intellectual and moral goals. What is the inner meaning of Balch's pacifist activism at Wellesley between 1915 and 1919? I suggest that it was an act she had prepared for, a part she had to take. To have conformed to the mentality of patriotic loyalty exhibited by most of her colleagues and her family would have been to lose her own internal path to self-development. In the end, the peace movement allowed Balch to find her own inner peace. Thus, the bold but satisfying statement, in her late seventies: "I did what I wanted with my life."[8]

When she was fifty-two, Balch's academic career came to an end. Another way to view this, however, is to see that her sense of herself as a powerful instrument had finally, belatedly, crystallized. Had she been a man, she might have found her destiny earlier, with greater ease, with less drift. To us then, Emily Balch, like the civic radicalism she espoused, is of more than political value. As a brilliant woman intellectual who bore the indefiniteness of her life with grace and stamina and who converted her "unfixed life" into a mixed blessing, she leaves us a legacy of spiritual, intellectual, and psychological growth. She found a way to capitalize upon her intellectual and personal sense of isolation; she converted her dependency on her father's economic generosity into an independence of judgment; she used her status as a single woman to take a controversial political stand. To serve "not in a fixed way" had been her desire, and in the World War I era she found a way to achieve that aim.

To explore the process by which Balch defined herself, I will draw a social-psychological portrait of Balch's development from childhood through midlife, moving along the life course from childhood and adolescence into adulthood. Diaries, letters, autobiographical notes, and heretofore unutilized family papers will be tapped. The major conflicts Emily Balch faced at each stage will be presented: first, parental themes from her early years within a supportive family culture; next, her conflict between the "monster" of egotism and the moral code of self-lessness (that in various guises appeared as another type of "monster"); finally, her feelings of drift and despair as an educated woman over how to shape her adult identity and to settle upon a rewarding career. It should be noted that these themes recur at each stage of Balch's development, causing her constantly to reassess herself and her progress toward finding her larger purpose.

Throughout the first four decades of her life, Emily Balch remained devoted to the belief that she was expected to accomplish a large mission. To comprehend this drive is to understand better why she took her pacifist stand in 1919 and why she did not ultimately fight harder for her Wellesley reappointment.

"Fortunate, in Her Family": Childhood through Early Adolescence

Emily Greene Balch's family background is crucial to understanding her identity. Vida Scudder said of Balch that she was fortunate in her family.[9] Emily was born in 1867 in Jamaica Plain, Massachusetts, the third daughter (after Annie and Bessie) to Francis Balch and Emily Noyes Balch (first cousins). Emily Greene Balch was reared in a protected, middle-class Victorian household. Her family was part of a large circle of Boston Brahmins who favored public service. Several aunts who remained single and grandparents either lived with or nearby Emily Balch when she was growing up. There was a break in years between Emily and her younger siblings, Frank, Alice and Maidie.[10]

Emily Greene was immediately seen as being special. Childhood poetry composed by her sisters talk about her as winning "name and fame."[11] Her father spent long hours talking, walking and reading with her and in her adolescence was fond of seeing her as a "Joan of Arc."[12]

The dominant tone of the household was set by her father, a graduate of Harvard. His frail health caused him to be released from duty in the Civil War. By profession he was a lawyer and executor to Charles Sumner, the abolitionist senator. To Emily, he was "the most unselfish person I ever knew."[13] A friend described him as a mixture of "Jesus Christ, Abraham Lincoln and Santa Claus."[14] He was known throughout his life by business associates and friends as a peacemaker.

Francis Balch took a great interest in Emily, saw her unique qualities, shepherded her to Bryn Mawr, and, while offering to make his daughter his law partner should she want to pursue law, prophetically determined that she was destined for greater things. His sponsorship and support seem to have exempted her from the usual difficulties of ambitious women of the 1890–1920 generation, many of whom claimed that they had to struggle to get educated. Jane Addams's father, for example, refused to allow her to attend Smith College because it was far away, and she had to settle for Rockford College, nearer to her home in Illinois. Nevertheless, Balch's diaries and letters reveal the strain she felt in separating from her father. Indeed, while she studied in Europe after gradu-

ating from Bryn Mawr, her father, who encouraged her studies, also
wrote constantly of how he "yearned to get a glimpse of her."[15] And
when she tried, after graduating from Bryn Mawr in 1889, to make a
career for herself, she often had to confront how her choice to leave
Boston might "pain papa."[16]

In many ways, Francis Balch represented the selfless life. And what
of her mother, Ellen Noyes Balch? According to Emily, her mother
was "the center of my life," until her death when Emily was seventeen. Indeed, an examination of Balch's early life and even later career
through her diaries and autobiographical fragments makes it clear that
not enough has been made of her intimate connection to her mother.[17]

In Emily's mind, her mother was associated with pleasure, with bodily
experiences, good and bad. Emily tells us that the best time of her life
was when she was quarantined with scarlet fever with only her mother to
nurse her. "My love for my mother had a passion in it; I never could get
enough of her."[18] In an autobiographical fragment, written in her eight-
ies, Balch recalled that once when her mother was nursing her youngest
sister, and her breast seemed too dry, Ellen Noyes called to Emily to suck
at her breast. Emily recorded that she was too old for this to be "natural"
and that she felt "disgusted." Yet, she noted poignantly, "I can still
remember to this day the taste of my mother's milk."[19]

Emily emphasized the fact that her first self-conscious moment came
in a conversation she had with her mother about feeling competitive
toward a girlfriend. She discussed with her mother this "nagging desire
to be first." She also recalled that her "first decision to disobey" was her
refusal to stay in the nursery with her younger siblings and nurse upon
smelling suffocating sulfur fumes. Balch noted with pride this first act of
disobedience, and it was somehow associated with successfully crossing
her mother. For this act she was neither punished nor praised.[20]

When her mother died of Bright's disease, Emily was bereft. She
recorded nothing in her diary, yet the aftermath of this loss can be seen
in many ways. One direct result was that Emily's father assumed dispro-
portionate weight in the household. His personality dominated, and
some of the children suffered. Somehow, also, the daughters were fatally
tied to home, and the family inevitably started to "cling together."
Balch's older sister Annie assumed the surrogate-mother role; on her
fell most forcefully the family claim. Balch felt even more that she had
to redeem herself, for she had been designated special and her sister
sacrificed.[21]

In addition to family culture, another great formative influence on Balch was her religious life. The Balches were Unitarians. When Emily Balch was ten, Charles Fletcher Dole came to preach at the Unitarian Church at Jamaica Plain. "He asked us to enlist . . . without limitations or any holding back, in the service of goodness, and . . . to meet the demands of this service, whatever its cost." She accepted this challenge, stating: "*I consciously dedicated myself as genuinely as a nun taking her vows,* and in spite of endless weakness, wrong doings, blunders and failures, I think I never abandoned in any degree my desire to live up to it." Only gradually did she come to recognize that total selflessness was not required. Eventually she embraced the full value of each individual self and the "rightness of building on that foundation."[22]

In many ways, as Daniel Walker Howe has pointed out, this was the classic struggle of the Unitarian conscience: to reduce the self and yet use the self to add virtue to and reform society.[23] There is still another way to view Balch's dilemma. Paradoxically, the male models in Emily's life represented selflessness and service, values we have come to think of as female. But in the late Victorian era through the First World War, many men like Francis Balch and Charles Dole extolled reform. Often in their lives, sometimes by dint of failing health but also by way of temperament, or love of beauty, and devotion to reform, they began to approximate a female persona. Some even followed, either in vocation or avocation, what might be called a "feminized" path. (Hence Francis Balch's love of botany and his long walks with Emily describing the flowers but prohibiting picking.)

What Emily had lost in her mother was not so much a female model of selflessness, for her father stood for this quality, but rather a real physical female presence, the pleasure and pain of a female body. While the men around her acted in a classical female way and demanded the reduction of self, her mother had represented the realization of self. Balch, who remained single and did not scorn that state, still felt she had missed some physically elemental aspect of life and paid tribute in later life to marriage, sexuality, and motherhood. This can be seen as a paean to her mother and her mother's way of life. Hers was a search not only to free herself from her father's house but also to live in her mother's house. She was seeking some reconciliation with her mother throughout her early adulthood. And her primary but broken attachment to her mother

may account for her inability to transfer this female love to another
female figure, as did many of her Wellesley peers, for example, who lived
in "Wellesley marriages."[24]

Historians of this generation of college-educated women, in an effort
to explain the psychic toll of the family claim, lay much stress on
the suffocation women endured in having to submit to their families.
Daughters were commonly called home and often expected to follow
their mother's paths. Hence Carroll Smith-Rosenberg has written about
a breach between generations of women during the turn of the century,
as college-educated women renounced their mothers' lives and made
themselves into "New Women."[25] Still, we should also be sensitive to
the opposite psychological tendencies and results: in some ways, women
who had been promoted by their seminary-educated, transitional-era
mothers, who had been exempted from domesticity or had exempted
themselves from it, felt ungrounded as well as guilty at the loss. They
experienced great emptiness and yearned for more of their mothers.
While Smith-Rosenberg argues that psychological estrangement led to
repudiation, alienation, and conflict between mothers and daughters,
such a breach could also end up in the desire to romanticize or to repli-
cate in some form their mothers' existence, or possibly to redeem it.[26]

We see this process in a short story Emily wrote while at Bryn Mawr
about a mother who is a "Modern Martyr." The mother in this story has
extraordinary mystical powers to heal the sick by taking on the patient's
or friend's illness. The mother weakens but the friend or stranger is
healed. The father, in contrast, stands by, watching rather impotently as
the mother martyrs herself for her friends and the community. The
mother is the heroine of society—not the father. And it is the mother in
a domestic, female, nursing role who is praised and endowed with
superordinary powers. Nonetheless, in consequence of her traditional
female role, she dies, leaving the child bereft. In this story, Emily ele-
vates her mother and her mother's world but demonstrates how the
mother's lot meant self-obliteration, leaving no model and a void for the
next generation.[27]

You can read here, too, that Emily's mother, in bearing eight children
and rearing six, in a marriage to a financially successful but sickly husband, paid a price in the sapping of her physical strength in motherhood, a fate that no Balch except Alice replicated.[28]

In the psychoanalytical school of object relations, D. W. Winnicott
discusses the "good enough mother" who provides a protected environ-

ment but also watches the child move out of the safe environment into autonomy and independence. In an extraordinary philosophical statement, written in the World War II period in another context, Balch herself suggested this concept. Balch attempted to explain her outlook on life and in turn illuminated her search not so much for a melding of the two worlds, of father and mother, of autonomy and dependence, but for the capacity to contain both at one time: "Chesterton says somewhere that antiquity taught the golden mean between extremes, but that Christianity teaches to hold, to experience at the same time, opposites in their full intensity, not refusing either, not fusing them, but somehow having both. He makes the +, with its junction of vertical and horizontal, a symbol of this." She wondered how much this feeling, this attitude, was due to the cooling-off period of her old age, to anesthesia to world horror, and "how much to something I am more responsible for."[29] Here we see the completion of her earlier struggle to find a way to hold on to her mother and follow her father.

Reading and the Intellectual Life

In addition to family culture and religion, much of Emily Greene Balch's early development—and particularly the formation of her intellectual being—can be attributed to her passion for reading. Hers was a reading family, and her mother told stories aloud at night and recited poetry, a tradition that Emily herself sustained. She loved words and from an early age found herself in books. The kinds of messages the stories conveyed are also, for our purposes, of import. She noted that the stories revolved around a heroine with a mission. She found the plots filled with "selfconsciousness but also a perfectly genuine conviction of the need of purposefulness in living. This theme of the person with a mission, which came to be the subject of so much raillery, has also genuine and useful overtones."[30]

As historian Barbara Sicherman has noted, for this generation of women, reading was more than a means of escape—the tales of the text often became part of everyday life. For women, this was one way to have adventure. For Balch, reading heroic tales provided inspiration and aspiration.[31]

A reading of Gogol's *Taras Bulba* led Balch to this passionate prose: "Oh, to be a wild Kossack! Fight hard and drink hard and ride hard. Out in the wide steppes or wilder Setch. A new world is opened to us, a new life, a new nation, a new time. Have I been dreaming? Our clothes grow strait. Oh, for a horse between the knees, my blood boils, I want to fight, strain, wrestle, strike. Not a nice time for women then. Never so good a time as now." She thought she "must have some Indian or Gypsy blood, I have such a longing for wild life at times and this strange wonderful book makes it all." Balch yearned to be "brave and have it all known, to surpass and be proud, oh the splendour of it!"[32] Reading, then, could engender consuming emotions about heroic deeds, and it could unleash erotic feelings. It was a potent resource pushing Balch out of passivity, rather than, as it is customarily considered, a passive activity.

Bryn Mawr College, Graduate Work, and Social Work (1886–1896)

In 1886, escorted by her father, Emily arrived at Bryn Mawr. Bryn Mawr was important to her for a number of reasons. It supported her intellectualism because it was filled with bluestockings. It led to her study of political economy and sociology with Franklin Giddings. Giddings stressed the altruism in human beings and talked of the coming of an ethical society if elites would act responsibly. It was at Bryn Mawr that Balch rejected, in Jane Addams's terms, "lumbering her mind with literature."[33] She sought to use her learning for a social purpose and "not to get lost in it for its own sake."[34] At Bryn Mawr, too, Balch found renewed support for her specialness. Her best friends there labeled her "Em-blem" and paid tribute to the powers of her mind and to her moral integrity.[35] Lucy Salmon, historian and teacher, encouraged Balch not to settle into teaching if she could afford to pursue another career line.[36] At graduation she won the first European fellowship, given to her for "beauty of moral character." At first she rejected this award but was then prompted by her family—and particularly by her sister Annie—to "put aside her Puritan conscience" and take the fellowship.[37] Annie, the surrogate mother in the Balch household, thus reenforced what Balch's own mother, Ellen Noyes, might have said: put the self into being, pay tribute to the self, do not renounce one's creativity.

Balch's struggles with the self and with upholding its unique point of view are well illuminated in a revealing undergraduate essay she wrote entitled, "The Disadvantages of Conventionality." In it she rehearsed the need for conformity at one level in society, so that not a lot of energy would be wasted in trying to create unique responses to everyday problems. But in almost all larger questions—and in particular in moral issues—she argued that "unconventionality must snap the chain and substitute a new and higher practice."[38] She wrote "even when conventionality does not lead men to do or think less nobly than they otherwise would, it tempts them not to think for themselves at all, *not to really live at all.*" Balch felt that conformity should liberate the mind and conscience to be free for things of importance. "*Whatever simply swims with the stream and goes whither it is carried is not a living thing, but a mere block.*"[39]

In many respects this is a philosophical defense of her childhood and adolescence, when she rejected playing with dolls, sewing, and wearing nice dresses. In this essay Balch defended the iconoclast, the pioneer. Yet, she painfully admitted: "Society on the contrary not only punishes the man who fails through trying to live understandingly, but even the man who succeeds and leaves the model which she herself copies in the next age—punishes too with the bitterest punishment that man can inflict, isolation."[40]

Written in 1888 or 1889, this undergraduate essay was a kind of moral manifesto that anticipated Balch's career as an outcast. In the First World War, as a pacifist, she found herself bitterly isolated from patriots, her best friends at Wellesley, and some of her family. In the Second World War, although she continued to serve in WILPF, she broke with many members who were absolute pacifists over her support of aggression against Hitler, in the service of a larger moral victory.

Concomitant with the essay about conformity that she submitted to her teachers at Bryn Mawr, there appeared in her diary another equally strong discourse with herself: "November 1889: Today, yesterday, the day before yesterday, the smart of mortification. Alone I had petted and rejoiced in my monster that makes his home within me. Grown bold therefore he stuck out his ugly phiz in public and shamed me. Well for me that I see him in his true aspect and am ashamed. So I may come to get the mystery of him and kill him dead after years of trial. (This referred to besetting Egotism.)"[41]

Only another month had passed when she admitted on January 29, 1890: "*It has always been my desire to be known, a truly vulgar ambition.*" She went on to chronicle how this feeling continually cropped up. She revealed that as a child she kept a record equal to a "highly eulogistic biography." In her head she would say, "Emily now rose and walked quickly across the floor and took her seat by the table." She regarded it as a bad habit that lingered and was difficult to defeat; she attributed her "miserable self-consciousness to it."[42]

At this stage of early adult development, how could Emily Balch reconcile the ambitious self with selflessness? How was self-gratification and ego to be balanced with service? One attempt at this appeared in a poem she recorded in her diary in 1892 and that reappeared in a somewhat altered form in her published book of poems, *The Miracle of Living*. She noted: "I have seen a Truth which if I can live it will be well," and then the poem:

> I said Oh God I would give away
> Myself and my life on any day
> I would give my pleasure and give my pain
> If thou wouldst make the commandment plain
> God answered thou thyself must see
> The need and the opportunity
> If thou hast a self to sacrifice
> Thou canst do no good in any wise.[43]

Calling upon God to solve the puzzle of what to do with one's life, as well as the advice to heed an inner voice, can be seen as characteristic of Unitarians. It was, however, also customary for women of the 1800s to cast their ambitions in the form of a call from God. Balch knew that she had to summon herself, to plan, and to pledge herself to act powerfully. But doubt and despair descended. On May 15, 1893, she wrote in her diary:

Always questioning—what to try to do, what to fit myself for, how to plan. Fixed as to general field of interest now, the social one, for 4 years, still no more definite rather less so in detail. I am so disappointed in myself and my powers or at least achievement. I believe I can do better than I have yet. One difficulty is to absolutely shut out ambition as a motive and keep up the standard of requirement I feel I should. I want to do work with the same intensity, concentration, and skill as a physician. To work as hard, whether as long or not, as if for money, if it is not for money viewed. One difficulty is that so much of what I should like to try, would . . . take me from home in separating me from Papa, and is moreover necessarily done under a conflicting strain of duties and expectation on the part of others.[44]

Here she was referring to her sisters, particularly Annie, on whom fell most profoundly the family claim.

"What the Idea of a Woman's Life Should Be"

After graduating from Bryn Mawr, Balch went to Europe to travel and study. She studied poor laws in Paris but felt terribly adrift and unfocused. On October 1, 1893, Balch wrote in her diary: "Beginning of tenth year without mama." On one level, perhaps the conscious one, it was her father whom she referred to as her standard and guide. Nonetheless she betrayed a lingering sense of loss of her mother, for the next day, on October 2, 1893, Balch declared in her diary:

I have felt for a long time in such an *impasse* with no future which I could foresee, nothing definite enough to work for, torn between the desire to be useful, to use my faculties to do what I ought at present and what I must probably in future in regard to money making, and at the same time not to pain Papa with absence or dislike plans or trouble Anne and Frank with too great singularity if it might be I could conscientiously avoid it. My practical course seemed barred by lack of theoretical conclusions as to what the idea of a woman's life should be. . . .[45]

Here Balch exposed her anxiety and uncertainty over what adult role a well-educated woman could pursue. While she took a few graduate courses at the University of Chicago, she never pursued a Ph.D. Like Jane Addams, Vida Scudder, Charlotte Perkins Gilman, and other brilliant women of this generation, Balch's path seemed blocked or ill-defined. For some women this kind of impasse led to drift and despair, but it could also lead to creative breakthroughs.

Finally, Emily Balch convinced herself that she had direction. She decided upon settlement-house work at Denison House, a social settlement for immigrants in Boston, and work in Boston charities, along with research for the Women's Educational and Industrial Union. She reflected: "It seems to me on the whole to promise usefulness. I distrust it because it savors so of the pinmoney making gentlewoman. God knows I would gladly be [a] chiropodist if that seemed best."[46]

During this stage of development, and well into her forties, Emily Balch was concerned with money and its meaning. She was in conflict over earning money that might deprive another of employment. As a sociologist and economist by training, Emily Greene Balch well recognized that most women were dependents of their families and of society. She felt financially dependent on her father and yearned for a position that would bring her independent income. And yet, in a revealing passage in a letter to her father about his supporting her until his death, she recognized the value of his status and showed her awareness of the benefits of her class position. The 1895 letter reads in part:

I do not want to live on your earnings all my life and hope I shall not, but at the same time I feel that it is very possible that I may be in positions where the being not wholly dependent on my situation may be most welcome and make frankness and independence of expression easier. Look for instance at Professor Bemis with wife and children and no special ability, losing his position at Chicago because (I have reasons besides newspaper talk to believe) his views as to labor organization displeased the rich men who have given so freely to the University.

Balch understood that free expression and freedom of intellectual and political inquiry could be effective. She therefore reconciled herself that taking "a sum, not enough to live on but enough to give one time to turn round, to wait awhile for the right place to open, is a thing to be very thankful for."[47] This is an extraordinary statement in light of what happened to Balch in 1919! Balch, who had earlier in her career in 1906 declared herself a socialist, comprehended that her political and socialist stands could cause her problems as a college teacher. She wanted to keep her options open, to be able to take a controversial stand and not have to elevate institutional loyalty over private conscience.

In 1896, Emily Balch fortuitously met Wellesley College professor Katharine Coman on a ship returning from Europe. Coman offered Balch a chance to read papers in economics. This temporarily rescued Balch from her displacement and drift. She joined the economics department at Wellesley, even though she felt her preparation, which included graduate work in France, Chicago, Berlin, and Radcliffe, had been "scrappy." She held no Ph.D.[48]

In 1899, Emily Balch was called to investigate the shoemakers' strike at Marlboro, Massachusetts. She later lent money to help form a union. Caroline Hazard, Wellesley's president at that time, said that this loan was the reason that she had been kept on as a mere assistant without promotion. Balch replied: "I consider that reason very creditable, I mean, very creditable to me." She added, "This impertinence, if it was that, had no ill consequences I think."[49]

In 1900, she was part of a Wellesley band of professors who protested the taking of "tainted" money (money accumulated from questionable business practices) from the Rockefellers. These women considered resigning, but in Vida Scudder's words, short of "fleeing to a hermitage," where could they find an institution more suitable to their intellectual endeavors and hospitable overall to their reform demands?[50] Balch remained at Wellesley.

Over the years, Balch created a number of new courses in economics and sociology. She taught about woman as consumer, she pioneered a course in immigration. She enjoyed promoting fieldwork in the city of Boston and integrating new ideas from the social sciences with social activism. Still, she felt restless. On April 19, 1903, she recorded: "The same sickening round-heartsick dawdle and demur with the work there and I perfectly conscious, perhaps even exaggeratedly conscious, of the enormity of my failure—I long for some kind of springboard to take off from with some momentum." Later, she recorded the familiar code of her generation: "Service is life."[51]

The Midlife Crisis: To Be "Ripe, Not Rigid or Superannuated"

As Emily Balch passed her mid-thirties and into her early forties, this uneasiness with her career, and the feeling that she had not met her father's standard nor her ultimate destiny haunted her again. On August 10, 1904, she inquired of herself in her diary: "Can I get training for religious work? without abandoning my profession? Could I learn to write and to speak. I do not feel at all sure I have anything to say worth writing. Is it worth speaking then? Speaking is a rare gift and needs cultivation. I do not know how far my thinking I can speak is a vanity."[52]

She worried lest this possible path "surprise either my family or friends." Yet she knew that if religious work was worth doing, it must be settled upon without considering too many external factors. Balch was in turmoil. "I do not *want* to do social service work or alliance work nor P.O. [Protestant Overseas] mission work. . . . I fret over whether I ought not to do at once something very much bigger."[53]

In the period 1904–6 Balch was due for her first sabbatical leave from Wellesley College. As she neared forty, Emily experienced a spiritual, intellectual, and psychological crisis. She yearned to use her remaining years fruitfully, "if only I can be ripe and not rigid and superannuated." As a younger woman, she had felt she should do more specifically religious work, possibly intermingle it with teaching. She had not then felt adequate to the task. As she ended her thirties she felt "steadier and less yeasty"; she had arrived "at an age where if I were ever to serve in this way I might be fitting myself at once."[54]

Mercedes Randall, a pacifist-activist who interviewed Balch and later compiled her biography, reported that Balch's idea of starting a religious order had become a kind of daydream, a romance, even a play. When in church she would fantasize about an unconventional church, organized and run by herself. However, she faced many obstacles, especially the handicap of being a woman, especially "if I were that woman, and my lack of magnetism." She still felt strongly, however, and did not want to rule out religion as a vocation. She consulted with Charles Dole and her friend Helen Cheever. Finally, she rejected this path.[55]

As of 1907, then, Emily Greene Balch had tried to be a social science analyst and had given up the idea of earning a Ph.D. She had tried a reform career at Denison House social settlement but left it for the career of teaching, which she termed "the long arm of the lever."[56] She found this wanting and herself inadequate at times and then toyed with starting a religious sect. Earlier she had praised the intensity displayed by physicians. She had the opportunity to follow her father's law practice but, based on her father's recommendation, passed up the chance to be his partner in his law firm.

One feels that at midlife, Emily Greene Balch was sitting under the proverbial "fig tree," to borrow an image from Sylvia Plath, trying to determine what to be.[57] None of these paths seemed to suit her. And yet according to family lore, friends at Bryn Mawr, teachers, and herself, she had seemed destined for more.

With all of this drifting, as she termed it, how did she sustain herself internally and psychologically? We can see that religion sustained her, as did reading, both of which enriched and informed her intellectual and spiritual life. She had a wonderful resiliency. Also, she had respect for, and somehow heeded, her inner dragons of ambition and ego, even while she sought to restrain these forces.

When the telegram came from Jane Addams asking Balch to join the women at The Hague and to enter wider international service, Balch sensed not only that this was her duty but that this was her way out of

"THE SIMPLEST OF NEW ENGLAND SPINSTERS"

stalled starts and a stymied feeling about her past careers. Later in life she would state that "I am no princess, but the simplest of New England spinsters, who for one accidental moment acted with powerful men."[58] Perhaps World War I was simply the accident of fate that propelled Balch forth; but we should be wary of accepting her self-effacing explanation. Women of this Progressive generation, even the most gifted women, saw themselves drifting and often spoke of their actions and choices in the passive voice. To us it often seems that they kept themselves afloat in some ingenious and clever manners.

As was the case for other pacifists, Balch's creed was shaped by Progressive Era thinking. She saw war as a threat to the values of social change. She had been against war since her adolescence. Moreover, she was not afraid of ridicule, nor of risking her reputation. Also, she had a strong spiritual nature. She joined with Jane Addams and other women to develop a plan for a conference of neutral nations that would negotiate peace. She was an emissary of the Women's Peace Party to Scandinavia and Russia. Later she talked to President Woodrow Wilson. While Wilson ultimately brought the United States into the war, her conversations with Wilson were important because the liberal principles she outlined for international agencies and conflict resolutions stimulated his thinking about a new diplomacy of world politics. With Jane Addams and Alice Hamilton, Balch co-authored *Women at the Hague.*[59]

In 1916, she took part in the International Committee on Mediation in Stockholm, supported by Henry Ford. Later, she rued the misrepresentation of the Ford mission that she felt the press perpetuated. Balch defended the "small deeds" approach of the Ford Peace Ship in attempting to make peace and to make history.

Emily Greene Balch was not afraid of ridicule nor of risking her reputation. She claimed that it was useful for elite women to be ridiculous because one could say what needed to be said and what important people, especially men in government positions, refrained from saying.

In February 1917, the United States broke off diplomatic relations with Germany. Balch tried to keep America out of the war. She was one of the founders of the Emergency Peace Federation, a group considered very radical, who tried to keep pressure on the government to remain neutral. Balch played the role of liaison between diverse radical peace advocates and liberal and conservative pacifists. Her family and some friends opposed her support of the radical segments of the peace movement. In 1919 the trustees of Wellesley College decided not to reappoint her after twenty years of teaching. She refused to make an academic freedom case, always hating controversies. Still, she did write Wellesley's President Pendleton that she felt she had been denied a job because of her pacifist and perhaps socialist activity. Like other pacifists, Balch felt the pain of loneliness and declared that "it is a hard thing to stand against the surge of war-feeling.[60]

Balch served as paid international secretary of WILPF in Geneva until 1922. She lobbied for enlarging its membership and helped to establish its structure. After 1922, she traveled independently and worked as a WILPF volunteer until 1931, when she succeeded Jane Addams as president of the American section.

By losing her job at Wellesley, Balch found her larger mission, her own form of sainthood. As a Wellesley college professor, Balch knew, at one level, that the tide might turn for her if she sustained a pacifist stance. The radicals at Wellesley had come perilously close to being terminated or to resigning before. It is true that the college granted her two unpaid leaves to pursue her pacifist activities, but trustees' records show that they did not approve of the cause she was going to work for.[61]

Perhaps Balch simply miscalculated the mood among the Wellesley Board of Trustees, which had recently added more businessmen. She could not know, for example, that by deferring a decision they had only to wait until her five-year contract ran out and then just "nonreappoint her," rather than terminate her in mid contract. After Wilson declared war in 1917 the pacifist creed was widely seen as a betrayal of national loyalty. An unfavorable sequence of events combined to put Balch in the worst position vis-à-vis the college and the renewal of her professorship.[62] Still, it is hard not to feel that she had prepared for her martyrdom. She had foreseen the need to be financially independent in order to take controversial political stands as a faculty member. As an undergraduate she had derided the disadvantages of conventionality. The peace movement, with Jane Addams at the helm, was undeniably to Balch a heroic crusade, one that equaled the chivalrous adventures that she had read about in literature and admired as a young woman. It was a legitimate vehicle by which to pay back the investments made in her by her father, sisters, friends, and teachers. In this act she was also able to remember her mother by reenacting martyrdom, her sacrifice. As a single woman, Balch asserted, unencumbered by family, it was incumbent upon her to take risks, to sacrifice her professional place for peace.

At the age of fifty-two, Emily Greene Balch had come to her own

"THE SIMPLEST OF NEW ENGLAND SPINSTERS"

inner freedom. She assumed her father's peacemaker mantle. And yet in likening herself to him, she did not repudiate her mother. Rather, she memorialized her with an act of personal sacrifice that also invoked a consciousness of self. In this moment of risk and of service to her inner voices—all of them—Balch discovered a steely self and displayed the moral steadfastness others had always attributed to her. Her calculated disobedience cost her her academic job, but when offered the chance to act heroically in the real world—not the world of fiction, her imagination, or her diaries—she cast away her self-doubts and in so doing became genuine to herself, at last.

Notes

I would like to thank the American Historical Association for awarding me a Beveridge Grant to do research on Emily Greene Balch and the American Association of University Women for a postdoctoral research fellowship. I also thank the Mary Bunting Institute, Radcliffe College, where I spent a semester doing my research and writing. I profited from the editorial advice of Susan Porter.

1. Emily Greene Balch, untitled autobiographical fragment, Balch Papers, Swarthmore College Peace Collection (henceforth cited as SCPC).
2. Balch as quoted in Mercedes M. Randall, *Improper Bostonian: Emily Greene Balch* (Boston: Twayne Publishers, 1964), 313.
3. Emily Greene Balch, "Working for Peace," *Bryn Mawr Alumnae Bulletin* 13, no. 5 (May 1933).
4. Quoted in Randall, *Improper Bostonian,* 48. On Balch and the Nobel Peace award, see Patricia A. Palmieri, " 'A Private Citizen of the World': Emily Greene Balch, 1867–1961," in *The Nobel Peace Award from 1901 until Today,* ed. Michael Neumann (Munich: Edicion Pacis, 1991).
5. Jane Addams, "The Subjective Necessity of Social Settlements," in *The Social Thought of Jane Addams,* ed. Christopher Lasch (New York: Bobbs-Merrill, 1965). On the choice between marriage and career, see, for example, Marjorie Dobkin, ed., *The Making of a Feminist: M. Carey Thomas* (Kent, Ohio: Kent State University Press, 1979).
6. Jill Conway, "Women Reformers and American Culture, 1870–1930," *Journal of Social History* 5, no. 2 (Winter 1971–72): 164–77.
7. Helen Cheever as quoted in Randall, *Improper Bostonian,* 437.
8. Emily Greene Balch, as quoted in Frances Burns, "Curious Experience to Be Center of a Myth, Says Nobel Winner," *Boston Globe,* March 6, 1947. In her commitment and her devotion to her cause, Balch resembles the philosopher Simone Weil.

9. Vida Dutton Scudder, "Emily Greene Balch," typescript, Balch Papers,
SCPC.

10. See Randall, *Improper Bostonian*, chapter 1, "The Neighborhood of Boston."

11. "To Emily—1887," poem written by Balch siblings in family poetry book, "Memories of Our Little Past" (unpublished volume in author's possession).

12. Francis Balch to Emily Greene Balch, April 12, 1896, Balch Papers, SCPC.

13. Balch as quoted in Randall, *Improper Bostonian*, 49.

14. Ibid.

15. Francis Balch to Emily Greene Balch, March 8, 1896, Balch Papers, SCPC.

16. Emily Greene Balch journal entry, October 2, 1893, Balch Papers, SCPC.

17. My thoughts about this mother-daughter relationship have been shaped by Nancy Chodorow, *The Reproduction of Mothering* (Berkeley: University of California Press, 1978).

18. Emily Greene Balch, as quoted in Randall, *Improper Bostonian*, 44.

19. Emily Greene Balch, autobiographical fragment, Balch Papers, SCPC.

20. Emily Greene Balch, autobiographical fragment, Balch Papers, SCPC.

21. Personal interview by the author with Balch's niece, Ellen Eppelsheimer, Concord, New Hampshire, January 25, 1988.

22. Emily Greene Balch, as quoted in Randall, *Improper Bostonian*, 48–49. Emphasis added.

23. Daniel Walker Howe, *The Unitarian Conscience: Harvard Moral Philosophy 1805–1861* (Cambridge, Mass.: Harvard University Press, 1970).

24. Patricia A. Palmieri, *In Adamless Eden: The Community of Women Faculty at Wellesley*, chapter 8, "A Colony of Friends," (New Haven: Yale University Press, 1995).

25. Carroll Smith-Rosenberg, "The New Woman as Androgyne: Social Disorder and Gender Crisis, 1870–1936," in *Disorderly Conduct: Visions of Gender in Victorian America* (New York: Alfred A. Knopf, 1985), 245–96.

26. In this interpretation, I have benefited from reading Diane Kahn, "Restitution for Mother's Lost Opportunities through Career Choice" (paper presented at Fifth Berkshire Conference on the History of Women, Vassar College, 1981). See also Linda W. Rosenzweig, *The Anchor of My Life: Middle-Class American Mothers and Daughters, 1880–1920* (New York: New York University Press, 1993).

27. Emily Greene Balch, "A Modern Martyr," typescript, Balch Papers, SCPC.

28. Personal interview by author with Ellen Eppelsheimer, January 25, 1988.

29. Balch as quoted in Randall, *Improper Bostonian*, 390. Donald Woods Winnicott, "The Observation of Infants in a Set Situation," *Through Pediatrics to Psychoanalysis* (New York: Basic Books, 1975).

30. Emily Greene Balch as quoted in Randall, *Improper Bostonian*, 45.

31. Barbara Sicherman, "Sense and Sensibility: A Case Study of Women's

204   Reading in Late-Victorian America," in *Reading in America: Literature and Social History,* ed. Cathy N. Davidson (Baltimore: Johns Hopkins University Press, 1989), 201–25. Also Barbara Sicherman, "Reading and Ambition: M. Carey Thomas and Female Heroism," *American Quarterly* 45, no. 1 (March 1993): 73–103.

32. Balch as quoted in Randall, *Improper Bostonian,* 69.

33. Jane Addams, *Twenty Years at Hull-House* (1910; reprint, New York: New American Library, 1981), 63.

34. Emily Greene Balch, journal entry, January 7, 1888, as quoted in Randall, *Improper Bostonian,* 68.

35. Louise Elder to Emily Greene Balch, September 1, 188[9?], Balch Papers, SCPC.

36. Randall, *Improper Bostonian,* 86.

37. Anne Balch to Emily Balch, n.d., but probably 1889, Balch Papers, SCPC.

38. Emily Greene Balch, "The Disadvantages of Conventionality," undergraduate essay, Balch Papers, SCPC.

39. Ibid. Emphasis added.

40. Ibid.

41. Emily Greene Balch, journal entry, November 1889, Balch Papers, SCPC.

42. Emily Greene Balch, journal entry, January 29, 1890, Balch Papers, SCPC. Emphasis added.

43. Emily Greene Balch, poem recorded in diary, 1892, Balch Papers, SCPC.

44. Emily Balch, journal entry, May 15, 1893, Balch Papers, SCPC.

45. Emily Greene Balch, journal entry, October 1, 1893, Balch Papers, SCPC.

46. Emily Greene Balch, journal entry, October 1, 1893, Balch Papers, SCPC.

47. Emily Greene Balch to her father, 1895, as quoted in Randall, *Improper Bostonian,* 97.

48. For a discussion of Balch's postgraduate training and academic career at Wellesley, see Palmieri, *In Adamless Eden,* chapter 5, 90–91.

49. Emily Greene Balch as quoted in Randall, *Improper Bostonian,* 109.

50. Vida Dutton Scudder, *On Journey* (New York: E. P. Dutton, 1937), 182–83.

51. Emily Greene Balch, journal entry, April 19, 1903; Emily Greene Balch, "Education and Life," June 23, 1909, Balch Papers, SCPC.

52. Diary entry, August 10, 1904, Balch Papers, SCPC.

53. Emily Greene Balch, journal entry, 1904, SCPC.

54. Emily Greene Balch as quoted in Randall, *Improper Bostonian,* 394.

55. Randall, *Improper Bostonian,* 395.

56. Balch as quoted in Burns, "Curious Experience to Be a Center of a Myth."

57. Sylvia Plath, *The Bell Jar* (New York: Bantam Books, 1981), 62–63.

58. Emily Greene Balch, "I am no princess, . . ." Balch Papers, SCPC.

59. Jane Addams, Alice Hamilton, Emily Greene Balch, *Women at the Hague*
(New York: Macmillan Co., 1915).

60. Emily Greene Balch, "Working for Peace," *Bryn Mawr Alumnae Bulletin* 13, no. 5 (May 1933): 13–14.

61. Board of Trustees Minutes, 1915–1919, Wellesley College Archives.

62. For a full discussion of Balch's termination from Wellesley College see Palmieri, *In Adamless Eden,* 240–44.

BEYOND SERVANTS AND SALESGIRLS

Working Women's Education in Boston, 1885–1915

LAURIE CRUMPACKER

In turn-of-the-century Boston, a number of interconnected institutions were concerned with the education of working women. This chapter looks at the way that two such organizations responded to what they saw as the needs of two groups of working women: domestic servants and salesclerks. The Women's Educational and Industrial Union (WEIU, founded in 1877) and Simmons College (incorporated in 1899) worked closely together on common goals—to upgrade the position of working women through education and improved opportunities for self-maintenance.[1]

Two of the Union's major programs, the School of Housekeeping and the School of Salesmanship, became part of Simmons College during its first ten years of operation. The Union had founded the School of Housekeeping in 1897 to improve the situation of domestic servants, and it had opened a School of Salesmanship in 1905 to increase the efficiency and better the lot of department store clerks. In 1903 and 1915 respectively these schools became the Departments of Household Economics and Education for Store Service at Simmons College. In this process, a reform agenda that had emerged from mid-nineteenth-century transcendental thinking became a model of political expediency and culminated in a vocational college curriculum.[2] At the same time, training programs originally designed to reform conditions for working-class women evolved into courses that provided career oppor-

Students watching demonstration in Prince Retailing Room, Simmons College. Courtesy, College Archives, Simmons College.

tunities for middle-class women. This transition and the forces among workers and reformers that shaped it are the subjects of this study.

This chapter will demonstrate that the WEIU's training programs for domestic servants and salesclerks followed different trajectories. The program for servants failed ultimately because middle-class reformers were unable to hear and respond to their foreign-born servants' concerns. Reformers wanted to train their servants to be more efficient and assumed that trained servants would be rewarded with increased status and better pay. But servants had different goals: they wanted more independence, respect, and time to themselves. Because their goals differed so markedly from reformers' prescriptions, servants had to struggle on their own to achieve their major objective of shifting from live-in schedules to day labor.[3] Responding to servants' lack of interest, reformers at the Union's School of Housekeeping shifted their focus away from training unwilling domestics to teaching middle-class women how to manage day help and perform household tasks more efficiently themselves.

SOCIAL REFORM AND POLITICAL ACTIVISM

Unlike the servants' courses, however, the training programs for sales-women continued for several decades, largely because they were designed with the clerks' own wishes in mind. Because middle-class women did not feel so distant from the mostly native-born salesclerks, they listened to clerks' complaints and set up programs that more nearly met their needs. Salesclerks saw these training programs as advantageous because they led to the desirable ends of better pay and promotions. For these reasons, clerks were more interested in training than domestic servants who could anticipate no such gains. These programs for department store clerks also attracted reformers because improving working conditions for saleswomen did not threaten middle-class domestic arrangements in the same way that reforms for servants appeared to.

The history of training programs for servants and saleswomen exposes positive and negative impacts of professionalization on early twentieth-century women's work.[4] Professionalization worked well for many middle-class women who used their expertise in domestic matters, especially childcare, to establish a "female dominion" and a series of new semiprofessions especially for women.[5] But "professional" attitudes also separated professional women from working-class women and problematized the cross-class relationships that reformers hoped to maintain with their working-class students and clients.[6] Ultimately female professional dominions perpetuated separatism and gender inequality as well as much of the class inequality left over from the nineteenth century.

Class separations intensified as political realities and new opportunities perceived to be connected with the achievement of woman suffrage encouraged middle-class women to develop alliances with men of their class. Sarah Deutsch points out in a recent article that these alliances changed the language of women's reform movements even as they may have improved some women's prospects for effecting social change. Altering their focus around the turn of the century, many women's reform organizations decided to concentrate on "chang[ing] the city and not just the individual woman."[7] The Simmons and WEIU experiences document middle-class women's evolving political pragmatism and alliances with male reformers. However, histories of these organizations also show that forces like class divisions, middle-class women's professional aspirations, and working-class women's desire for respectable, decent-paying, and autonomous work were probably the most important factors in changing the character of working women's education as the twentieth century began.

The Women's Educational and Industrial Union, founded in 1877, was a prototype for women's exchanges that opened in seventy-five cities between the 1870s and the 1890s.[8] Like other women's exchanges, the Boston Union was begun by middle- and upper-class women to offer aid to the poor women who were crowding into cities in the last quarter of the century. But, in contrast to most of the other exchanges, its "seven earnest women" founders had in mind not merely an exchange but a more diversified organization, "an experimental succoring agency for many of the difficult problems of living that confront urban dwellers."[9]

The Boston Union's dual purposes were explicit in its original designation as an educational *and* industrial union. As a united front, a union, middle-class women would educate themselves about other urban women's problems and reach out to working women with educational initiatives, work opportunities, and social services. Founder Harriet Clisby hoped the Union would "[r]each forth in every direction to aid, strengthen, and elevate women by drawing them into a condition of unity. . . . [It would] pioneer in any educational, industrial and social movement that seemed likely to improve the condition of women generally."[10] Explicit in the Union's guidelines was the provision that no woman should be excluded from its services because of economic circumstances, race, ethnicity, or creed. The Union included among its directors Alice Goldmark Brandeis, a Jewish woman and wife of Supreme Court Justice Louis Brandeis; Josephine St. Pierre Ruffin, a leader in the National Association of Colored Women; and Mary Kenney O'Sullivan, an Irish-American labor leader. But while the Union's principles were inclusive of all women, its practices yielded mixed results.

One goal for the primarily middle-class members of the WEIU (like Jane Addams, Lillian Wald, and other leaders in social work) was the creation of useful occupations for women of their own class. Their access to servant help freed some of their time, and their education and exposure to reform movements provided direction for much of their energy. The founders of the WEIU said they felt "obliged to provide spiritual encouragement for themselves [in order to] break away from the immense imprisonment of life which was stifling them."[11] The Union's motto, "A Union of all for the good of all," implied both the founders' own need for meaningful work and the nineteenth century's

optimistic notion that all women, simply by virtue of their womanhood, were sisters who could band together for their common good.

The Union's first seven standing committees reflected the founders'
ideas about how they might best serve working women. There was a
Finance Committee for fundraising and budgeting, a Committee on
Social Affairs in charge of the library and reading room, a Committee
on Moral and Spiritual Development to present lectures, and an Industrial Employment Committee to investigate employment opportunities
and train women for "appropriate" work. The Committee on Hygiene
and Physical Culture presented lectures on "the laws of life" and, for a
short time, sponsored a free clinic for indigent women; the Education
Committee discussed "true ideas affecting questions of human interest";
and the Protection Committee offered legal aid, usually for domestic
servants whose rights had been violated.[12]

In spite of the Union's lofty intentions, seeds of class division were
present from the beginning. There was never any question of who were
the "helpers" and who required help. Membership on the board of
directors and committees was reserved primarily for middle- and upper-
class supporters while recipients of services—from trade training to sub-
sidized food and lodging—were needy working-class women or middle-
class women who had fallen on hard times. There were even separate
lunchrooms for members and for clients. From the start it was clear that
members would set policy and decide the types of training available, the
morally edifying or practical subjects for lecture series, the salaries
of employees, consignment reimbursements, and other matters of policy in the Union's trade shops, classes, and other programs. Working
women were to benefit from services but not contribute their own
organizing talents.

Union leaders were not unaware of the possible divisions caused by
class differences. In the 1880s, Union president Abby Morton Diaz
repeatedly defended the Union against charges that "it benefits the well-
to-do and neglects the poor."[13] The Union, she insisted, did not represent the "rich reaching down to help, [nor] the poor reaching up to be
helped but meet[]s all women's needs—working heart to heart."[14] She
maintained that by taking a personal interest in their progress, the
Union helped women to help themselves. In 1880, she advised members: "Let there be no distinction felt. . . . It is right that differences exist
for we need them . . . but possibilities of highest spiritual growth lie in
the harmonious blending of all varieties of human life . . . that each may

serve and receive for the good of each and the whole."[15] While this optimistic attitude about class interactions was eventually to prove the undoing of a number of the Union's initiatives, at least during its early years the Union's activities and appeal were seemingly unhampered by class conflict. In fact, during the last quarter of the nineteenth century, the Union was extremely successful in attracting both members and clients. Within a year of its founding it had four hundred members, and by 1889 the number had grown to fourteen hundred. In 1896, the WEIU claimed to serve fifteen hundred women each day, and the following year it expanded into two adjoining buildings at 164 Boylston Street.[16]

In keeping with their emphasis on aiding working women, early in the WEIU's history members had expressed concern over what was then called "the servant problem." This was a term used in the popular press to describe middle-class housewives' problems with hiring and retaining live-in domestic help. Working-class women were in great demand as workers, and whenever possible they chose occupations other than domestic service. Housewives who employed one or two live-in servants therefore had considerable trouble filling places. Although they evinced real concern over problems faced by servants, the unavailability of household help may have been the primary reason for Union members' extreme concern with the "servant problem."[17]

The WEIU's efforts in this area had begun in 1877 with its Industrial Employment Committee, whose charge was to run an employment bureau to place women in what Union members believed to be respectable and secure situations. In 1885 this office was divided into two branches, one for the placement of domestic servants and the second an "Appointment Bureau" (or business branch) to secure for "trained women . . . positions of responsibility and power."[18] The Appointment Bureau was a success, but the domestic employment branch was more problematic, closing periodically, mostly because there were always more employers seeking domestic help than servants looking for situations.

As with most of the Union's reform activities, the goals and practices of the Domestic Employment Bureau changed over time. Its original objective had been to place young women, particularly those from immigrant families, with middle-class families so that they might avoid factory work, poverty or, worst of all, prostitution. Union members believed that going "out to service" in a "good" family would help settle and Americanize those who were new to this country and would also aid any women with "morally questionable" pasts. The Union's 1892 *Annual* *Report* was enthusiastic: "When women take a kindly interest in those who work hard for them, then will the millennium dawn upon our hearthstones."[19]

By the end of the century, however, more and more young, white, native-born women were choosing factory or department store work over domestic service. In 1897, when Union members noticed that the supply of potential servants was not meeting the demand of house-holders, they organized a Domestic Reform League, which lasted until 1910. The League's goals reflected Progressive Era beliefs in investigation and analysis: "The objects of the League are the scientific and careful consideration of present conditions; the awakening of the interest of women in the largest aspect of the problem; recognition by the employer that fair conditions should be given for faithful service; and by the employee that interested and efficient service must be given in exchange for fair wages and just conditions."[20]

Although the Domestic Reform League launched investigations to determine why young women were not going into domestic service, its other practices did not substantially change the work done previously by the Domestic Employment Bureau.

The Union had shown that it cared about the welfare of servant women through its attempts to reform employment bureaus and help servants collect their wages. But members were also acting out of self-interest because in order to pursue reform activities, they needed competent domestic servants to keep their own households running. Union members believed a well-run home to be the foundation of a stable society. Businessmen and community leaders needed a home base to escape from what was even then termed the "rat race" of public life. A competently managed and smoothly functioning home would train the next generation of males in efficient business practices and females in the management of their own homes. The well-run home, Union members assumed, depended on live-in servants who could be trained to the tasks and preferences of a particular household and who would always be on call when needed. Day servants were plentiful, because many women wanted the freedom of living on their own or returning to their families at night, but this arrangement seemed inefficient and undesirable to many middle-class women. This impasse between employers and employees was an important aspect of the "servant problem."

Union investigators were influential around the country in documenting the dimensions of the "problem." In 1900, under the auspices of the Domestic Reform League and the Union's Research Department, Mary E. Trueblood published a study comparing domestic service with other kinds of jobs available to Massachusetts working-class women. She noted that all the single live-in domestics in her study were foreign born, compared with only a portion of those workers she met in shops, restaurants, and factories. She also found that household workers worked longer days (10.6 hours) and more days per week than other workers, who at least had their evenings, Sundays, and a half day on Saturday off. Trueblood observed that while house workers' wages, including their board and room, were higher than those of shop girls and waitresses, they were lower than those of factory workers.[21] But the greatest contrast between domestic workers and other workers in her study lay in the area of satisfaction and contentment. Trueblood concluded that

In the shoe factories, shops and restaurants many of the girls seem to enjoy their work. No doubt . . . the association with others doing the same work accounted for it in part. They knew, too, that their work . . . would end at a fixed time. It was particularly noticeable in these three occupations that the girls respected themselves, their work and their employers. They seemed to feel themselves a part of the commercial world and [that] they were helping to do a large thing. . . . Of servants [however] very few seemed satisfied with their employment, but in no case was the objection to the work itself. Those receiving the best pay were often the most dissatisfied. Truly no amount of money can compensate a self respecting person for the loss of a reasonable amount of free time and independence.[22]

Had Union organizers listened to these workers, they would have understood that the "servant problem" had less to do with the nature of the work or its wages than with its inordinately long hours, isolation, lack of autonomy, and status. As one factory worker summed it up, "I don't like the idea of only one evening . . . and every other Sunday [off] . . . I also think that going out [in service] makes a girl stupid in time. . . . She never reads and does not know what is going on in the world. . . . The domestic after she marries gets careless. . . . She has lived in such fine houses that her small tenement has no beauty for her."[23] Even the Union used denigrating language about domestic service when comparing the Domestic Employment Bureau with its other branch, which it called the Bureau for "higher employment."

Clearly Union members did not hear servants' real concerns because by the end of the century, while they continued to provide legal aid to servants who were unfairly treated on the job, they were focusing more of their efforts on legislative regulation. A Union report after 1910 lamented that women and children in factories had legislative protection, but "the 80,000 domestic workers [had] no protection even in their search for work."[24]

This shift to legislative remedies reflected the changing emphasis of many Progressive reformers who, during this period, turned to the state for remedies when other reform efforts seemed to have failed. Union organizers also felt empowered by widespread acceptance of their investigative efforts and by women's growing political power. In Massachusetts, for example, women had gained school suffrage in 1879 and were drawing closer to the achievement of their other suffrage goals. For Union members legislative reform was becoming the most important new weapon in their arsenal; but, even so, they did not abandon their work with individual women.[25]

With legislative change slow and difficult to achieve, Union members sought more rapid and tangible results. They therefore decided, in 1897, to offer specialized training courses for domestics and housekeepers. The WEIU's School of Housekeeping had as its initial goal the "scientific study of the home and of conditions of daily living . . . [so] that the standard of living [might] be raised in all homes." They began a five-month course for servants, which included instruction in kitchen, dining room, parlor, chamber, and laundry work, and cooking. Students served a three-month probationary period with "intelligent women" who were supposed to aid them in their understanding of household tasks. The course for employers emphasized household management and offered study in public health, home construction, art, individual and child health, hygiene, nutrition, home nursing, and "the home in relation to society." "Such study," their brochure concluded, was "absolutely necessary to the development of a better citizenship, of a greater country, [and] a nobler race."[26]

While many housewives applied, the number of interested servants declined rapidly after the first year. Union leaders explained that servants had little incentive to seek training because with or without spe-

216   cial courses, domestics were in great demand. Servants offered other reasons for their lack of interest. One said, "Those schools are not for us; no one ever finds out what we want to learn; they start out with a theory and everything must fit that, and we won't fit—that's all."[27]

Because of low enrollments, the WEIU dropped the course for domestics after two years and added a new course designed to prepare housewives to improve their own household management and college graduates to work "professionally" in social service, teach home economics, or manage an institution. This group studied sociology and economics, dietetics, building construction, drainage, heating and ventilation, public health principles, and municipal sanitation. In keeping with the evolution of the home economics movement, the School of Housekeeping was educating women either to reorganize their own homes or to earn a living by applying household management skills in a larger and more public context.[28]

The redesigned School of Housekeeping was fast becoming a professional school for the study of domestic science (household economics) rather than a place to learn the "art" of housekeeping. With these changes, Union leaders were aware that their efforts had altered radically from earlier attempts to improve the situation of domestic servants through training courses. They defended this change, however, in typical Progressive language as "modern" and "scientific." Moreover, they maintained that the turn away from "remedial" measures toward investigation, professional education, and legislation would act as a "preventive" for the social problems plaguing householders and servants alike.[29]

Although the new School of Housekeeping was more popular than the old, it was still expensive to maintain, and Union leaders claimed that by 1902 it had "drained their treasury." They were relieved therefore to sell the School to Simmons College, which used it as the nucleus for a Household Economics Department. The Union's 1902 *Annual Report* justified the sale, stating, "The Union had dared in faith and ignorance to undertake the work. . . . Tangible results were meager, the most valuable contribution to the community having been the constant emphasis on the social significance of the home."[30] The sale appeared to satisfy all parties: Simmons was pleased to have an already successful program among its early departments; and the Union felt that it had made an important contribution to reform by linking the home to larger social issues. Forgotten in the celebration were the servants whose problems had originally inspired the Union's domestic reform endeavors.

SOCIAL REFORM AND POLITICAL ACTIVISM

At the WEIU, the educational programs of middle-class women had, in this case, failed to reach across class lines to aid their servants. Imprisoned within their own class-based notions about domesticity and appropriate female work, reformers believed that time spent in middle-class homes was edifying for servants. They did not understand servants' oft-expressed desire for more independence, their desperate need for more free time, and their clear preference for day labor over live-in work. Until the early twentieth century, most middle-class women were convinced the well-run home depended on live-in help; thus, their own self-interest interfered with their ability to hear their servants' requests. As the makeup of the domestic workforce changed from native-born white to foreign-born, ethnic, and racial minorities, white middle-class women became even less able to identify with these workers and their needs and therefore less likely to succeed with cross-class attempts at reform.[31]

Recognizing the need to redirect their reform efforts, WEIU members saw Simmons College as embodying many of their ideals and thus as a logical new home for the School of Housekeeping. Simmons and the WEIU shared a history that went back to 1867, when Boston clothing manufacturer John Simmons drew up his will. Simmons appeared to be motivated by a concern for working women similar to that which spurred the founding of the WEIU. It was after all with the help of hundreds of poorly paid needlewomen that Simmons had produced the first ready-made men's suits and made his fortune. His will earmarked five hundred thousand dollars in Boston real estate to endow "[a]n institution to be called Simmons Female College, for the purpose of teaching those branches of art, science and industry best calculated to enable the scholars to acquire an independent livelihood."[32] One of his executors suggested that Simmons's motivation may have been "to make a return to that class of women by whose labor he had laid the foundation of his fortune."[33]

When Simmons died in 1870, Catharine Beecher and others close to the WEIU's founders were consulted about the kind of "female college" that should be established.[34] However, fate intervened when the Boston fire of 1872 destroyed the downtown Boston buildings that composed Simmons's legacy. His executors sold the land and reinvested the money from the sale, but the fund did not reach the original half million dollars until 1899. The college was incorporated in that year and opened its doors to students in 1902. The fortunes of the WEIU and Simmons

College converged immediately when Simmons purchased the Union's School of Housekeeping in 1903.

Like Union members, Simmons's leaders believed women should be self-supporting and that the most appropriate careers for women extended their nurturing work beyond the home. Simmons's first dean, Sarah Louise Arnold, often used this rationale to defend women's education against its detractors. In a 1908 lecture aptly entitled "Reconcilement of Cross Purposes," Arnold explained:

It may not be the privilege of every woman to devote her life to children of her own; nevertheless, in every woman who is truly prepared for her work in the world, the spirit of the mother is regnant;—and the task which will most appeal to her will have in it generous caretaking for the lives of other children. . . . In all our conceptions of the education of women, this function, this privilege, this right, must take precedence.[35]

Arnold maintained, as did WEIU members, that women did not work primarily for self-fulfillment but rather to sustain themselves and their families if they did not marry, were widowed, or otherwise experienced hardship.

Simmons's first programs reflected this balance between the perceived needs of working women for self-maintenance and society's demands that women's work be appropriately maternal and domestic in nature. Seeking also to avoid direct competition with male professionals, Simmons's earliest departments included Household Economics, Secretarial Studies, General Science (for teachers and laboratory technicians), Library Science, Social Work (1904), and Salesmanship (1912). While all these courses of study on some level followed a maternalist model, home economics most clearly embodied the private values of the home brought into the public world of work. As Simmons's first president, Henry Lefavour, said, "The work of this department bears an intimate relation to the main purposes for which the college stands."[36]

Despite its maternalist links, home economics as a field was not in conflict with the needs and goals of career women; in fact, they used it to further their professional status. With most social science and science professorships closed to them, household economics allowed women like MIT's Ellen Swallow Richards and Simmons's Susan Myra Kingsbury to publish and teach in the sciences and social sciences as long as they labeled their work "home economics." Home economics departments even offered business courses under the name of "Institutional Management." In universities, settlement houses, and women's unions, leaders of the home economics movement advanced their own careers as they followed Women's Christian Temperance Union leader Frances Willard's advice to "make the whole world homelike."[37]

Keeping pace with the national movement in domestic science, Simmons College continued to professionalize the work begun by the WEIU's School of Housekeeping. By 1910, household economics at the college was described as "[a] four-year program [which leads to] the degree of Bachelor of Science, and affords preparation for . . . management, for teaching, or for individual research. . . . [It] permits an emphasis on science, education, institutional management or social work."[38] In addition to completing the college's general requirements (in English, languages, philosophy, and other subjects), household economics students took courses in the sciences (physics, biology, chemistry, physiology, bacteriology, and dietetics), the social sciences (history, sociology, economics, and psychology), the technical subjects of cooking, sewing, accounting, and other household "arts," and, depending on their specialization, education or institutional management. Women who majored in home economics were clearly preparing for lives as professionals whether they chose to use their knowledge in or out of their homes.

The professionalization of domestic science in many ways appeared to solve the "servant problem" for middle-class women. Domestic science suggested that housewives who used the newest developments in household technology to lighten their housework would no longer need servants. Indoor plumbing, vacuum cleaners, semiautomatic washing machines, electric refrigerators, stoves, hot water heaters, telephones for ordering goods, and automobiles for shopping changed the nature of household duties. In addition, canned and processed foods, manufactured soaps, and bakery-baked breads and pastries further decreased the amount of manual labor required to maintain middle-class homes. Although studies of household technology show that women spent the same number of hours doing housework even with these advances, the work was different in nature; therefore, middle-class women were beginning to think that housework could be accomplished without the aid of live-in help. These changes in middle-class life caused most reformers to turn their attention away from domestic service and welcome the modern conveniences of domestic science.[39] The transformation of the WEIU's School of Housekeeping into Simmons College's Department of Household Economics was a significant manifestation of these changing perceptions about housework and the roles of housewives and servants.

During the same era, middle-class women spent an increasing number of hours shopping in the department stores that had been designed to attract their business. The difficult working conditions of the clerks who served them captured some of these women's attention as had their servants' plight in earlier years. A movement to improve conditions for saleswomen therefore grew up during the Progressive Era, but it followed a pattern of development rather different from attempts to ameliorate the situations of domestic servants.

Reformers were drawn to the plight of salesclerks for some of the same reasons they were concerned about domestic workers. Working conditions in department stores were deplorable. Wages for clerks were low (averaging five to six dollars a week), hours were long; and rules against talking, sitting, and taking breaks were rigidly enforced. Undercover surveillance by "service shoppers" and extreme penalties for breakage and "insubordination" were not uncommon. The majority of salesclerks were native-born women who started store work as teenagers with only grade school educations. Native-born women were attracted to this occupation because they thought it a step above domestic service. Clerking was not considered manual labor (clerks wore white collars); it offered finite hours (they went home at the end of the day and had Sundays off); and co-workers were usually white and native born. Because department stores were new, traditional class attitudes about subservience to "one's betters" were not yet as ingrained as in household service. Finally, because clerking jobs were inherited from the nineteenth century's largely male salesforce, some of the status of "men's work" remained attached to these jobs. In this period, then, department store employment was seen as a desirable job and a possible route to upward mobility. (Occasionally clerks became buyers or department managers or married a manager or customer.)[40]

The initial response of female reformers to department store conditions was twofold. The National Consumers' League, founded in 1899 by Hull House worker Florence Kelley, emanated from the social settlement movement. It harnessed women's roles as consumers, threatening boycotts of department stores and products sold or produced under adverse working conditions. The Consumers' League's powerful "White Paper" lists of offending merchants were mandates for the socially conscious to boycott offenders and often prompted department store managers and owners to improve working conditions for their employees.[41]

In response to reformers' concerns, many department stores sponsored "welfare programs," which offered employee lounges, lunch rooms, gyms, libraries, vacations, and savings plans. Social workers taught classes in hygiene, etiquette, and proper English usage with the implicit goal of altering the "class and cultural perspective of the salesperson."[42] These attempts to impose middle-class cultural norms often met with resistance from clerks, and welfare programs did not interest managers either because their primary goal was not reform but rather the systematization of their business practices. Seeing the interests of clerks and managers as related, WEIU social worker Lucinda Wyman Prince proposed training programs in "salesmanship" as an innovative approach to meet the needs of both groups.

Prince's salesmanship course, the first in the country, began at the WEIU in 1905. In preparation for the course, Prince worked briefly at a department store bargain counter to observe working conditions for herself. Legend has it that in one stint of a few hours, she sold more than any other clerk for the entire day. She used this experience and other "new" ideas about the link between training and efficiency to convince a number of Boston department store owners (notably at Filene's and Jordan Marsh) to sponsor a three-month training program for their employees. They would attend classes at the Union in the morning and then work behind the counter for the rest of the day; during their training period, they would receive a partial salary.

Prince promised employers that her training program would change "the whole mental attitude of the girls."[43] In this, her rationale was similar to that behind the early training programs for domestics. She believed that with training and acculturation, clerks would perform more efficiently and earn greater respect from customers and employers. Increased status would in turn command higher wages and improved working conditions. In 1907, she observed, "Four years ago I came to the conclusion that saleswomen as a whole were lamentably ignorant of responsibility and right thinking toward their work as a profession, of a regard for system and attention toward detail and of a knowledge of the goods which they sold."[44] A few years later, with her program firmly in place, Prince promised, "the girl behind the counter who continually chews gum and talks in terms of 'I says to him' is fading into the background. The future saleslady will be all efficiency and business." Prince concluded that her training would give salesclerks "a clearer perception of what business is, thus engendering the right attitude toward the work by which they live."[45]

Like the early training programs for domestics, Prince's program aimed to remedy deficits in the employees rather than alter in any material way the male-dominated store structure or the relations of capitalism with their inherent possibilities for exploitation. Her course approached the project of "making over" the individual woman by offering classes covering knowledge of stock, business arithmetic, the psychology and ethics of salesmanship, hygiene, wages (especially how to save and spend them wisely), and "how to live" (including the company one should keep, reasonable sleeping hours, and good nutritional habits). Correct English usage and grammar were emphasized throughout the course.

A rousing success, Prince's endeavor spawned hundreds of similar programs connected with department stores, high schools, and vocational schools throughout the country. In 1908, 145 of Prince's first 190 graduates reported a raise within a year (usually about two dollars per week). One merchant gleefully informed another that training programs made employees "want to make more money for themselves . . . and they'll make you rich while they are doing it."[46] Retailers were so grateful that they created an education department within the National Retail Dry Goods Association and made Prince its director.

The burgeoning of vocational training programs nationwide created a shortage of teachers in the new area of salesmanship. To fill this need, Prince convinced Simmons College in 1915 to begin a one-year program to train instructors in this new area. Boston merchants showed their support by helping to finance a separate building (29 Temple Place) for the School for Store Service, which would later become the Prince School of Retailing. The one-year certificate teacher-training program for women who already had college degrees included observation and selling experience in department stores, courses in educational theory, applied psychology, textiles (including visits to textile mills), economics, and practice teaching in the original training program for saleswomen. The retailing program was extremely popular at Simmons, and by 1939, under male direction, the School moved beyond teacher training to offer courses in business administration and advertising.

SOCIAL REFORM AND POLITICAL ACTIVISM

The salesmanship program was a success for both working women and their professional teachers for a number of reasons. First, unlike domestic servants, salesclerks might actually anticipate advancement in their work—from clerk to floor supervisor, assistant buyer or even, in rare cases, to buyer. Since these advances were usually based on "superior" skills, training programs geared to improve skills made sense to an ambitious clerk thinking about eventual promotion. Good evaluations also often meant that management granted saleswomen incentives (small bonuses) and wage increases.

In addition, salesclerks apparently felt less threatened by middle-class educators than domestic servants had. Unlike servants, they worked together with peers and perceived their group to be a "clerking sisterhood." Class and gender solidarity built self-esteem and allowed clerks to assert themselves and assure that training programs met their needs. Their associations with peers resembled the networks and church groups of African-American domestics. In both cases, group identity and support enabled individual empowerment whether through training programs or the organization of trade unions.[47]

Training programs may also have worked well for salesclerks because, while clerks represented different class backgrounds than reformers, they were usually not as diverse racially or ethnically as domestic servants. Middle-class women probably felt that training was most successful when the trainees were as similar as possible to their teachers. Therefore, in the eyes of reformers and educators, young white upwardly mobile working women held greater promise than foreign-born or nonwhite servants. Finally, as discussed earlier, both Simmons College and the WEIU were explicit about their goals to provide meaningful work for middle-class professional women as well as education for working-class students. Thus, the training program also appealed directly to reformers because they provided career opportunities for middle-class teachers like themselves.

This chapter's examination of the evolution of training programs for domestic servants and saleswomen raises intriguing questions about the growing ability of working-class women to articulate their needs and desires for improved working conditions. At the same time, it documents both the successes and failures of middle-class reformers who relied on education as a way to improve working-class women's lives. Attempts by WEIU and Simmons College educators to reach across class

lines were similar to endeavors by other Progressive Era women's organizations like the Women's Trade Union League (WTUL) and the
National American Woman Suffrage Association (NAWSA). Where successful, these tenuous alliances between working-class and middle-class
feminists, between women of color and white women, represented significant breakthroughs. But coalition building across class and race
barriers was as difficult for the two organizations studied here as it was
for the WTUL and NAWSA.[48]

Calling itself a "union of all for the good of all," the Women's Educational and Industrial Union had been explicit about coalition building during the nineteenth and early twentieth centuries. It supported
trade unions for working women and offered legal protection for these
women when they tried to exact just wages from employers who were of
the Union members' own class. Simmons College too made efforts at
cross-class outreach by keeping its tuition lower than at elite schools, offering scholarships to those in need, and welcoming Jewish and African-
American students when discrimination was still common at most other
colleges. But most important, like the WEIU, Simmons was committed
to educating women who needed to work for a living.

The leaders of Simmons and the WEIU, at least until World War I,
believed that gender solidarity could transcend class and racial divisions.
Relying on these beliefs, many Progressive women were successful in
establishing the female dominions discussed earlier in this chapter.[49]
Because they recognized the virtual impossibility of breaking into the
barricaded male professions, middle-class women found meaningful
work for themselves and for working-class women within a female
domain. These women espoused a doctrine of "social motherhood" that
maintained that domestic concerns should influence public policy.
They therefore insisted that women's roles as nurturers qualified them
uniquely for certain careers such as social work, nursing, teaching, home
economics, librarianship, and office work, all of which emerged as
women's "professions" during this period. And along with work opportunities, the female dominion created a more public sphere of influence
that allowed women to raise certain political issues in ways that could
not easily be ignored. School and municipal reform, food and drug
regulation, women's suffrage, protective legislation for working women
and children, and prohibition were on the Progressive reform agenda
and were kept alive by representatives of the female dominion.

Although this group of Progressive Era reformers could claim certain successes, many of their initiatives failed the very women they initially set out to aid. The different fates of the salesmanship program and the training program for domestic servants at the WEIU and Simmons can finally be attributed to the inability of middle-class white women to come to terms with race, class, and ethnic differences. They were instead developing new coalitions with men of their own class, like Simmons's first president, Henry Lefavour, who was also a member of the WEIU board. These cross-gender affiliations were becoming more popular because many Progressive Era reformers were more comfortable in alliances with men and women of their own class and believed that these alliances were more likely to be politically successful.[50]

Another barrier to cross-class coalitions was middle-class women's assertion of the superiority of their vision of family, home, and community. Such claims allowed some middle-class women to gain access to the public realm as long as they concentrated on matters considered appropriate for their sex. But middle-class women's ideas about domesticity were not necessarily appealing to nor achievable by rural, working-class, ethnic, or racial minority women. Class differences in domestic ideology and experiences were clearly a major factor in the misunderstandings between householders and domestic servants.

Also, because many women reformers saw their main opportunity for power or control emerging from their identities as women—their gender assignment to be nurturers or at least experts on motherhood and child care—most of them prescribed a limited sphere for all women, bounded by their capacity to be mothers. This view imposed severe restrictions on women's movement beyond prescribed nineteenth-century boundaries of the domestic sphere. For example, the leaders of the Children's Bureau advised breastfeeding for all new mothers for up to eight months. They also supported the concept of a family wage, so that women could stay at home to rear the many children they might have if they followed the Bureau's proscriptions against artificial contraception. The irony, according to Robyn Muncy, is that while white middle-class single women sometimes found liberation through social motherhood, their theories restricted married women of all classes to a narrowly defined domestic sphere.[51]

Further class conflicts emerged with the professionalization of women's work in such fields as domestic science and salesmanship training. The movement to professionalize many vocations during this period was both male dominated and middle class. One of its goals was to separate the professions from other kinds of less prestigious work and to erect barriers that assured that only an elite few would share the rewards of professional status. This mentality clearly discouraged outreach or coalition building with those beyond the professional inner circle, which was almost always white and middle class. Professionalism mandated exclusion and thus conflicted with earlier efforts of women reformers to bridge gaps between classes.[52]

With professionalization, middle-class women also faced a conflict between the scientific, objective language of the professions and the passionate, sympathetic, moral discourse that had informed definitions of women's sphere and organizing efforts during the nineteenth century. Penina Glazer, Miriam Slater, and others have pointed out that women, by the way their sphere was defined, were excluded from the language and trappings of traditional professionalism. Nevertheless, as Muncy and Deutsch show, some groups of women, especially those associated with the settlement house movement and, as this study shows, with the WEIU and Simmons College, appropriated these trappings and became "experts," establishing female strongholds in women's and children's affairs and in household economics.[53] Interestingly, because the WEIU and Simmons College established career paths for women outside of the traditionally male professions, they never competed directly with men for professional status. As a result, they were less likely to encounter significant male resistance and even found alliances possible with professional men.

The WEIU and Simmons experiences demonstrate that while establishing a female dominion allowed a certain amount of progress for working women of all classes, class conflict was always present and problematic even within the women's reform organizations most committed to collaboration. The WEIU's efforts to aid domestic servants foundered when the demands of these workers came into direct conflict with Union members' beliefs about family and community and with these middle-class women's perceived need for live-in help.[54] When faced with these conflicts, the Union shifted tactics and allied itself with the movement to professionalize household work through the study of home economics at Simmons College. In taking this step, they abandoned racially and ethnically diverse working women of the servant class in favor of upwardly mobile white women who were more similar to themselves.

The salesmanship training program followed a different trajectory.

SOCIAL REFORM AND POLITICAL ACTIVISM

Because salesclerks were largely white and native-born and engaged in white-collar work, middle-class reformers could understand and identify more readily with their concerns. Department store clerks were not present in middle-class homes, and therefore reform of their working conditions could not be perceived as nearly so threatening to middle-class homemakers as changes in the status of domestic servants. In addition, clerks gained strength and esteem from their perceived membership in a clerking network and therefore were in a better position to define their needs and ask for training programs that would serve them. Finally, clerks could actually look forward to promotions and improved working conditions if they enrolled in training programs; and middle-class women could find meaningful work as their teachers.

In each of the above instances, successful reform depended on the ability of working-class women to voice their concerns and influence the reformers interested in their plight. Isolated by their working situations in individual homes and further disempowered by societal denigration of domestic service as an occupation, household workers had little choice but to "vote with their feet." They simply did not enroll in training programs, which they saw as unrelated to their needs and incapable of providing for their advancement. Middle-class women, moreover, were unable to bypass their own self-interest and class-based "family values" to hear and respond to servants' problems and proposals. Saleswomen, on the other hand, responded well to training that they saw as providing for their needs for improved working conditions. They too "voted with their feet," and large numbers enrolled in courses. Middle-class mentors listened to clerks and store owners and became teachers in courses that served the needs of all three groups.

Ultimately, educational reforms during this period worked best for upwardly mobile, native-born, working-class women. Educators at Simmons and the WEIU took seriously these women's needs to be independent, and they were committed to using education as a means for them to gain access to new lines of work like social work, public health nursing, or laboratory technology. A Simmons education could upgrade a white-collar woman's job from typist to private secretary or librarian, from unskilled salesclerk to trained saleswoman or buyer, from hospital-based nurse to autonomous public health nurse, from volunteer charity worker to paid professional social worker, or from housewife to home economist, dietician, or institutional manager.

Middle-class women reformers also found more meaningful work

228 roles—especially as educators, managers, and political activists who combined research with advocacy. While these middle-class women rarely competed openly with men, they attempted what they saw as possible, and in doing so, they found self-supporting work for many women who needed it. It would remain for the next generation of working women, educated by the Progressive Era reformers, to extend women's dominion further into the public realm, define new political and career alternatives for women, and design many of the programs of today's welfare state.

Notes

Versions of this chapter were presented at the Duquesne History Forum (October 1989) and the Organization of American Historians' Annual Meeting (April 1991). This research has been supported in part by grants from the Schlesinger Library of Radcliffe College and the Simmons Fund for Research. I have received helpful comments from Susan Porter, Sam Bass Warner, Mary Frederickson, and Linda Rosenzweig.

1. The overlap among leaders of these two organizations includes Mary Morton Kehew, president of the WEIU from 1892 to 1918, a member of the first Simmons Corporation, and a founding member of the Women's Trade Union League. Other WEIU board members also at Simmons were Sarah Louise Arnold and Henry Lefavour, Simmons's first dean and first president; social work and social science innovators Frances Rollins Morse, Susan Myra Kingsbury, and Eva Whiting White; and chemist Ellen Swallow Richards. Social worker Lucinda Wyman Prince founded both the Union's School of Salesmanship and the Simmons School of Education for Store Service.

2. On the late-century shift in rhetoric and strategy at the WEIU from "transcendental" language and goals to political expediency, see Sarah Deutsch, "Learning to Talk More Like a Man: Boston's Women's Class-Bridging Organizations, 1870–1940," *American Historical Review* (April 1992): 379–404. Earlier scholars have also dealt with this theme; see especially, Aileen Kraditor, *Ideas of the Woman Suffrage Movement, 1890–1920* (New York: Columbia University Press, 1965), and Jill Conway, "Women Reformers and American Culture," in *Our American Sisters,* ed. Jean E. Friedman and William G. Shade, 3d ed. (Lexington: D. C. Heath, 1982), 432–43.

3. For more on this shift, see Elizabeth Clark-Lewis, " 'This Work Had an End': African-American Domestic Workers in Washington, D.C., 1910–1940," in *"To Toil the Livelong Day": America's Women at Work, 1780–1980,* ed. Carol Groneman and Mary Beth Norton (Ithaca, N.Y.: Cornell University Press, 1987), 196–212.

4. For this chapter I accept the description of the process of professionaliza-tion presented in Penina Glazer and Miriam Slater, *Unequal Colleagues: The Entrance of Women into the Professions, 1890–1940* (New Brunswick, N.J.: Rutgers University Press, 1987). Glazer and Slater suggest that, during the late nineteenth century, this process involved setting new standards, upgrading and lengthening training periods, and developing and controlling licensing and other "gatekeeping" requirements for the primarily male professions of law, medicine, science, the ministry, and academia. How this process excluded women and thus forced or enabled them to establish the "women's professions" of nursing, teaching, social work, and librarianship or the "semi-professions" of office management, home economics, laboratory technology, and others is discussed in more detail by Glazer and Slater and later in this chapter.

5. The term female dominion is used to describe a sphere of influence for women professionals such as social workers by Robyn Muncy in *Creating a Female Dominion in American Reform 1890–1935* (New York: Oxford University Press, 1991). In *The Physician's Hand: Work, Culture and Conflict in American Nursing* (Philadelphia: Temple University Press, 1982), Barbara Melosh posits a similar sphere of influence for nurses.

6. On attitudes and language common among professionals, see also Margaret W. Rossiter, *Women Scientists in America: Struggles and Strategies to 1940* (Baltimore: Johns Hopkins University Press, 1982) and Deutsch, "Learning to Talk."

7. Deutsch, "Learning to Talk," 397.

8. For more on the city exchange movement, see Sheila Rothman, *Women's Proper Place: A History of Changing Ideals and Practices, 1870 to the Present* (New York: Basic Books, 1978), 21, 86–87. On Boston's WEIU, see Karen J. Blair, *The Clubwoman as Feminist: True Womanhood Redefined, 1868–1914* (New York: Holmes and Meier, 1980), 73–91, and Deutsch, "Learning to Talk," 388–97.

9. Eleanor W. Allen, "Boston's Women's Educational and Industrial Union," *New England Galaxy* (Spring 1965): n.p.

10. Quoted in Agnes Donham, "The History of the Women's Educational and Industrial Union" (1955), unpublished typescript, WEIU Collection, Schlesinger Library (SL), 6.

11. Allen, "Boston's WEIU," n.p.

12. Donham, "History."

13. WEIU *Annual Report* (1886), 7, WEIU Collection (SL).

14. WEIU *Annual Report* (1881), 9, WEIU Collection (SL).

15. WEIU *Annual Report* (1880), 8, WEIU Collection (SL). See also Donham, "History," 28.

16. On the significance of the space occupied by Union buildings and their very desirable downtown location see Deutsch, "Learning to Talk," 389–90.

17. On the "servant problem," see David M. Katzman, *Seven Days a Week:*

Women and Domestic Service in Industrializing America (Urbana: University of Illinois Press, 1981), 223–65. See also Judith Rollins, *Between Women: Domestics and Their Employers* (Philadelphia: Temple University Press: 1985), 48–55. On the transition from live-in to day service, see Clark-Lewis, " 'This Work Had an End.' "

18. Donham, "History," 118.

19. *WEIU Annual Report* (1892), 36, WEIU Collection (SL). For more on the "family influence," see Susan Porter, "Independent Women and Dependent Children" (paper read at the American Historical Association, New York, December 1990).

20. *WEIU Annual Report* (1905–6), 27, WEIU Collection (SL). Office work was not usually open to young women who lacked high school training or sometimes the language proficiency essential for a "typewriter's" job. On the application of social science methodology to the study of domestic service, see also Faye Dudden, *Serving Women: Household Service in Nineteenth-Century America* (Middletown, Conn.: Wesleyan University Press, 1983), 236–42.

21. Statistics from Mary E. Trueblood, *Social Statistics of Working Women*, Massachusetts Department of Labor Bulletin, No. 18 (May 1910).

22. Quoted in Katzman, *Seven Days a Week*, 278.

23. Ibid.

24. Quoted in Donham, "History," 117.

25. The WEIU's evolving interest in public-policy concerns is discussed in Deutsch, "Learning to Talk."

26. *School of Housekeeping*, Brochure (1900), 2, *Simmons College Archives* (SCA).

27. Katzman, *Seven Days a Week*, 264.

28. For more on the home economics movement, see Dolores Hayden, *The Grand Domestic Revolution: A History of Feminist Designs for American Homes, Neighborhoods and Cities* (Cambridge, Mass.: Harvard University Press, 1981).

29. Donham, "History," 126. See also Deutsch, "Learning to Talk."

30. Donham, "History," 127.

31. On the changing nature of this workforce, see Rollins, *Between Women*, 48–59; and Clark-Lewis, " 'This Work Had an End.' " Scholars disagree about what happened to domestic servants after their "abandonment" by middle-class reformers. David Katzman suggests that only two constructive responses to the exploitation of this group of workers remained: legislative regulation and unionization, and that both proved as "illusory as any utopia." Domestic service was excluded from protective labor legislation during the Progressive Era and again in the Depression; and separate and isolated working situations have remained the major deterrents to the organization of unions by these workers. (See Katzman, *Seven Days a Week*, 262–65; Clark-Lewis, " 'This Work Had an End' "; and Rosalyn Terborg-Penn, "Survival Strategies among African-American Women Workers: A Continuing Process," in *Women's Work*

and Protest: A Century of U.S. Women's Labor History, ed. Ruth Milkman (New York: Routledge, 1985), 110–55.

32. Will of John Simmons, quoted in Henry Lefavour, "Founder's Day Address," *Simmons College Review* 3, no. 2 (December 1920): 55, SCA.

33. Attributed to Benjamin J. Brooks and quoted in Lefavour, "The Will of John Simmons," *Simmons Quarterly* 3, no. 1 (January 1911): 1–9, SCA.

34. For more on women's education during this period, see Lynn D. Gordon, *Gender and Higher Education in the Progressive Era* (New Haven: Yale University Press, 1990); and Barbara Miller Solomon, *In the Company of Educated Women: A History of Women in Higher Education in America* (New Haven: Yale University Press, 1985).

35. Sarah Louise Arnold, "Reconcilement of Cross Purposes" (1908), 5, SCA.

36. Henry Lefavour, *Annual Report of the President of Simmons College* (1908), SCA.

37. Quoted in Hayden, *The Grand Domestic Revolution,* 153.

38. *Simmons College Catalogue* (1910–11), 37, SCA.

39. The impact of technology on housework is the subject of Ruth Schwartz Cowan's *More Work for Mother: The Ironies of Household Technology from the Open Hearth to the Microwave* (New York: Basic Books, 1983); see esp. 69–191.

40. For more on the makeup of this workforce, see Susan Porter Benson, *Counter Cultures: Saleswomen, Managers, and Customers in American Department Stores 1890–1940* (Urbana: University of Illinois Press, 1988), 3–11. The popular movie *It* (1927), based on Elinor Glyn's novel and starring Clara Bow, presented the story of a shopgirl who eventually married the rich store owner.

41. On the National Consumers' League, see Nancy F. Cott, *The Grounding of Modern Feminism* (New Haven: Yale University Press, 1987), 87–88; and Muncy, *Creating a Female Dominion,* 150–51.

42. Benson, *Counter Cultures,* 142–46.

43. "Boston School for Saleswomen Attracts Country's Attention," *Boston Sunday Post,* May 2, 1907.

44. Ibid.

45. "Woman Owns and Manages Big School of Salesmanship," *Chicago Herald,* c. 1912, undated clippings, SCA.

46. Ibid.

47. Benson, *Counter Cultures,* 227–32; Clark-Lewis, " 'This Work Had an End,' " 210–12.

48. See, for example, Colette A. Hyman, "Labor Organizing and Female Institution Building: The Chicago Women's Trade Union League, 1904–24," in Milkman, *Women's Work and Protest,* 22–41; Nancy Schrom Dye, "Creating a Feminist Alliance: Sisterhood and Class Conflict in the New York Women's Trade Union League, 1903–1914," in Jean E. Friedman and William G. Shade, *Our American Sisters,* 393–410; Ellen DuBois, *Feminism and Suffrage: The Emergence of an Independent Women's Movement in America, 1848–1869* (Ithaca,

232   N.Y.: Cornell University Press, 1978), 21–52, 126–61; and Paula Giddings, *When and Where I Enter: The Impact of Black Women on Race and Sex in America* (New York: William Morrow, 1984), esp. 119–34.

49. On terminologies for feminisms of the Progressive period, see Nancy F. Cott, "What's in a Name? The Limits of Social Feminism; or Expanding the Vocabulary of Women's History," *Journal of American History* 76 (December 1989): 809–29; and Cott, *Grounding of Modern Feminism*, 215–39; Rosalind Rosenberg, *Beyond Separate Spheres: Intellectual Roots of Modern Feminism* (New Haven: Yale University Press, 1982), 28–51; and Gordon, *Gender and Higher Education*, 190–93. The establishment of "female dominions" is documented in Muncy, *Creating a Female Dominion*.

50. Deutsch, "Learning to Talk."

51. On limitations of "social motherhood," see Muncy, *Creating a Female Dominion*, 158–65, and Mimi Abramovitz, *Regulating the Lives of Women: Social Welfare Policy from Colonial Times to the Present* (Boston: South End Press, 1988), 181–213.

52. Glazer and Slater, *Unequal Colleagues*, 1–23.

53. Muncy, *Creating a Female Dominion*, 58–165; Deutsch, "Learning to Talk."

54. In a slightly later period, Phyllis Palmer examines the failure of middle-class employers to respond to the concerns of their servants. See Palmer, "Housewife and Household Worker: Employer-Employee Relationships in the Home, 1928–1941," in Groneman and Norton, "*To Toil the Livelong Day*," 179–95.

CONTRIBUTORS

HENRY F. BEDFORD, author of numerous articles and books including *Trouble Downtown: The Local Context of Twentieth Century America* (1978) and *Seabrook Station: Citizen Politics and Nuclear Power* (1990), received his Ph.D. from the University of Massachusetts (Amherst) in 1965.

NANCY BOWMAN is a Ph.D. candidate at the University of Maryland.

LAURIE CRUMPACKER, professor of history at Simmons College, received her Ph.D. from Boston University in 1978. She is the author of numerous articles and coeditor of *The Journal of Esther Edwards Burr* (1984) and *Second to None: A Documentary History of American Women from the Sixteenth Century to the Present* (1994).

PAUL R. DAUPHINAIS received his Ph.D. from the University of Maine in 1991. His chapter is part of a larger study of French-Canadians in New England.

POLLY WELTS KAUFMAN, lecturer in history at the University of Massachusetts (Boston), received an Ed.D. from Boston University in 1978. She is the author of many articles and several books, including *Women Teachers on the Frontier* (1984) and *Boston Women and City School Politics, 1872–1905* (1994).

234   PATRICIA A. PALMIERI is the author of several articles and *"In Adamless Eden": The Women's Intellectual Community at Wellesley* (1995). She received an Ed.D. from Harvard University in 1981.

SUSAN L. PORTER, an assistant professor of history at Simmons College, received her Ph.D. from Boston University in 1984. She has written several articles and a forthcoming book, *Gendered Benevolence: Orphan Asylums in Antebellum America.*

LINDA M. SHOEMAKER is a Ph.D. candidate at Binghamton University. She is the author of *A History of the Brookline Friendly Society* (1994).

RODGER STREITMATTER, professor of journalism in the School of Communications, American University, is the author of several articles in *Journalism History* and *Journalism Quarterly* about African-American women journalists. He received his Ph.D. from American University in 1988.

JAMES M. WALLACE, professor of education in the Graduate School of Professional Studies at Lewis and Clark College, is the author of many articles and *Liberal Journalism and American Education, 1914–1941* (1991) and the coeditor of *Ethical and Social Issues in Professional Education* (1994). He received his Ed.D. from Harvard University in 1966.

INDEX

Abbott, Grace, 106
Adams, John Quincy, 54
Addams, Jane, 185, 200–201, 210
African-American women
   as clubwomen, 7, 147, 151, 154,
      158–59
   and desegregation, 167, 179
   and integration, 154–57
   as journalists, 147–57
African-Americans on Boston School
   Committee, 182
Alfred University and Caroline
   Healey Dall, 123, 138–39
American Mount Coffee School As-
   sociation, 156
American Social Science Association
   and Caroline Healey Dall, 123,
   137–38
American Woman Suffrage Associa-
   tion, 165
Ames, Fanny Baker, 125
Anthony, Susan B.
   and Caroline Healey Dall, 122,
   125, 135–37

and Josephine St. Pierre Ruffin,
   155
antislavery movement, 150
   and Caroline Healey Dall, 122,
   130–32
apprenticeship of graduates of
   Boston Female Asylum, 17–26
Arnold, Sarah Louise, 228
   as dean of Simmons College, 218
   as supervisor in Boston Public
   Schools, 171

Balch, Emily Greene, 7
   background of, 187–93
   education of, 192–96
   and peace activities, 8, 185, 199–202
   as professor at Wellesley College,
   183, 197–201
   and settlement house work, 196–
   97
Beecher, Catharine, 128, 217
Boston Associated Charities, 103, 105
Boston Courant, Josephine St. Pierre
   Ruffin editor of, 151

Boston Female Asylum
  and choices of graduates, 22–34
  goals and attitudes of managers of,
    17–19, 32
  programs of, 19–22, 26–28
Boston Normal School, 168–69
  becomes Boston Teachers' College,
    174, 181
Boston School Committee
  service of women on, 165–67,
    169–78
  size of, 167, 178–79
Boston School for Social Work, 6
  alliance breaks down, 109
  founded, 99, 102
Brackett, Jeffrey, 100–102, 104–9, 111
Brandeis, Alice Goldmark, 210
Bryn Mawr College, 193–94

Cabot, Richard C., 113
Catholic women
  in public office, 165, 175, 178
  as teachers, 166, 168
  as voters, 167–68
Chapman, Maria Weston, 131
Cheney, Ednah Dow, 154, 156, 162
child labor, 71–72, 81, 85, 88, 95
Children's Bureau, 225
Clisby, Harriet, 210
Collins, Patrick, 169, 172, 177, 179
Coman, Katharine, 197
Curley, James Michael, 179

Dall, Caroline Healey, 7
  as author and lecturer, 135–37
  background of, 122, 125–29
  as founding member of American
    Social Science Association, 123,
    137–38
  marriage of, 131, 133–34
  religion of, 126
  in social reform, 130–34, 138–39
dame schools, 46

Davis, Paulina Wright, 132, 134
Denison House, 107, 196, 199
Diaz, Abby Morton, 211
Dierkes, Mary A.
  background of, 175–76
  serves on Boston School Commit-
    tee, 176–77
domesticity, 34, 96, 124, 218
  among French-Canadian women,
    73–78
domestic service
  of graduates of Boston Female
    Asylum, 22–30
  and the Women's Educational and
    Industrial Union, 208, 212–14
  See also wage work
Douglass, Frederick, 150
Duff, Ellen L., 170–71
Duff, Julia Harrington, 7
  background of, 168, 170
  serves on Boston School Commit-
    tee, 165, 169–78
  supports Boston women as
    teachers, 167–69, 174

Eastman, Crystal, 183
education of women, 46–47, 77, 87
  at Boston Normal School, 168,
    174
  and Caroline Healey Dall, 123,
    138–39, 141
  at Girls' Latin School, 166
  at Simmons College, 218–27
  at Women's Educational and In-
    dustrial Union, 210, 215–17
Eliot, Charles W., 103, 110
Emergency Peace Federation, 200
Equal Rights Association, 136
ethnicity, 7, 63–66, 167–71, 178–79
  and ethnic cooperation, 78

Fall River, 65–68, 72
family claim, 189–91

family economy, 20–21, 31, 88, 91, 92
  and child labor, 71–72
  among French-Canadians, 63–67, 71–78
family wage, 3, 31, 76, 93, 94, 225
feminization
  of social work, 99, 101, 109, 113
  of teaching, 44–45, 48
  in textile mills, 67
  See also women teachers
Fifield, Emily A., 7
  background of, 170
  serves on Boston School Committee, 169–74
Fitchburg, 64, 71, 73, 76–78
Fitzgerald, John F., 179
Fortune, T. Thomas, 150
French-Canadian women
  as homemakers, 72–78
  as textile workers, 63–67
Fuller, Margaret, 128–30, 133

Garrison, William Lloyd, 122, 131, 150
German-Americans, 175–76
Girls' Latin School, 166
Good Government Association, 169, 177
Grimke, Sarah, 128

Hale, Sara Josepha, 54
Hamilton, Alice, 200
Harrington, Walter, 177–78
Harvard University and the Boston School for Social Work, 6, 102–3, 109, 112–14
Hazard, Caroline, 197
Higgins, Alice, 103–4
Hill, Eliza Trask and Independent Women Voters, 167–68
housewives, 77–78, 89–90
Howe, Julia Ward, 136, 154, 162

immigration, 4, 63–66
Independent Women Voters, 167–68
Irish-American women
  as teachers, 165–69
  as voters, 167–68, 175

Kansas Relief Association, 150
Kehew, Mary Morton, 228
Keller, Elizabeth, 171
Kelley, Florence, 106, 220
Kingsbury, Susan Myra, 218, 228

League of Women for Community Service and Josephine St. Pierre Ruffin, 156
Lee, Joseph, 104
Lefavour, Henry, 103, 218, 225, 228
literacy rates, 72–73
Lowell mills, women workers in, 24, 66–71

Mann, Horace, 43, 45–46, 53, 56
marriage, 94
  among French-Canadians, 73–74, 78
  and graduates of Boston Female Asylum, 23, 25, 29–34
Massachusetts Bureau of Statistics of Labor, 66, 68, 69, 85, 96
Massachusetts Federation of Women's Clubs, desegregated by Josephine St. Pierre Ruffin, 155–56
Massachusetts Moral Education Association, 154–55
Massachusetts School Suffrage Association, 150, 154, 167
Massachusetts Woman Suffrage Association, 154
May, Abby W., 154, 162, 166
Morse, Frances Rollins, 104, 228
motherhood. See republican motherhood

National American Woman Suffrage Association, 224
National Association for the Advancement of Colored People, 156
National Association of Colored Women, 7, 151, 158–59
National Consumers' League, 220–21
National Federation of Afro-American Women, founded, 149, 151
needleworkers
    among graduates of Boston Female Asylum, 17, 24–28, 32
    See also wage work
New England Hospital for Women and Children, 155–56
New England Woman Suffrage Association, 154
New England Women's Club, 136, 154
New England Women's Press Association, 154
Nobel Prize for peace, awarded to Emily Greene Balch, 8, 185

Oliver, Henry Kemble, 85–87, 94, 96
orphans, 76
    in Boston Female Asylum, 17–21
O'Sullivan, Mary Kenney, 210

Parker, Theodore, 122
Peabody, Elizabeth, 129–30
Peabody, Francis, 103
Phillips, Wendell, 131, 133, 150
Prince, Lucinda Wyman, founds school for retailing, 221–23, 228
Prince School of Retailing, 222
professionalization
    of domestic science, 209, 225
    of salesmanship, 209, 220–21, 225
    of social science, 137–40

of social work, 6, 99–101
of teaching, 56–57
prostitutes, 91–93
Public School Association, 169, 172–75, 180

race and interracial cooperation, 154–57
republican motherhood, 2, 33, 53–54, 57
retailing, training for, 221–23
Richards, Ellen Swallow, 218, 228
Richmond, Mary, 106
Rose, Ernestine, 132
Ruffin, George Lewis, 149–50
Ruffin, Josephine St. Pierre, 7
    background of, 149
    as editor of Woman's Era, 147–49, 151–56
    founds Woman's Era Club, 148
    interracial activities of, 154–57, 210
    marriage of, 150

salary scales, 21, 89, 91, 94, 96, 109–10
of French-Canadian men, 68, 77
of teachers, 49–50
of textile workers, 67–70
Salmon, Lucy, 193
school attendance, 72–73, 76, 85
School of Housekeeping, 207, 215–17
    purchased by Simmons College, 218
    started by Women's Educational and Industrial Union, 207, 215–17
School of Salesmanship, 207
school suffrage, 178
    achieved by Massachusetts women, 166, 215
    and numbers of women voting, 167–68, 175
Scudder, Vida, 185, 188, 198

settlement house movement, 106–7, 196–99, 220

Severance, Caroline, 136

sewing trades. *See* needleworkers

Simmons College
  and Boston School for Social Work, 6, 102–3, 109, 112–14
  educational programs of, 8, 218–27
  founded, 217

single women, 23, 32, 90–91, 93–94, 96

sisterhood, 6–7, 124, 141, 154–56, 197–98, 210

Smith, Zilpha Drew, 105, 109–10

social class
  and cross-class coalitions, 224–25
  mobility, 20, 31

social motherhood, 224

social work
  beginnings of, 100–101
  as women's work, 99, 101, 109, 113

South End House, 106

Stanton, Elizabeth Cady
  and Caroline Healey Dall, 122, 128, 132, 136–37
  and Josephine St. Pierre Ruffin, 155

Stone, Lucy, 154–56, 162

Storrow, James Jackson, 172, 178–79

Stowe, Harriet Beecher, 155

Sumner, Charles, 122, 150

teachers
  Boston women as, 165–69, 174
  See also women teachers

ten-hour law, 88, 93

textile industry, 65–71

Thomas, M. Carey, 185

Todd, Mabel Loomis, 154, 162

Transcendentalism, 128–29

Truth, Sojourner, 155

Tubman, Harriet, 155

Unitarianism, 126–28, 170, 186, 190

U.S. Sanitary Commission, 150

vocational education, 207

volunteerism, 3, 18–19, 110

Wadlin, Horace, 86, 88–91, 96

wages. *See* salary scales

wage work
  of domestic servants, 21–30, 34, 88–89, 91
  in factories, 88, 95
  of needleworkers, 24–28, 32, 46, 71, 89, 92
  in textile industry, 63–78
  in women's professions, 91, 99, 224
  See also social work; teachers

Wald, Lillian, 106, 183, 210

Washington, Booker T., 150

Wellesley College, 183, 197–98, 201

Wells-Barnett, Ida B., 147, 156

White, Eva Whiting, 105–7, 228

widows, 21

Willard, Frances, 219

Williams, Fannie Barrier, 151, 155

Woman's Era
  and desegregation, 153–56
  and feminism, 152
  founded by Josephine St. Pierre Ruffin, 147
  as organ of National Association of Colored Women, 151
  and racial justice, 153

Woman's Era Club, 147, 154

woman suffrage, 133

women's education. *See* education of women

Women's Educational and Industrial Union, 8, 196
  purposes of, 210–11
  training programs of, 207–17

Women's International League for Peace and Freedom, 8, 185, 201

240

Women's Peace Party, 200
women's rights movement
  and Caroline Healey Dall, 122,
    131–37, 140
  and education of women, 56
  and Josephine St. Pierre Ruffin,
    152–54
Women's Trade Union League, 224

women teachers
  as inexpensive, 49–51, 57
  as morally desirable, 52–56
  See also teachers
Woods, Robert A., 104, 106–7,
    109–11
Worcester, 64–71, 74, 76–78
Wright, Carroll D., 86–92, 96